The 365 Day Children's
BIBLE
Storybook

The 365 Day Children's Bible Storybook

Published by Scandinavia Publishing House 2011
Drejervej 15, 3 DK-2400 Copenhagen NV, Denmark
E-mail: info@scanpublishing.dk
Web: www.scanpublishing.dk

Text copyright © Joy Melissa Jensen
and Scandinavia Publishing House 2011
Illustrations copyright © Gustavo Mazali
Design by Ben Alex
Printed in China
ISBN 978-1-4336-8003-8
All rights reserved

Scripture quotations are taken from the Holman
Christian Standard Bible ® Copyright © 1999, 2000,
2002, 2003, 2009 by Holman Bible Publishers. Used
by permission.

The 365 Day Children's
BIBLE
Storybook

Retold by Joy Melissa Jensen

scandinavia

Contents

The Old Testament

CREATION 6–7
ADAM AND EVE 8–11
CAIN AND ABEL 12–13
NOAH 14–17
**THE TOWER
 OF BABYLON 18–19**
ABRAHAM 20–29
ISAAC 30–31
JACOB 32–47
JOSEPH 48–73
MOSES 74–111
JOSHUA 112–129
JUDGES 130–135
DEBORAH 136–139
GIDEON 140–153
SAMSON 154–163
RUTH 164–169
HANNAH 170–171
SAMUEL 172–179
SAUL 180–185
DAVID 186–210
SOLOMON 211–215
ELIJAH 216–221
ELISHA 222–223
JONAH 224–229
DANIEL 230–241
ESTHER 242–252

The New Testament

JESUS' BIRTH 254–261
JESUS' CHILDHOOD 262–263
JOHN THE BAPTIST 264–265
JESUS' EARLY MINISTRY 266–283
JESUS' TEACHING 284–322
**JESUS' HEALINGS
 AND MIRACLES 323–357**
JESUS' LAST DAYS 358–395
JESUS' RESURRECTION 396–407
THE EARLY CHURCH 408–419
SIMON PETER'S MINISTRY 420–425
PAUL'S MINISTRY 426–445

The Old Testament

DAY 1
God Makes Heaven and Earth
Genesis 1:1-19

In the beginning, God created heaven and earth. The earth was a dark and empty place. There was only a roaring black ocean covering empty land. The Spirit of God called out in the darkness, "Let there be light!" Suddenly light shone down and created the first day.

On the second day, God said, "Let the sky be separated from the ocean." And the ocean and the sky obeyed God's command.

On the third day, God said, "Let the water be all in one place, and let dry land appear. Let there be plants and trees so the earth may be filled with living things." The water and earth obeyed. Trees spread their big leafy branches, and little flowers and plants sprung up out of the ground to greet the sun.

On the fourth day, God said, "Let the moon and stars shine at night, and let the sun shine by day. These lights will mark the seasons and shed light on the earth." God looked around and saw that all He had done was good.

DAY 2

God Creates the Fish, the Birds, and the Animals

Genesis 1:20-25

On the fifth day, God said, "Let the ocean be filled with sea creatures!" Just then, the water began to churn with life. Great whales lifted their mighty heads. Dolphins jumped and splashed in the sunlight, and little sea crabs scuttled along the sea floor.

God saw that all this was good, so He said, "Let the sky be filled with creatures of the air!" Seagulls swooped in the breeze along with butterflies and buzzing insects. God created all of them, big and small, and to each He gave His blessing. God was happy with the creatures of the sea and the air.

On the sixth day, God said, "Let the deserts and valleys and mountains be filled with animals!" And that's what happened. Elephants trumpeted loudly, giraffes stretched out their spotted necks toward the trees, and porcupines waddled on the ground with their prickly bodies. The earth was home to animals of all shapes and sizes, both wild and tame. God loved watching them play with each other. He was very pleased and blessed each and every one of them.

CREATION

DAY 3
Adam and Eve
Genesis 1:26–2:3, 18-25

God looked around at all the animals of the earth, and the animals of the sea and sky. Something was still missing. So God said, "I will create man. He will be special because I will make him in My image."

Then God took a handful of soil, and out of it He made Adam. God loved Adam. He even let Adam name all the animals. But God said, "It isn't good for man to be alone."

So God took Adam's rib while he was asleep, and out of it He created the first woman. Her name was Eve. She was the perfect partner for Adam, and Adam loved her.

God gave Adam and Eve His blessing. He said, "The earth is filled with animals you may rule over and many good plants and fruits you may eat. Fill the earth with your children and care for all the living creatures!"

After God had finished creating the world, He created the seventh day as a special day of rest.

DAY 4
The Garden of Eden
Genesis 2:8-17

God had placed Adam and Eve in a garden called Eden. The Garden of Eden was a lush and colorful paradise. Plump, ripe fruit grew from the trees, flowers blossomed, and waterfalls crashed down with clear, cool water.

In the middle of the garden, God placed a tree called the Tree of Knowledge. The fruit eaten from this tree gave the power to know the difference between right and wrong. God told Adam and Eve that they could eat from any of the trees in the garden, except for the fruit from the Tree of Knowledge. "If you eat from that tree," God warned, "you will die."

ADAM AND EVE

DAY 5
Adam and Eve Disobey God
Genesis 3:1-7

One day a snake slithered up to Eve as she was walking in the garden. He hissed at her. "Eve," he said, "why don't you take a bite from that juicy piece of fruit hanging from the Tree of Knowledge?" Eve remembered what God had said. "God told us we must not eat fruit from that tree," she replied. To this, the snake answered, "That is only because the fruit will allow you to know the difference between right and wrong. God doesn't want you to be as wise as He is."

The snake made Eve curious. "What would be the harm in one tiny bite?" Eve asked herself. So she sunk her teeth into the fruit and tasted it. Then Eve handed the fruit to Adam, and he also took a bite. For the first time, Adam and Eve looked at each other and realized they were both naked. They were embarrassed and quickly covered themselves up with the biggest fig leaves they could find.

DAY 6
Out of Eden
Genesis 3:8-24

That afternoon, Adam and Eve heard God walking in the Garden of Eden. They were frightened because they knew they had disobeyed Him. They hid behind the trees and plants, hoping God would not discover what they had done. But God knows all things.

God called out to Adam, "Why did you disobey what I said and eat the fruit from the Tree of Knowledge?"

Adam answered, "Eve was the one who took the fruit. It's her fault!" And Eve said, "But it was the snake who told me to take the fruit. So it's the snake's fault!"

God loved Adam and Eve very much. He was disappointed that they did not listen to His command but chose to listen to the sneaky snake instead. He gave Adam and Eve some animal skins to cover themselves. Then He cast them out of the Garden of Eden. From then on, they had to work hard for their food.

DAY 7
Cain and Abel
Genesis 4:1-16

Adam and Eve had two sons. The older son was named Cain. He farmed the land. The younger son, Abel, was a shepherd.

One time when the brothers were still young men, they made an offering to show God how much they loved Him.

CAIN AND ABEL

Cain saved part of his harvest grain and offered it to God. Abel killed the firstborn lamb from one of the sheep. He butchered the lamb, cut off the best parts and offered them to God. God was pleased. He accepted Abel's offering, but He didn't accept Cain's offering.

Cain was filled with jealousy toward his brother Abel. So God said to Cain, "Why are you upset? If you do what is right, I will accept your offering!" But Cain wasn't listening. He was too busy trying to figure out a way he could get back at his brother.

A few days later Cain said to his brother Abel, "Let's go for a walk."

Abel followed his brother far off into the fields and over the rocks. When Cain was certain that they were all alone, he picked up a rock and hit Abel over the head with it.

Later that day God called out to Cain, "Where is Abel?" Cain answered, "How should I know? Am I supposed to look after my brother?" But Cain could not fool God. "Why have you done this terrible thing?" God asked him. "You've killed your own brother. From now on you will be without a home."

So Cain had to leave his family. He wandered around from place to place, never really belonging anywhere.

CAIN AND ABEL

DAY 8
Noah Builds an Ark
Genesis 6:5-22

The world God made quickly filled with more and more people. God saw all their bad deeds. They cheated and stole and lied. God was disappointed in their behavior. He was sorry that He had made them. So He decided to start over.

God planned a great flood. He would let rain pour down until it drenched the land and drowned the people. But there was one man who pleased God. This man was good and kindhearted. His name was Noah.

God told Noah about His plan to flood the earth. "You have made me happy," God said to Noah. "Because of that, I will save your family from the flood." Then God told Noah to gather up the thickest, strongest lumber he could find. He wanted Noah to build a boat, called an ark. God said, "Make it big enough to hold your family and big enough to hold one male and one female of every kind of animal on earth."

Noah did just as God asked. He worked all day and all night, hammering wood planks together and building the biggest boat the world had ever seen.

DAY 9
The Great Flood
Genesis 7:1-16

The ark was finally finished. Noah made sure to have a special place ready for each kind of animal. He packed the ark full of food and supplies. Then the rain began—first a pitter-patter and then a torrent. The land was covered in water. The time had come for God's great flood.

Noah went into the ark with his wife and children. Then the animals marched inside. Two by two, the animals crawled into their stalls. Everyone was glad to be safe on Noah's ark. Noah made sure his family was on board. Then he counted all the animals. Yep, everyone was there. They were ready to go! The flood rose higher, and God closed the door to the ark.

DAY 10

Forty Days and Forty Nights of Rain
Genesis 7:17-24; 8:1-19

Rain poured down for forty days and forty nights. The flood was so deep that it covered the highest mountain peaks! Nothing on earth survived. Only Noah, his family, and the animals were saved. God was watching over them.

When it stopped raining, Noah sent out a raven in search of land. The raven came back, unable to find a place of dry land anywhere. So Noah sent out a dove. The dove returned, just like the raven. But when Noah sent the dove out a second time, it returned with a branch from an olive tree. The bird had found land! Then Noah sent out the dove one last time. But this time the dove never returned.

"I have ended the flood," God said to Noah. "You can leave the ark now." So Noah opened the door and called everybody out of the boat. Each of God's animals stepped off the boat, stretching their legs and sniffing the clean fresh air. It felt good to walk on dry land after so many days on the swaying, shaky sea.

DAY 11
The Rainbow's Promise
Genesis 9:1-16

God gave a blessing to Noah and his sons. He said to them, "May you have many children and grandchildren! This will be the land I will give to your families for generations to come. I saved you from the flood because you have been faithful and obeyed My commands. Now I will make a promise that I will keep forever. I will never send another flood to destroy the earth again."

Just then, a beautiful rainbow full of bright colors shone in the sky. God said, "The rainbow will be My sign to you that I always keep My promises. Every time you see a rainbow, remember I am with you. I will never leave you again."

NOAH

DAY 12
The Tower of Babylon
Genesis 10:32–11:9

Noah's sons, Shem, Ham, and Japheth had children. And their children had children too. Soon the world was filled with people again. Some of them settled in a place called Babylon. The people in Babylon decided to build a tower so high that it would reach heaven. "We will be famous," they said to one another.

But when God saw the tall tower, He was not pleased. He saw that the people of Babylon were no longer humble servants. Instead, they were proud—believing they could reach the heavens with their high tower. He punished the people by giving them each their own language. No one could understand each other anymore because all the languages created a confusing babble of sounds! The tower could no longer be finished. They were too busy arguing in all their different languages.

DAY 13
God Chooses Abram
Genesis 12:1-9; 13:1, 18

Abram was one of God's special people. He lived in the city of Haran. One day God said to Abram, "Leave the place that you come from, and go to the land I will show you." Abram trusted God with his whole heart. He loaded his camels with all his belongings, and left home with his wife, Sarah, and his nephew, Lot, and all their servants. They traveled through the desert hills with only God as their guide.

When Abram and his family came to the land of Canaan, God said, "This land is yours! It will belong to your family forever. I will bless you and all the people in your family that come after you. Everyone on earth will be blessed by your life!" Abram felt very thankful, so he set up an altar in the desert where he could worship God. Then Abram and the rest of his group journeyed onward. Finally they came to a place they liked and pitched their tents and settled.

DAY 14
The Promise of God
Genesis 15:1-6; 17:1-17

Abram was growing older. God had given him many things—a good wife, land, and animals. But there was one thing Abram wanted that God had not

given him. Abram wanted to have a child with his wife Sarah. They had tried to have a child before, but God had never blessed them with one. Now they had wrinkles and gray hair. They had given up hope of ever being parents.

One evening God said to Abram, "Your name will be changed to Abraham because you will be the father of many nations. Look at all the brilliant night sky! Can you count the stars? That is how many descendents you will have!" Abraham said, "I trust You, God! You have already given me everything I could ask for. But how can I be the father of many when I have no children?" God answered, "You will have a son with your wife, Sarah. And everything you have will be his." Abraham could hardly believe it. But he had faith. He got down on his knees and thanked God.

ABRAHAM

DAY 15
Three Travelers

Genesis 18:1-14

One hot summer afternoon, Abraham was sitting outside his tent when three travelers came by. Abraham saw them, and he jumped up and called out to them, "Come, let me get you some water to wash your tired feet!" Then Abraham ran back to the tent. "Sarah!" he called, "would you make some bread for our guests?" Sarah got cooking while Abraham went out in search of his best calf to serve with some milk and yogurt. The men gathered around under the shady trees sharing a drink and talking. Sarah was listening by the tent door.

One of the men said, "Abraham, your wife will give birth to a son soon." When Sarah heard this, she laughed to herself. "Why did Sarah laugh?" God asked Abraham. "Doesn't she think she can have a child in her old age? I am God, and nothing is too difficult for Me! I promise by this time next year, you will already have your baby boy."

23
ABRAHAM

DAY 16
Good People in a Wicked City
Genesis 18:16-33

The three travelers got up to leave. Abraham walked with them. God said to Abraham, "I have heard that the people of Sodom and Gomorrah are doing all kinds of evil things. I have heard that many of them sin and carry out wicked deeds. I am going to see if all of this is true. What do you think, Abraham?" Abraham thought about it. Then he turned to God and said, "What if there are fifty good people living in Sodom? Are you going to destroy those in the city who are righteous?" God answered, "I will save the city for fifty good people." Then Abraham asked, "What if there are forty good people?" And God told Abraham, "If there are forty good people, I still won't destroy the city."

Abraham thought for a moment. Then he said, "God—what about twenty good people? Will you destroy the city if there are twenty good people?" God told Abraham "If there are twenty good people, I still won't destroy the city." But Abraham was still not satisfied. "And what if there are only ten good people?" Yet again God told Abraham, "If there are only ten good people, I won't destroy the city."

Then God went on His journey toward Sodom and Gomorrah, and Abraham turned back to his tent where Sarah was waiting.

DAY 17
God Saves Lot and His Family
Genesis 19:1-29

Noah's nephew, Lot, lived in the city of Sodom. Two angels came to warn Lot of God's plan to destroy the city. Lot invited them into his home for the night. The angels told Lot, "God has plans to destroy the city of Sodom because it is turning into a dark and evil place. Your

family has been faithful and good. You will be saved by God's grace."

A group of men from Sodom had gathered outside Lot's home to attack the two angels. The angels bolted the door and said, "Lot, take your family and all your relatives and leave now. God plans to burn this wicked city! Quick, leave before the city turns to ash!" Lot bundled up his family in cloaks to protect them from the sooty ash. They hurried and stumbled over the rocks and escaped from the burning city. God had not forgotten his promise to Abraham. He saved Lot and his family.

DAY 18

Isaac Is Born

Genesis 21:1-7

God kept His promise to Abraham and Sarah. He gave them a healthy baby boy. They named him Isaac. Isaac was a beautiful baby. Abraham was very proud. Sarah looked up at her husband and said, "Who would have guessed that we would have a son in our old age? I will never laugh at God's promises again. Now I think it's silly I ever doubted God at all!" Isaac was a good baby, and they both loved him dearly.

As Isaac grew older, Abraham and Sarah spent a lot of time with him. Abraham taught Isaac all about God's wonderful world. Sarah went on long walks with the young boy. She pointed out the animals and plants and taught Isaac their names. Abraham and Sarah knew Isaac would grow up to be a strong servant of God.

DAY 19
Abraham Obeys God
Genesis 22:1-18

After several years had passed, God decided to test Abraham's trust and obedience. God said to Abraham, "Go get Isaac, your son whom you love so dearly. Take him to the high mountaintop of Moriah and kill him on an altar as a sacrifice in honor of Me."

Abraham's heart nearly broke with sadness when he heard God's words. He had cared for Isaac, played with Isaac, and taught him all kinds of things. Now God was asking him to sacrifice his child! But Abraham was filled with faith and love for God. He knew that his only choice was to obey.

Abraham got up early the next morning and chopped wood for the altar. He tied the wood into bundles. Then he told Isaac to come with him up the steep mountain.

Abraham and Isaac were out of breath by the time they reached the top. Abraham took the wood and coals and made an altar in the spot where God had told him to sacrifice Isaac. Then Isaac said, "Father, we have the coals and the wood, but where is the lamb for the sacrifice?" Abraham answered sadly, "God will provide the lamb, son." Abraham knew that God had intended Isaac to be the sacrifice, but he just couldn't bring himself to tell his son.

Abraham tied up Isaac. But just as he was about to kill him, the voice of God called out, "Stop, Abraham! Don't kill Isaac! Now I know that you were willing to sacrifice the most precious thing that belonged to you. You trusted Me and obeyed my command. Because of this, I will bless your family forever." Abraham sighed with relief. He saw a ram nearby and sacrificed it to God instead. Then Abraham and Isaac went home with happy hearts, grateful to God.

ABRAHAM

DAY 20
A Wife for Isaac
Genesis 23:1-2; 24:1-27

Many years went by, and Sarah had passed away. Abraham knew that soon he would be called up to heaven too. Before he died, he wanted to find a good wife for his son Isaac. Abraham called one of his most trusted servants to him. "Go to the land where I was born," Abraham told him. "My brother Nahor lives there. Find a good woman among his people for my son Isaac to marry."

When the servant arrived he was worn out from his long journey. He rested with his camels near a well. There, a woman named Rebekah was filling her water jar. The servant asked her for a drink. "I'll be glad to give you a drink," she answered. Then she saw the servant's thirsty camels and kindly offered them some water as well. Abraham's servant had brought along some gold bracelets to give as gifts, and he placed them on Rebekah's arm. "Thank you for your kindness," he told her. Then he said, "Tell me, who is your family?" Rebekah replied, "My father is Bethual, the son of Milcah and Nahor."

Abraham's servant knew that he had found the right woman for Isaac. Not only was Rebekah kind and generous, she was also Abraham's relative. The servant told Rebekah that he had come on behalf of her uncle Abraham. So she invited him back to her home to stay with her family.

DAY 21
Isaac and Rebekah
Genesis 24:28-67

Abraham's servant told Rebekah's father why he had come. "I have been sent to find a wife for my master Abraham's son, Isaac, among his relatives." Then the servant said, "Rebekah has impressed me with her gentle kindness. I would like her to come back with me and be Isaac's wife!" Rebekah's brother and father knew that this was God's plan. They were sad to see Rebekah go, but they were happy for her also.

Isaac was walking out in his father's field when the servant and Rebekah approached on their camels. Rebekah spotted Isaac right away. There was something special about him. "Who is that man walking out there?" Rebekah asked. The servant replied, "That's Isaac—the man you will marry!" So Isaac and Rebekah were married. They loved each other dearly, and Abraham could die happily knowing that Isaac had a family of his own.

DAY 22
Esau and Jacob
Genesis 25:19-26

Rebekah and Isaac wanted to have children, but God did not give them any. Isaac prayed for God to give them a child. Finally God answered his prayer. Rebekah became pregnant. She knew that she was pregnant with twins because she could feel them fighting with each other inside of her!

One day God came to Rebekah and said, "You will be blessed with two boys. But just like they are fighting inside of your womb, they will fight as they grow older too. They will separate into two different nations. The younger son will be strong and great. The older son will be his servant."

After nine long months of carrying the babies, Rebekah gave birth. The first baby was covered with bright red hair! They named him Esau. The second baby came out just behind, holding onto his brother's heel. They named him Jacob.

JACOB

DAY 23
Esau Makes a Promise
Genesis 25:27-34

Jacob and Esau were very different. Esau was an excellent hunter, while Jacob stayed at home. Esau was his father's favorite son, while Jacob was his mother's favorite son. Because Esau was older, he had certain birthrights that Jacob did not have.

One evening, Jacob was cooking a stew at his camp. Esau was out on a hunt when he smelled the delicious food wafting up from the pot. "That red stew you're cooking smells good, brother. May I have some?" Esau asked. "Yes," Jacob said, "I will give you some of my stew if you promise to give me something in return."

"What do you want?" asked Esau who was growing hungrier by the minute. He was happy to agree to anything. "Give me your birthrights," replied Jacob. Esau quickly reached for the bowl of stew. "Sure, why not?" Esau said without a thought. "What good are they to me, anyway?" Then he gulped down the soup, while Jacob smiled to himself. He knew that he had tricked his brother.

DAY 24
Isaac Blesses Jacob
Genesis 27:1-40

Isaac was now old and blind and close to dying. Before he died, he wanted to give his older son, Esau, a special blessing. It was his birthright as the elder son. Because Rebekah loved Jacob better, she wanted Jacob to have the blessing instead of his brother.

"Go to your father," Rebekah said to Jacob one evening. "He will think you are your brother, Esau, and he will give you his blessing!" But Jacob said, "My brother is a hairy man, and I am not. If my father finds out I am tricking him, he will curse me!" Rebekah was a clever woman. She quickly took some goat skins and wrapped them around Jacob's arms.

Then Jacob went to his father and said, "It's me, Esau." Isaac reached out and felt his hairy arms and believed that he was telling the truth. He laid his hands on his son's head and gave a blessing that endowed him with strength and courage. This blessing meant that God would be with him forever.

When Esau came home he rushed in to see his father. "Father, it's Esau—I'm home from my hunt, and I've brought you some meat!" Isaac suddenly realized he had given his blessing to the wrong son! Esau and his father were upset, but it was already too late. Jacob had God's blessing.

DAY 25
Rebekah Sends Jacob Away
Genesis 27:41-45

Esau was furious at his brother Jacob for tricking him. He had forgotten about the promise he had made to Jacob to give him his birthrights. He thought Jacob had unrightfully stolen his blessing. He boiled inside with anger toward Jacob. He decided that after his father died, he would kill Jacob.

When Rebekah found out what Esau planned to do, she ran to Jacob. "Jacob, my son!" she cried. "Your brother Esau is angrier with you than he's ever been! He is just waiting for the time when he can kill you! Listen carefully and do what I say. Go to the home of my brother Laban in the town of Haran and stay with him for a while.

When it is safe, I'll send for you to come home again."

Jacob packed his things and prepared to leave his home. Rebekah sent Jacob off on his long journey with a mournful wave good-bye. She was sorry to see her beloved son leave.

DAY 26
Jacob's Dream
Genesis 28:10-22

Jacob traveled over hot deserts and dry plains. He was worn out and stopped just before nightfall to find a good place to sleep. After he found a good spot, he lay down and rested his head on a rock for a pillow.

That night Jacob had a brilliant dream. He saw a stairway that reached from the ground up to heaven. God's angels were going up and down the stairway. God spoke to him and said, "Jacob, I have been with your father and your grandfather. Now I am with you. I will give you and your family the land on which you are now sleeping. Your descendents will be as many as the specks of dust on the ground! I will never leave you or the people that come after you!"

Jacob woke up early the next morning feeling rested and peaceful. He remembered his dream. Then he stood the rock he had used as a pillow on its end. He poured olive oil on the rock in honor of God. Then Jacob kneeled down and prayed, "Watch over me, Lord God, and I will worship You forever."

DAY 27
Jacob Works for Laban
Genesis 29:1-14

At last Jacob came to the land where his uncle lived. He looked out into a field and saw some shepherds by a well. He walked over to them and asked, "Do you know a man named Laban?"

"Yes, we do," they said. "And here comes his daughter Rachel with her sheep." The shepherds pointed to a girl who was heading toward the well. Jacob told Rachel that he was the son of her aunt Rebekah. Rachel was amazed and ran off to go find her father. Jacob went with her.

When Laban heard about Jacob, he ran out and kissed him. He put his arm around Jacob and said, "You are family. Stay here with us as long as you please." So Jacob stayed and lived with Laban and his children. He helped Laban by watching over his animals.

DAY 28
Jacob Marries Leah and Rachel
Genesis 29:15-30

One day Laban said to Jacob, "It isn't right for you to work without pay. What can I give you in return?" By this time Jacob had fallen in love with Rachel. Her sparkling eyes made him happy. So he told Laban, "If you let me marry Rachel, I will work seven years for you." So Laban and Jacob made an agreement.

Jacob worked seven years for Laban. He didn't complain once, and he always did his best. The time did not seem very long for Jacob because he was so in love with Rachel.

At last the day came for the wedding. Laban prepared a big feast with lots of friends and family. But when Laban brought out the bride, it was Leah, and not Rachel. Jacob panicked. He turned to Laban and said, "Where's Rachel? I worked seven years for her, not Leah!"

Laban told him, "In our country the older daughter must marry first. You can marry Rachel. But you'll have to work seven more years for me."

So Jacob married Rachel too. But he had to work seven more years for Laban.

DAY 29
Jacob Runs Away
Genesis 31:1-21

Jacob worked many years for Laban. But he had many children with his wives, and he was eager to start his own life.

Laban had several sons. They were jealous of their brother-in-law Jacob. "Jacob is richer than any of us," they complained. "But if it wasn't for our family, he wouldn't have anything at all."

Laban and his sons became less and less friendly toward Jacob. The Lord came to Jacob and said, "Go back to the land of your family, and I will bless you."

So Jacob sent for Rachel and Leah. He told them, "I have worked a long time for your father. Never once have I cheated him. And I've always done what was best for his sake. But every day I feel less welcome here. Now the Lord has come to me and told me what to do. It's time for me to return to Canaan."

Rachel and Leah said, "Do what the Lord asks, and we will go with you. You are a good man. But our father is treating all of us like strangers."

One day while Laban and his sons were out working, Jacob loaded the camels with all his possessions. Leah and Rachel gathered their children together and prepared to leave. Rachel went back and grabbed one last thing. She took her father's precious statue and hid it in her sack. Then the group left before Laban could see that they had gone.

DAY 30
Laban Catches Up With Jacob
Genesis 31:22-42

When Laban found out that Jacob had run away, he was furious. Then he saw that his precious statue was missing. So he rode after them, searching the countryside high and low. Seven days later he caught sight of them in the hill country of Gilead. But God appeared to Laban in a dream and said, "Don't say anything to Jacob—not a promise or a threat."

Laban was too angry to listen. He stormed in on Jacob's camp and yelled, "Why have you run away with my daughters like a kidnapper? And why have you stolen my statue like a thief?"

But Jacob stayed calm. He told Laban, "I left without telling you because otherwise you would not let us go. As for your statue, we haven't taken it. Go ahead, search our tents." Laban searched every tent, but he did not find anything.

Rachel had hidden the statue under a cushion, and she was sitting on top of it.

"I'm not a thief," Jacob finally told Laban. "In the last twenty years, I've never stolen a single thing from you. I worked fourteen years just to earn your daughters. Then I had to work another six years to buy your sheep and goats. All that time you tricked me out of my pay. God saw that I was in trouble, and He has helped me. He is on my side, and He has told me what to do."

DAY 31
An Agreement Is Made
Genesis 31:43-55

Laban told Jacob, "God has told me not to hurt you. And I cannot take my daughters from you because they are your family now. So let's make an agreement. We will pile up some large rocks in this place. These rocks will remind us that the Lord watches over both of us, even when we are apart from one another. I won't come after you or try to steal my daughters back. But you must promise to take good care of them and

my grandchildren too. Remember the Lord is watching us, and He will make sure we keep our agreement."

Jacob sacrificed an animal to the Lord to show that he would keep the agreement. Then together, Jacob and Laban ate the meat and spent the night on the mountain. In the morning Laban got ready to leave. He hugged and kissed his daughters and grandchildren. Then he went back to his home.

DAY 32
Jacob Wrestles a Stranger
Genesis 32:1-32

As Jacob was getting closer to Canaan, he sent messengers to find his brother Esau and tell him they were coming. He had not seen Esau for a long time. He was afraid Esau would still be angry with him. So he told the messengers to tell Esau, "Master, I'm your servant. I have been living with our uncle Laban all these years. Now I am coming home, and I hope that you will welcome my family when we arrive."

When the messengers returned, they told Jacob, "We've gone to your brother. He's coming this way with four hundred men!"

Jacob started to tremble. He was convinced that his brother was going to attack him and his family. So he divided his people and all his animals into two groups. "Each group should travel separately," he told them. "That way if one group is attacked, the other one can escape." Then Jacob prayed, "Lord, when I first crossed the Jordan River, I only had a walking stick. But now I have two large groups of people with me. You have given me so many blessings. Now please watch over me and my family."

The next day Jacob picked out his best goats and sheep. Then he picked out his fattest cows and his strongest donkeys. He said to his servants, "Take these animals to Esau. Tell him they are a gift from his brother." After the first herd was sent, Jacob sent a second and a third herd on to Esau. He told each messenger to say the same thing.

That night Jacob could not sleep. He kept thinking about Esau and his four hundred men. "Let me take you somewhere else," he told his family. "It's too dangerous to travel with me." So Jacob led them across to the other side of the river. Then he went back and slept alone.

Just before the sun rose, a man came and wrestled with Jacob. Jacob struggled and fought against Him. When the man saw that He could not win, He touched Jacob's hip and threw it out of joint. The sun was beginning to rise in the distance.

The man said, "It's morning; let go of Me."

But Jacob refused. "I won't let go of You until You bless me."

The man asked, "What's your name?"

"My name is Jacob," he answered.

"Jacob," said the man. "you have wrestled with God and you have won. Your name will now be changed to Israel."

"But who are You?" Jacob asked in amazement.

"Don't you know who I am?" the man asked. He laid His hands on Jacob and blessed him. Jacob got up and left, but he was limping because of his hip.

"I have seen God face to face," Jacob said. "And I am still alive."

DAY 33
Jacob Meets Esau
Genesis 33:1-17

Later that day Jacob saw Esau coming toward him. Behind Esau were hundreds of men. "Quick," Jacob told the children, "go to your mothers!"

Jacob went in front and bowed down seven times. Then he watched as Esau ran toward him. But instead of attacking Jacob, Esau hugged and kissed him.

"Whose children are these?" Esau asked as he looked around at Jacob's family.

Jacob answered, "These are the ones the Lord has kindly given me."

Then Esau said, "Thank you for the animals you sent. But I already have plenty, brother. Keep them for yourself!"

"No," Jacob insisted. "You have accepted me and treated my family with kindness. Please keep them as a gift from me."

"Okay," said Esau. "Shall we go now?"

Jacob answered, "I have my children and my animals. And you know how hard traveling is on them. Why don't you go on ahead, and we will meet again."

So Esau went home while Jacob and his family camped at a place called Succoth. It was there that Jacob built a house for his family and shelters for his animals.

DAY 34
Joseph's Dream
Genesis 37:1-11

Jacob had many sons. But his favorite son was Joseph. When Joseph was a teenager, he helped take care of the sheep with his older brothers.

One day Jacob gave Joseph a gift. It was a coat so colorful and bright that it was impossible not to stare at Joseph when he wore it. His brothers were jealous. They knew their father loved Joseph more than he loved them.

One evening Joseph had a dream. He told his brothers about it. "We were tying up bundles of wheat in a field. My bundle stood up, and your bundles bowed down to it."

His brothers scoffed, "So you think you'll rule over us, do you?"

Joseph had another dream. He told his brothers, but they just laughed and made fun of him again. So Joseph went to tell his father.

"The sun and the moon and eleven stars bowed down to me," he explained.

"What can it mean?" his father asked. "Will your mother and I and your brothers one day bow down to you?" Joseph didn't know. But Jacob kept thinking about his son's dream.

DAY 35
Joseph Is Thrown into a Well

Genesis 37:12-24

One day Joseph's brothers had taken their sheep to graze in a pasture near Shechem. Jacob told Joseph, "Go and find out how your brothers are doing."

So Joseph searched and found his brothers in a place called Dothan.

When Joseph's brothers saw him coming, they pointed and laughed. "Look," they said, "it's the dreamer! Why don't we throw him into a pit full of wild animals, then we'll see what happens to those dreams."

Reuben was one of Joseph's brothers. He tried to protect Joseph. "Let's not kill him," he said. "Let's just throw him into a dry well." Secretly Reuben planned to go back and rescue Joseph after his brothers had gone.

As soon as Joseph walked up to them, they tackled him to the ground and tore off his colorful coat. Then they drug him across the desert and threw him into a dry well so deep that he could not get out.

DAY 36
Joseph Is Taken to Egypt
Genesis 37:25-35

Joseph's brothers went back to their camp to eat. They heard a caravan rolling by and looked up. It was a group of Ishmaelites heading toward Egypt. Their camels were loaded with spices and perfumes they were going to sell in the marketplace.

Judah, one of Joseph's brothers, said, "What will we get out of throwing Joseph in a well? If we can sell him to these traders, we'll make some money. And after all, Joseph is our brother."

So the brothers ran back and pulled Joseph up out of the well. They sold him to the Ishmaelites for twenty pieces of silver. Then they watched the caravan rattle away down the road. "What are we going to say to our father?" they asked each other.

So they came up with a plan. First they killed a goat. Then they dipped Joseph's coat in the blood. When they came home, they tried to look very sad. They held up Joseph's coat and showed their father. "Isn't this Joseph's coat?" they asked him.

"Yes!" Jacob cried out. "He must have been torn to pieces by some wild animal!"

Then he hung his face in his hands and cried. The brothers tried to comfort him, but it was of no use. He told them, "I will be sad until the day I die."

DAY 37
In the House of Potiphar
Genesis 39:1-6

Meanwhile Joseph had finally arrived in Egypt. The Ishmaelite traders sold him to a man named Potiphar who was one of the king's most important officials. He kept Joseph in his house as a servant. While Joseph did his work, Potiphar watched him very closely. There was something special about Joseph. It was as if everything he did turned out to be a success. This was because the Lord was with Joseph.

So Potiphar made Joseph his personal assistant. He put Joseph in charge of his house and all of his property. Because of Joseph, Potiphar became rich.

53
JOSEPH

DAY 38
Joseph in Prison
Genesis 39:7-20

Joseph was not only smart; he was also strong and handsome. After a while, Potiphar's wife began to take an interest in him. "Come be with me," she said to him one day.

But Joseph told her, "Potiphar has put me in charge of everything he owns. The one thing he hasn't given me is you. So why would I want to sin against God and take you from him?" Then he turned around and left.

But Potiphar's wife didn't give up. She kept begging him to be with her. Joseph tried to ignore her. But one day she found him alone in a room. She caught him by his coat, but Joseph wriggled out of it and left the room.

Potiphar's wife yelled, "I've just been attacked—help, help!"

The servants came running in, and she held up Joseph's coat. "Look!" she cried. "Joseph has just attacked me. Here's his coat to prove it!" When Potiphar came home, his wife told him the same lie she had told the servants. He was outraged and threw Joseph in prison where all the criminals were kept.

JOSEPH

DAY 39
Joseph Interprets Dreams
Genesis 40:1-23

Some time later, the king's cook as well as his servant had made the king angry. He threw them into the same prison that Joseph was locked up in.

One night while they were sleeping in their cell, the servant and the cook had strange dreams. They woke up puzzled. They wondered what the dreams meant.

"God knows the meaning of dreams," Joseph told them. "Tell me your dreams, and I will tell you what they mean."

So the servant told him, "I saw three branches ripe with grapes. I squeezed the juice from them and served it to the king."

"In three days you will be forgiven," Joseph told him. "You'll serve the king just like you used to do. But when these things happen, tell the king about me and help me get out of here."

Then the cook said, "What about my dream? I was carrying three bread baskets on my head. The top one was full of food and the birds were pecking at it."

"In three days the king will have you

killed," Joseph told him. "And the birds will come and peck at your body."

Sure enough, everything happened just as Joseph said. The cook was killed. And the servant went back to serving the king at the palace. But he completely forgot to tell the king about Joseph.

DAY 40
The King's Dreams
Genesis 41:1-32

Two years later, the king of Egypt had two separate dreams that frightened him. He called in his magicians, but they did not know what the dreams meant. So he called in his wise men, but they did not know either. That's when the servant remembered Joseph.

"Your majesty," he said, "when I was in prison there was a young Hebrew there who could tell the meaning of dreams. Everything he said came true."

The king was willing to try anything. He sent for Joseph. Joseph shaved and changed his clothes. Then he went in to see the king.

The king told him, "I was standing on the banks of the Nile River in my dream. And then I watched as seven fat, healthy cows came up out of the water. But seven sick cows came up out of the water too. They ate the healthy ones. I also dreamed that seven full heads of grain were swallowed up by seven dry heads of grain."

"This is what your dreams mean," Joseph told the king. "There will be seven years of plenty. You and your people will have everything that you need. But then there will be a famine. For seven years Egypt will not have enough to eat. People everywhere will go hungry."

DAY 41
Joseph Is Made Governor over Egypt
Genesis 41:33-46

Joseph then told the king, "Don't be frightened by your dreams. God has let you know what will happen. Now let us prepare for it. First, put someone wise in charge of Egypt. Then make sure part of every harvest is saved. Extra food can be locked away in storehouses. When the time comes for the famine, we will be ready."

The king was impressed. "Joseph has the spirit of God in him," he told his officials. "No one could possibly handle this better than he can. Joseph will be in charge of Egypt from now on."

Then the king took off his royal ring and put it on Joseph's finger. He put a gold chain around Joseph's neck. And he let Joseph ride in a chariot next to his own. Whenever the people saw Joseph coming, they shouted, "Make way for Joseph!" He became the governor of Egypt, and everybody loved and respected him. But during this time he did not forget about the king's dreams. He made sure that everyone was prepared for the hard times ahead.

DAY 42
Seven Years of Famine
Genesis 41:47-57

During the first seven years, Egypt had the largest harvests they had ever seen. There was so much to eat that the people didn't know what it felt like to be hungry. Trying to count the grain was like trying to count the sand on a beach. But Joseph insisted that a part of every harvest remain untouched. Then he had the grain gathered and locked into storehouses.

Finally, the seven years of plenty came to an end. The harvests grew smaller and smaller until there was nothing at all. The animals were thin and bony from not eating. And soon the people began to starve. They went to the king and begged him for help. "We're hungry," they said. "We need something to eat." So the king sent the people to Joseph.

Joseph opened the storehouses and grain poured out. The people were able to eat again. But the famine had spread into lands far beyond Egypt. People were starving in other countries. So they came on long trips to Egypt in order to buy grain from Joseph.

DAY 43
Joseph's Brothers Go to Egypt
Genesis 42:1-24

Meanwhile in Canaan, Joseph's brothers and father were also starving.

Jacob told his sons, "Go to Egypt and buy some grain for us." So the ten brothers left for Egypt. But Jacob didn't let his youngest son Benjamin go. He loved Benjamin just as he had loved Joseph. He was afraid of letting Benjamin go anywhere and he always kept him at home.

The brothers traveled across the desert and into Egypt. They went to the governor and bowed before him. But they didn't realize that the governor was their very own brother.

Joseph recognized them right away. "You are spies," he told them angrily.

"No, we're not!" they replied. "We are from a family of twelve brothers. But one is dead, and the youngest is at home with our father."

"Let's see if you're telling the truth," Joseph said. "Go home and get your youngest brother. Bring him back here to me. If you don't, I will put you to death."

The brothers whispered to one another in their own language, "We are being punished by God because we were cruel to Joseph. God saw how we paid no attention to his cries and sold him like an animal long ago."

Joseph understood what they were saying, and he turned away and cried.

DAY 44
Joseph's Brothers Return to Canaan
Genesis 42:25-38

Before the brothers left for Canaan, Joseph had their sacks filled with grain. He secretly put the money they had paid for it back in their sacks as well. Then the brothers left for Canaan to get Benjamin.

When they stopped to rest, one of them opened up their sack to feed his donkey. A pouch full of silver coins was lying on top of the grain. "Why has my money been returned?" he asked the others. "It's right here in my sack."

The other brothers turned as white as ghosts. "Why is God doing this?" they said. "I am sure we paid for our grain. But now the governor will call us thieves!"

When they arrived home, the brothers told their father everything. "We must take Benjamin to Egypt," they explained. "That's the only way the governor will believe that we are not spies." They also told their father about the money they found in their sacks.

Jacob replied, "I'm an old man. My beloved Joseph was eaten by wild animals, and now you want to take Benjamin. I won't let him go."

So the brothers had to stay in Canaan and could not return to Egypt.

DAY 45
Jacob Lets Benjamin Go
Genesis 43:1-23

The grain that Joseph had given his brothers was running low. Jacob told his sons, "Go back and buy some more food."

"But father," they replied, "if we dare go back, we must bring Benjamin with us."

So Jacob agreed to let them take Benjamin. He also piled their bags full of special gifts like perfume, honey, and pistachio nuts. "Give these to the king and give him double the money for the grain. If he is angry with you, these things might help."

Then the brothers left for Egypt. When they arrived at the palace, they told the servant their story, saying, "Last time we came to Egypt, we paid money for the grain we bought. But when we stopped on our journey, we found the money right back in our sacks. We don't know how it got there, but we have brought the money back to you."

The servant said to them, "God must have put it there, because I received every coin you paid."

The brothers were confused. But they followed the servant inside and waited to speak with the governor.

DAY 46
Joseph and Benjamin
Genesis 43:24-34

The servant told Joseph that his brothers had arrived. So Joseph had the servant give them water to wash their feet and food for their donkeys. He came out to his brothers and they laid the gifts they had brought at his feet. Then they bowed down to him.

"How is your father?" Joseph asked them.

"Our father is alive and well," they replied.

Joseph looked at each of their faces, and then he spotted Benjamin. "This must be the youngest," he said, "the one you told me about." The other brothers nodded. Joseph walked up to Benjamin and said, "God bless you, my son." He loved Benjamin most of all, and his eyes began to fill with tears. He left the room so that his brothers wouldn't see him crying. Then he washed his face and took a deep breath. He came out and said, "Let's eat!"

The brothers were seated from the eldest to the youngest. "How does he know our ages?" the brothers wondered. But they said nothing. They ate and drank and had a good time. Whenever they were served a portion of food, Joseph made sure Benjamin got five times as much as the others.

DAY 47
The Stolen Cup
Genesis 44:1-13

The time came for Joseph's brothers to return home to their father. Joseph filled their sacks with grain. Then just like before, he had the money they paid for the grain put back in their sacks. He also had his own silver cup hidden in Benjamin's bag. He wanted to test his brothers and see if they had changed for the better.

Early the next morning, Joseph's brothers left on their donkeys. But just as they were leaving the city, Joseph told his servant, "Go after them! Ask them why they have stolen my silver cup after I have been so good to them."

The servant caught up with the brothers and did just as Joseph told him. "Why have you stolen my master's silver cup?" But the brothers didn't know what he was talking about.

"Why would we ever do such a thing?" they said. "We would never steal your master's cup. And if you find it among one of us, kill whoever took it. And the rest of us will be your master's slaves."

So the servant looked through each of their sacks. Finally he got to Benjamin's sack and opened it. Joseph's silver cup was laying right on top. Joseph's brothers couldn't believe it. Their hearts sank, and they ripped their clothes and cried. Then they went back to the governor.

DAY 48
Judah Pleads for Benjamin
Genesis 44:14-34

When the brothers came back to Joseph, they immediately threw themselves at his feet.

"We can't prove we are innocent," said Judah. "So we are now your slaves."

But Joseph told him, "No, I only want the man who has stolen the cup to stay with me. The rest of you can go home."

"Please, Sir!" Judah begged. "You have as much power as the king himself. I am only your slave. Don't get angry if I

JOSEPH

speak. Once I told you we were a family of twelve brothers. Two of those brothers are the sons of Rachel, my father's favorite wife. My father loves those sons very much. Long ago the oldest went missing. My father thinks he was eaten by a wild animal. He is still grieving over that son. And now there is only Benjamin left. I promised my father I would bring him back safely. Please— take me instead of Benjamin and let my brother go home. Otherwise my father will surely die of a broken heart. I couldn't bear to see my father so sad."

DAY 49
Joseph Tells the Truth
Genesis 45:1-15

Joseph knew it was time to tell his brothers who he was. "Come up close to me," he told them. His brothers obeyed, but they didn't understand why he had tears in his eyes. Then he spoke, "I'm your brother Joseph! You sold me long ago to the Ishmaelites. But don't blame yourselves for what you did," Joseph continued. "The Lord was with me. He has let us meet again. Even though you were cruel to me, it worked out in a wonderful way. The Lord let me save you and many other people from going hungry. Go home and tell your father his son is alive and that God has made me a ruler of Egypt!"

Joseph's brothers could not believe it. Their faces lit up with joy. They were grateful to their brother for forgiving them. Joseph went over to Benjamin first. They cried and kissed each other. Then Joseph hugged and kissed each one of his brothers.

He had not seen them since he was a boy, so they had a lot to say. They sat and talked together for several hours.

DAY 50
The King Welcomes Joseph's Family
Genesis 45:16-28

The king found out that Joseph's family had come to Egypt. He was pleased and told Joseph, "Have your brothers return to Canaan. Give them some extra wagons for their wives and children to ride back in. But be sure they bring your father. Tell him he does not have to bring anything. I will make sure he gets all the best things in Egypt."

So Joseph's brothers went back to Canaan. They told their father, "Joseph is alive, and he has become a ruler of Egypt!" But their father would not believe them. "It can't be true," he said. So they told their father everything Joseph had said. He still did not believe them. Then several wagons pulled up. "Look, Father!" his sons said. "The king has sent these for us to ride back in. Do you believe us now?"

Jacob saw the wagons and realized it was true. He clapped his hands together and cried, "My son Joseph is alive! And I will get to see him before I die."

DAY 51
Joseph's Family Settles in Egypt
Genesis 47:1-12

When Joseph's family had arrived in Egypt, he took them to meet the king. The king asked his brothers, "What does your family do for a living?"

"We are shepherds," they replied. "We have always raised sheep. But these days our pastures are dried up. There is no more grass for our animals to graze on."

"Stay here in Egypt," said the king. "The land of Goshen has green grass and good soil. You can raise your flocks there. I will even put you in charge of some of my own animals."

Then the king turned to Joseph's father. "How old are you?" he asked.

"I have lived a hundred and thirty years," Jacob told him. "I've had to move from place to place all my life. But so did my parents and grandparents."

Then Jacob laid his hands on the king and gave him a blessing.

Joseph helped his family settle in Goshen. He made sure that each brother had a piece of land and every single family had plenty to eat.

DAY 52
Jacob Blesses Joseph's Two Sons
Genesis 48:1-2, 8-22

Jacob was old and nearly blind. Joseph knew that his father would die soon. So he brought his two sons, Manasseh and Ephraim, to be blessed by their grandfather.

The boys stood by their grandfather's bed. "I can barely see you; come closer," Jacob told them. So Manasseh came up to Jacob's right side, and Ephraim came up to his left. Jacob kissed and hugged both of them. "I never thought I would see you again, Joseph," Jacob said. "And now here I am with your two sons!"

Jacob held out his arms to bless them. But just before he did, he crossed his arms and put his left hand on Manasseh and his right hand on Ephraim.

Joseph said, "Wait, Father! The older boy is supposed to be blessed by your right hand. You made a mistake."

Jacob replied, "Trust me, Son. Manasseh will become great. But your younger son Ephraim will be even greater. His family will become many nations."

Then Jacob told Joseph, "I am about to die. But God will be with you. He is going to give us the land He has promised. But in the meantime, I'm giving you the hillside I captured from the Amorites."

DAY 53
Joseph's Promise
Genesis 50:15-21

After Jacob died, Joseph's brothers started to worry. They thought that Joseph might still be angry with them.

So they sent Joseph a message, saying, "Before our father died, he reminded us of all the cruel things we did to you. He has told us to ask you for forgiveness. Please forgive all the terrible things we did. We sinned, but we are still your brothers."

Joseph read the message and cried. Just then his brothers came in and threw themselves at his feet. "We are your servants," they said.

Joseph wiped the tears from his eyes and said, "Don't be afraid of me. I have no right to be angry with what God has decided. It's true you tried to harm me, but God made it turn out for the best. I promise I will take care of you and your children."

Joseph's brothers knew that Joseph had truly forgiven them, and he would keep his promise.

DAY 54
Slavery in Egypt
Exodus 1:6-14

While Joseph was alive, the Hebrews lived in peace. But many years after Joseph died, a new king ruled over Egypt. This king did not know about all the good things Joseph had done. He wanted the Hebrews out of Egypt. "They have taken over our land," he complained. "Soon they will take over our people too."

So the king forced the Hebrews to be slaves. They had to work all day. They had to mix cement and carry bricks and build entire cities. It was hard work, and they were not treated very well. But even though the work was miserable, their families grew larger and spread throughout the land. This just made the Egyptians hate them even more.

DAY 55
The King's Order
Exodus 1:15-22

The king called in Shiphrah and Puah to see him. They were midwives who helped women give birth to their babies. He told them, "I want you to kill every baby boy among the Hebrews." The midwives were shocked, but they agreed to the king's demand.

When the time came for a Hebrew woman to give birth, the midwives hoped the child would be a girl. But if it was a boy, they still would not kill the child.

The king knew the women had disobeyed his orders. "Didn't you hear me?" he asked them angrily. "I told you to kill all the Hebrew boys!"

The women made up a story. "Your majesty," they told him, "Hebrew women have their babies much quicker than Egyptian women. By the time we arrive, it's already too late to kill them." So the king sent out a command all over Egypt saying, "As soon as a Hebrew boy is born, he must be thrown into the Nile River!"

MOSES

DAY 56

Moses Is Born

Exodus 2:1-4

During this time there was a man and a woman from the tribe of Levi living in Egypt. The woman had just given birth to a baby boy. When she heard the king's order, she panicked. She loved her baby; he was her pride and joy. So she searched her house and found a spot where she could hide him and kept him hidden for three months. During this time the king's officials were roaming the country. They were killing every baby boy that belonged to the Hebrews.

The woman decided she had to find a better hiding spot. So she gathered some long reeds and weaved a basket out of them. She put her baby in the basket. Then she sneaked down to the riverbank, and she let the basket float among the bulrushes on the water. Miriam, the baby's older sister, had followed her mother down to the river. Her mother went back home but Miriam stayed crouching down in the grass. She wanted to watch over her brother and see what would happen to him.

DAY 57
Saved by a Princess
Exodus 2:5-10

That evening the king's daughter was heading down toward the river to bathe. As she approached the riverbank, she saw something floating on the water. "Quick, go and fetch that basket!" she called to her servant. The servant waded into the river and carried the basket back to the princess. They were surprised to see a little baby boy inside. His cheeks were rosy from crying. "The poor child!" exclaimed the princess. "He must be one of the Hebrew babies." The princess picked up the baby, and she rocked him in her arms until he fell asleep.

Miriam had been watching the whole thing. She went over to the princess and said politely, "Your majesty, I can see that you love this little baby. Perhaps I could find a woman to care for him until he is old enough for you to keep him."

The princess smiled at Miriam. "Yes, that's a fine idea," she said. So Miriam took her little brother back to their mother. She raised the boy until he was old enough to be adopted. Then she took him to the princess. "He's yours now," the boy's mother said. "What will you name him?" The princess said, "His name will be Moses."

DAY 58
Moses Stands Up for a Slave
Exodus 2:11-15

Moses grew up in the palace. He had the best of everything. At mealtimes he had plenty to eat. And he wore only the finest clothes. One day Moses took a walk outside of the palace grounds. He saw the Hebrews slaving away under the hot sun. Then he noticed that one of them was being whipped by an Egyptian slave master. Moses was furious and ran over to save the man who was being beaten. He grabbed the slave master with both hands and killed him. Moses tried to hide the body in the sand. But someone found out about what he had done. Everybody began to gossip about Moses. The king was so angry that he sent his men to arrest Moses and have him killed. Moses had to run away. He did not stop until he crossed the border and reached the land of Midian in the desert.

DAY 59
Jethro Welcomes Moses
Exodus 2:15-21

Once Moses arrived in Midian, he was tired and thirsty. He sat down by a well and had a drink of water. Just then, the seven daughters of a priest named Jethro came to the well to give water to their sheep and goats. But a group of shepherds tried to bully them. Moses stood up for the girls and chased the shepherds away. Then Moses offered to water the women's sheep and goats himself. They thanked him and went back to their father's house.

"Why did you take so long?" he asked when they came in. The women told their father about the shepherds who bullied them. "But a young Hebrew helped us," they explained. "And he even watered our flocks."

"Why didn't you invite him home?" Jethro replied. "We must return his kindness and let him stay with us."

The girls went back to find Moses. They invited him to come and live with them. So Moses stayed with Jethro, and he even married one of his daughters named Zipporah.

DAY 60
The Burning Bush
Exodus 3:1-10

One day Moses was guarding Jethro's sheep and goats on the mountainside. He was wandering along the trail when suddenly, something incredible happened. He saw a bush light up in flames. As he stepped closer to get a better look, he noticed that the bush was not burning up. Then the voice of God called to Moses from the bush, "Moses, I am here to tell you what I plan to do. I have not forgotten My beloved people. I know that they are suffering as slaves in Egypt. They have prayed to Me, and I will answer their prayers. I have something special in store for them. And I have chosen you, Moses, to lead My people out of Egypt. You will bring them safely to the land I have promised your ancestors. Now go to the king, and ask him to free My people."

DAY 61
Moses Can Perform Miracles
Exodus 3:6, 11; 4:1-9

Moses was frightened. He hid his face behind his hands. "But why have You chosen me?" he asked God.

"Don't worry Moses," God replied. "I am with you! Throw your walking stick on the ground." Moses obeyed. When the stick hit the ground, it turned into a slithering snake at Moses' feet. "Now pick the snake up by the tail," God said. Moses bent down and grabbed the tail. The snake went stiff and turned back into a walking stick.

Then the Lord said, "Now put your hand under your shirt." Moses obeyed. When he pulled his hand out again, it was ghostly white and covered with scales. Moses was scared, so he put his hand under his shirt and took it out again. Now it was normal. God said, "These miracles will show everyone that I have sent you to save My people. If they still do not believe you, take some water from the Nile River. Pour it on the ground, and I will turn the water into blood before their eyes."

DAY 62
Aaron and Moses
Exodus 4:10-17, 27-31

"Lord," Moses said, "if I go to the king, he will not listen to me. Besides, I am not a good speaker. I stutter, and I talk too slowly."

So the Lord said, "Your brother Aaron is a good speaker. He will speak for you. I will be with both of you and tell you what to say."

So Moses met Aaron on the mountainside. They greeted each other with a kiss. Moses told Aaron everything God had said. Aaron agreed to go with Moses and see the king. But first they met with the Hebrew leaders.

"The time has come for the Lord to lead his people out of Egypt! And Moses is the man God has chosen to lead them," Aaron told them. The leaders did not believe them. "We've been in slavery for hundreds of years!" they said. "Why would God free us now?"

To show them it was true, Moses took his walking stick and threw it on the ground. The men jumped back in surprise when the stick turned into a snake. Then Moses performed the other miracles. The leaders realized that Moses and Aaron were telling the truth. They bowed down on the ground and thanked the Lord for His goodness.

DAY 63
"Let My People Go"
Exodus 5:1-5; 7:3-13

Moses and Aaron traveled to Egypt and arrived at the king's palace. They stood before him and said, "God has appeared to us, and He has asked that you let His people go!" But the king barely even looked at Moses and Aaron.

"Why should I obey this God of yours?" he snarled. "Go away." Aaron threw the walking stick on the ground, and it turned into a snake. The king thought they were just playing a trick. He called in his magicians, and they used their secret powers to make snakes out of sticks too. Then Aaron's snake swallowed the other snakes. But the Lord had made the king stubborn.

"You're wasting my time and everyone else's too," he told Moses and Aaron. "Go away! I will not let your people go."

DAY 64
Blood and Frogs
Exodus 7:1-5, 14-25; 8:1-15

Moses and Aaron felt discouraged. But the Lord came to them and said, "I will bring ten plagues on Egypt, one after the other. These horrible things will not happen to the Hebrews because I will keep them safe."

Then God told Moses and Aaron to take the walking

stick and hold it out over the Nile River. They obeyed and watched the water turn into blood. The fish in the water died, and people had to walk around pinching their noses from the awful stink. Not a drop of clean water was left anywhere in Egypt. When the king saw this, he began to worry. But he still refused to let the people go.

Now God sent the second plague—frogs. They went hopping and croaking down streets and right into people's homes. Not even the king could get away from them. Frogs jumped on his dinner table and slept on his pillow. "Please," the king begged Moses and Aaron, "I will let your people go!

Just get rid of these frogs!" Moses prayed, and God made all the frogs die. But once the king saw that things were back to normal, he still did not let God's people go.

DAY 65
Gnats and Flies
Exodus 8:16-32

The Lord said to Moses, "Take the walking stick and strike the ground with it. I will turn all the dust into gnats, and they will swarm all over Egypt." Moses obeyed. And the sky became black with little buzzing gnats. Gnats landed in people's hair and covered the animals.

"What's the big deal?" said the king. "My magicians can turn dust into gnats too." But when the magicians tried, they could not do it.

"God must have done this," they told the king. But the king didn't listen.

Then the Lord said to Moses and Aaron, "Go to the king and say, 'The Lord commands you to let His people go.' When he refuses, I will send another plague upon Egypt." They obeyed. But just like God said, the king wouldn't listen. So the Lord sent millions of flies to infest Egypt. People had to swat them away all day long. They could not get any work done, and they couldn't sleep at night. The king begged Moses and Aaron, "I will do whatever you ask, as long as you get these flies out of here!" So Moses prayed, and God took the flies away. But the king was not telling the truth. He still refused to let God's people go.

MOSES

DAY 66
Disease and Sores
Exodus 9:1-12

The Lord sent Moses to the king again. "If you don't let God's people go," Moses said, "He will bring an awful disease on all your animals." The king was stubborn. He still would not let the people go.

So the very next day, God sent a disease on the Egyptians' animals. Their horses and donkeys, camels and cattle, sheep and goats—all got sick and died. The people could no longer get meat or milk. There were no donkeys or camels to carry heavy loads. And they had no wool to use for warm blankets and clothes.

Next God commanded Moses and Aaron to scoop up ash from the stove. Then He sent them to the king. Moses threw the ash into the air, and it turned into a disease. The Egyptians and their animals became covered with sores. Their skin was spotted like a leopard, and they were covered with oozing blisters. Even the king's magicians were too miserable to get out of bed. But the king still refused to let God's people go.

DAY 67
Hail and Locusts
Exodus 9:13-35; 10:1-20

Then God told Moses, "Stretch your arms toward the sky. I will send the worst hailstorm in the history of Egypt." So Moses lifted his arms up, and the sky grew dark. Thunder rumbled loudly. Lightning flashed through the black clouds and struck the ground. Then God sent hail. The hailstones fell like heavy rocks—they pounded the earth and flattened the harvests. The king was terrified. He sent for Moses and Aaron and told them, "I will let your people go if you get rid of this hail!" But after God stopped the hailstorm, the king still didn't keep his promise.

"How much longer are you going to disobey the Lord?" Aaron asked the king. "Your people are suffering. Your animals have died. Your country is a disaster."

"All right, all right," said the king, "you can go, but only the men." Moses and Aaron refused the king's offer. They knew that God wanted all of them to leave Egypt, not just some of them. So the Lord sent a wind full of locusts. They ate everything, and there was not a single flower or green plant left in Egypt. The king still refused to let the people go.

DAY 68
Darkness and Death
Exodus 10:21-26; 11:1-8

Now the Lord told Moses, "Stretch your arms up to the sky. I will cover Egypt with darkness thick enough to touch." Moses obeyed, and blackness covered everything. No one could see anything at all. The people stayed inside their homes and did not come out for three days. The king called Moses and Aaron to him and said, "All right! You may go, but you must leave your animals behind."

"No," Moses said. "We will all go together, even the animals."

Then the Lord said to Moses, "I will send one last punishment on the king of Egypt and his people. This time the king will not only let you leave, he'll chase you out."

Moses went to the king and said, "The Lord has asked you to let His people go, and you have refused. Tonight He will pass over Egypt. Everywhere He goes, the firstborn son in every Egyptian family will die. No family will be left out, including your own son. When this happens, you will know it, because there will be so much crying that you will have to cover your ears. But the Hebrews will

88
MOSES

have no reason to cry. You will know that the Lord is with His people, and you will let us go."

DAY 69
God Keeps His Promise
Exodus 12:1-41

The Lord told Moses and Aaron to speak to His people. They told them, "The time has come for the Lord to lead our families out of Egypt! He has asked you to celebrate with a special Passover meal. Cook a young lamb and eat it with bitter herbs and bread. After you have finished eating, put some blood from the lamb on the doorposts. Have sandals on your feet and walking sticks in your hands. There will be a long journey ahead."

The people did everything God told them to do. During the night God moved through the houses of the Egyptians, and every firstborn son died. But He passed over the houses that had blood on the doorposts.

Before dawn, the whole country was crying for their lost sons. The king's son died too. He called for Moses and Aaron. "Get out of here," he told them, "and never come back!"

Everything happened just as God had said. Finally the Hebrews were free! Moses called all the people together and they finally left.

DAY 70
The Exodus
Exodus 13:17-22; 14:1-4

God led His people through the deserts of Egypt. He never left them. During the day He appeared as a cloud leading the way before them. At night, He lit up their path in the form of a flaming light. The people walked a long way, and when they came to a place called Etham near the border, they needed a rest. They set up camp, but God told them to turn back and camp in a different spot. He wanted the king and His army to chase after Israel. He was going to show His great power and help the Israelites win. The people obeyed, and camped where God led them. Then they pitched their tents, tied up their animals, and went to sleep.

DAY 71
The King's Chase
Exodus 14:5-14

The king of Egypt got the news that the Hebrews were leaving his country. "Look what we've done!" he shouted to his men. "We let them go, and now we'll have no slaves." He had already forgotten about the plagues the Lord had sent on the Egyptian people. Every horse-drawn chariot was loaded with soldiers. The king led them on a chase to capture the people of Israel.

Finally they caught up with them at their camp. When the Hebrews saw the chariots heading towards them, they were frightened and ran to Moses. "You brought us out of slavery only to die here in the desert," they moaned, "and now the king will kill us all!" But Moses knew that the Lord had a plan. "Don't be afraid," he said. "You will see God work His miracles. Have faith! God will take care of us."

DAY 72
The Parting of the Red Sea
Exodus 14:15-31

God told Moses, "Tell the people to start heading toward the Red Sea. When you get to the water, hold your walking stick out. I will part the waters, and you will be able to march across to the other side." So Moses led the people toward the sea. As they approached the shore, Moses held his walking stick out.

The waters began to part straight down the middle and build up like two mighty walls on either side. Israel crossed through the Red Sea. The Egyptian army was amazed. They followed right behind in their chariots.

Once Moses reached the other side, he waited until all the people had safely crossed over. Then he held out his walking stick above the water, and the waves crashed together again. The Egyptian army drowned with their chariots in the wild, foamy waves.

DAY 73
Water for the Thirsty
Exodus 15:1-27

The Israelites celebrated their victory. The Lord had saved them! They sang out, "Praise the Lord for His great victory! He has thrown the horses and their riders into the sea." Moses' sister Miriam shook her tambourine and began to dance and sing. The other women joined in and praised the Lord with their songs.

After many hours of rejoicing, Moses led the people into the Shur Desert. They walked for three days without water. The people were tired and thirsty.

Finally they found some water at a place called Marah. But as soon as they took a drink, they spit it out again. The water tasted bitter and had a horrible aftertaste. "What are we going to drink?" they asked Moses. But Moses didn't know, so he prayed. God told Moses to throw a piece of wood into the water. Moses obeyed, and the water turned clean and fresh. The people drank as much as they could. Then they filled up their casks and walked on.

That evening, they came to an oasis with twelve springs and seventy palm trees. They stopped there and camped for the night.

DAY 74
Food for the Hungry
Exodus 16:1-31

The people walked through the desert a long time. They were heading toward Mount Sinai across the western edge of the desert. The sun beat down on them, and they were running out of food. "It's a shame we're not slaves in Egypt anymore," they began to complain. "At least we had bread and meat and a chance to sit down. Out here we'll starve!"

God spoke to Moses and said, "I have heard My people's cry. Tell them I will send food from heaven. Then they will know I am God, and they will trust in Me."

That evening a flock of quail landed in the campsite among their tents. The people roasted the birds and ate the delicious meat. Then they went to sleep. The next morning they woke up to a sound like falling rain. When they peeked out of their tents, they saw the ground was covered with little white flakes. "What is this?" they asked each other. Moses answered, "This is the bread God has given us to eat today." The people called the bread "manna." It tasted like sweet wafers made with honey. The people gathered up the manna and ate till they were full.

DAY 75
The People Doubt God
Exodus 17:1-7

The Lord led the people, and they traveled onward. But their water supply had already run out, and they were getting thirsty again. "We need something to drink," the people complained to Moses. "Do you want us to die of thirst?" Moses didn't know when they would find water again. He bowed his head in prayer. "Forgive the people, Lord. They are impatient. But it's true, they do need water."

God told Moses, "When you get to the rock at the foot of Mount Sinai, hit it with your walking stick. I will make water pour out of it."

Moses trusted God and led the people to the rock. But the people were still complaining bitterly, saying, "Is God really with us? Is Moses telling us the truth when he says

God will bring us water?" Finally they reached the rock. Moses struck it with his stick, and just as God had promised, water poured out. They drank it and felt strong again. But they still doubted God. So Moses named that place Massah, which means "testing," and Meribah, which means "complaining."

DAY 76
At the Foot of Mount Sinai
Exodus 19:1-20

Two months had passed since the people of Israel left Egypt. The people camped at the foot of Mount Sinai. Moses went up to the top to pray to God. God told Moses, "I have cared for you just like a mighty eagle cares for his young. If you continue to obey Me, Israel will be My holy nation. Go and tell the people this good news."

So Moses went back down the mountain. He told the people what God had said, and the people promised to love and obey the Lord. They stayed at the camp three more days and celebrated God's goodness. But on the third day, they woke up to storm clouds. There was thunder and lightning, and black smoke covered the top of Mount Sinai. Then the people heard the sound of a horn blast. Moses called the people together, and he took them to the foot of the mountain. They looked up and saw a fire on top of the mountain. Then God told Moses to climb the mountain and meet Him there.

DAY 77
The Ten Commandments
Exodus 20:1-17; 31:18

When Moses reached the top, God spoke to him. "I am God, the One who has brought you out of slavery in Egypt," He said. "These are My Ten Commandments:
  Do not worship any god but Me.
  Do not worship idols and false images.
  Do not swear and misuse My name.
  Remember the seventh day—the
    Sabbath, and keep it holy.
  Respect your father and mother.
  Do not murder.
  Be faithful in marriage.
  Do not steal.
  Do not tell lies about others.
  Do not want anything that belongs to
    someone else."
  When God had finished speaking to Moses, He gave him two stone tablets with the Ten Commandments carved into them.

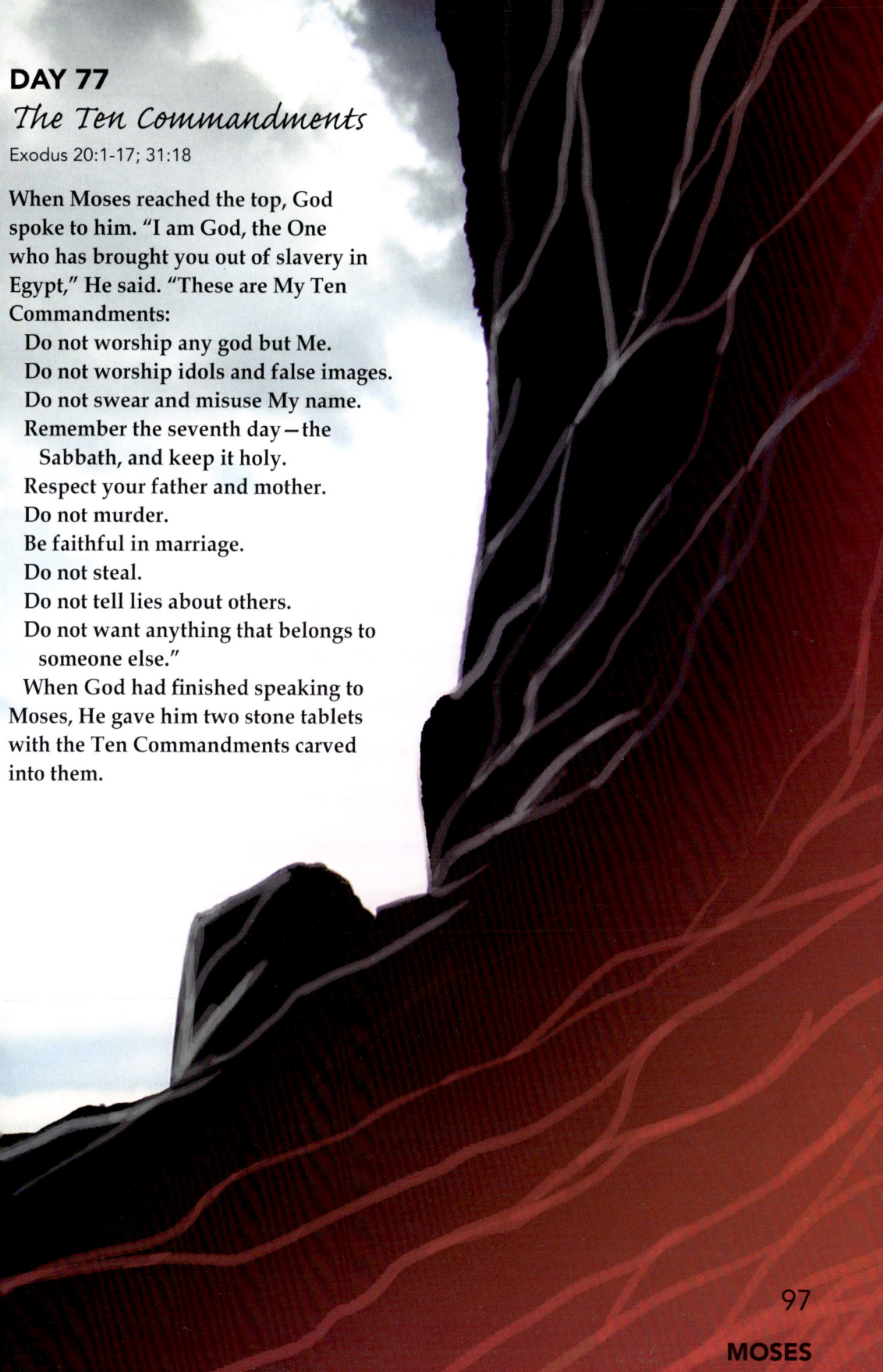

DAY 78
God's Promises for Israel
Exodus 23:20-33

God said to Moses, "I will send an angel ahead of you on your journey. The angel will bring you to the land I have prepared for your people. There are people already living in this land. But these people worship false gods, and they will try to get you to worship their gods. Don't make any agreements with them. You must remain faithful to Me. If you do, I will bless your land. Your valleys will flow with milk and honey; your fruit will grow plump and sweet; your crops will always be plentiful. I will take away sickness among your people. New babies will be born, and people will live happy lives into old age." These are the things God promised Moses and the people of Israel.

DAY 79
The People Agree to Obey God
Exodus 24:4-11

Moses wrote down everything the Lord told him. He was eager to tell the people of Israel. But first he wanted to build an altar to worship God. He woke up early the next morning and set up twelve large stones, one for each of the twelve tribes. Then he burned special offerings and sacrificed bulls. Finally he called all the people together. He read to them aloud from the Lord's Ten Commandments. When he finished, the people shouted, "We will obey the Lord!"

Moses took some of the blood from the sacrifices and sprinkled it on the people. "With this blood the Lord makes His agreement with you," Moses told them. Then Moses and Aaron went up to the mountain together with some of the leaders. God met them on the mountain. Under His feet was something like a jewel blue pavement, bright as the sun. The leaders of Israel were amazed. They thought that if they saw God, they would die. But they didn't die, so they stayed on the mountain and ate and drank.

DAY 80
The Golden Calf
Exodus 32:1-12

While Moses was on the mountaintop, the people down below began to feel restless. "Why is Moses taking so long?" they complained. "He may as well have died up there!" The people went to Aaron and said to him, "We need a god to worship. We can't wait any longer for Moses." So Aaron asked the people to give him all their gold jewelry. Then Aaron melted the jewelry down and molded it into a golden calf. The people began to worship the calf as a god. "This is the god that brought us out of Egypt!" they cheered as they danced around the golden calf and bowed down before it. Then they ate and drank and celebrated their new god.

The Lord saw all of this, and He was angry. "Go and see what the people are doing!" He said to Moses. "They are already disobeying Me. I'm angry enough to destroy them!"

Moses pleaded, "Please, God, don't harm them. Otherwise the Egyptians will laugh and say You saved us just to destroy us."

DAY 81
Moses Destroys the Idol
Exodus 32:15-20, 30-32

Moses ran back down the mountain still holding the Ten Commandments. Finally he came to the foot of Mount Sinai where his people were dancing around the statue of a golden calf and worshipping it. "Why are you worshipping a dead statue?" Moses shouted. "The one true God is with you. Have you forgotten Him already?"

Moses was so angry, he threw the stone tablets on the ground, and they shattered into little pieces. Then Moses marched over to the golden calf and ground it up into dust. He threw the dust into the

101

MOSES

people's drinking water. Then Moses ordered the people to drink it. He did not want any trace left of the false idol.

The next day Moses prayed for the people. He asked God to forgive their sins. God listened to Moses, and He promised to stay with the people of Israel.

DAY 82
God Shows Mercy
Exodus 33:12-23; 34:28-30

Moses prayed to the Lord, "You have chosen me to lead Your people. But I still don't know who will help me. Let me know Your plans. Then I can obey you. Remember You have chosen the nation of Israel to be Your people."

The Lord replied, "Be at peace. I will go with you."

Moses said, "If You go with us, everyone will know that You love Your people. Everyone will say that the nation of Israel is blessed."

The Lord told him, "You've made Me happy. And you've always obeyed Me. Because I am your friend, I will do just as you have asked."

Moses said, "Lord, since You are pleased with me, let me see You!"

The Lord answered, "You cannot see My face. But I will hide you in the rock's cleft and put My hand over your eyes. Once I pass by, I will take My hand away. You will see My back. And My glory will pass over you."

After forty days and forty nights on the mountain, Moses finally returned to the people with two new stone tablets. The people were amazed and dared not go close to him. His face was shining with the glory of God.

DAY 83
The Second Ten Commandments
Exodus 34:1-10

God told Moses, "Be ready in the morning. Come up to Mount Sinai and bring two stone tablets with you. I will write the Ten Commandments on the tablets like the first ones that were broken. But don't bring anyone with you."

Moses cut two stones. Then he carried them up to the mountain. The Lord came down in a cloud and stood beside Moses.

"I am the Lord," He said. "I love My people, and I forgive their sins."

Moses bowed to the ground and prayed, "God, if You are pleased with me, go with us. Let us be Your people."

God replied, "I promise to be with you. And I will perform miracles for you. The people in your land will see My great works and know that I am the Lord."

103

MOSES

DAY 84
The People Grumble About Being Hungry
Numbers 11:4-20

The people of Israel left their camp at Mount Sinai. But they had not traveled very far before they began to complain again. "This manna is getting boring. Where is our meat?" they whined. "We might've been slaves in Egypt, but at least we had fish and garlic and melons."

The Lord heard everything they said. They were not thankful for the food He gave them. "God," Moses prayed, "My people keep whining for meat. But where can I get it for them? You made me responsible for all these people, and yet they're not my children. How am I supposed to help them?"

God answered Moses, "Tell the people not to worry. I have been among them and heard them complain. Tomorrow they will get more meat than they could ever eat."

DAY 85
The Lord Sends Quail
Numbers 11:31-35

God sent a strong wind over the sea. The wind carried a whole flock of quail into Israel's camp. There were so many birds that they began to land on top of one another until they were piled up three feet high. The people rushed around trying to get as much as they could. They stuffed them into bushels. They took the biggest quail and roasted them. But before they could sink their teeth into the meat, God's anger shook the camp. He had been watching the people's greedy ways. Some had not thanked God before they began to eat. Others complained they had no wine or fruit to eat with it. So the Lord sent a disease into the camp to punish the people. The ones who had been selfish died. The others buried them. They called the place "Graves for the Greedy." Then they packed up their camp and traveled on to a place called Hazeroth.

DAY 86
Miriam and Aaron Are Jealous of Moses
Numbers 12:1-15

Moses was a humble servant of God. He never thought he was better than anyone else. But his brother and sister were jealous of him. Miriam and Aaron gossiped about Moses behind his back. "Who does Moses think he is?" they asked. "Why does he get all the glory?"

The Lord heard them say these things about their brother. He was disappointed and called them at once to the sacred tent. God came down in a cloud and stood before them. "I am the Lord," He said. "Moses is My servant and the leader of My people. He has been faithful to Me. Why are you putting him down?" Then God left, but He was angry.

Aaron turned to Miriam and stepped back in fright. She had turned as white as snow. The Lord had given her leprosy. Aaron ran to Moses. "Brother!" he cried. "We have talked badly about you. But don't let God punish us for the foolish things we've said. Save Miriam from this horrible sickness."

So Moses prayed to God, "Please forgive my sister and heal her."

God answered, "I will do as you say. But first you must make her stay outside the camp for seven days as punishment."

So the people of Israel stayed at their camp for seven days until Miriam returned.

DAY 87
Twelve Men Are Sent into Canaan
Numbers 13:1-24

God told Moses to choose one leader from each tribe of Israel. He told Moses, "Send the twelve men ahead to explore the land of Canaan. This is the land I am giving to you and to the people of Israel."

So Moses chose twelve men. "Find out everything you can about Canaan's land," Moses instructed them. "Return and tell us about the land and the people. And bring back some fruit so we can see how well things grow."

The twelve men agreed and left for Canaan. As they went through the Southern Desert, the scouts came to the town of Hebron. They found three tribes living there. Then they went to a valley with huge vineyards and trees bursting with fruit. The men cut off a bunch of grapes. The bunch was so heavy and full of juicy purple grapes that two men had to carry it! They also took some pomegranates and figs. They called the place "Bunch Valley."

DAY 88
The Twelve Scouts Return
Numbers 13:25-33

After forty days of exploring the land of Canaan, the twelve men returned back to camp. "Canaan is an amazing land," they told the people. "Just look at the size of this fruit!" The men passed around the grapes they had brought with them. "But the people there are strong, and the cities have high walls all around them. There are tribes living along the sea and down in the valleys and all over the desert."

The people began to worry. "How can we capture this land?" they asked each other. "There are too many people living there already." But Caleb wasn't worried. He was one of the Israeli leaders. "Let's take the land," he said. "I know we can do it!"

"There is no way we can take the land," the other men told him. "We saw the people there, and they are like giants. They were so big that we felt as little as grasshoppers."

MOSES

DAY 89
Moses Speaks to Israel
Deuteronomy 8:1-18

Moses heard the people doubting, so he spoke to them, "Don't you want to go into the Promised Land? Have you already forgotten how your God has led you through the desert full of snakes and scorpions? He wanted to test your faith, so He made you go hungry. But He never left you. He sent manna from the heavens for your hunger. Then He poured water out of a rock for your thirst. God knows that His people need more than food and drink to live on. So He gave you the precious words He spoke. He is bringing you to the land He has promised your ancestors. It is a land with wheat and barley, and vineyards and orchards. We have already seen the size of the fruit that grows there. There will be plenty to eat and drink! But after you have had your fill, don't be proud. Don't forget you were once slaves in Egypt. The Lord was the One who set you free. The Lord gives you strength."

DAY 90
The Last Days of Moses
Deuteronomy 34:1-10

The people journeyed onward and camped at a place called Moab.

God led Moses on ahead across the Jordan River, while the others stayed behind. God took Moses to Mount Nebo. From the top Moses could see far and wide across the horizon. He could see the cities in the north. He could see the Mediterranean Sea far out west. And he could see the valleys in the South. Then God said to Moses, "This is the land I promised Abraham, Isaac, and Jacob that I would give to Israel. I have let you see it. But you cannot enter into it with your people. Now it's time for you to come and be with Me."

So Moses died in Moab. He was one hundred and twenty years old. Israel stayed at their camp and wept for Moses for thirty days. He had been their leader and God's special servant. They never forgot the amazing things Moses did for Israel.

DAY 91
Joshua Becomes the Leader of Israel
Joshua 1:1-9

Joshua had been Moses' special helper. God came to Joshua and said, "Now that Moses is gone, you must lead the people across the Jordan River into the Promised Land. Wherever you go, I will give you that land."

Then God said, "I will be with you, just as I was with Moses. Be strong and brave. Remember what Moses taught you. Read the Book of Law and obey My words. Think about what My words mean, and try to understand them. If you obey Me, there will be no reason to be afraid. I will be there to help you wherever you go."

So Joshua became the new leader of Israel.

DAY 92
The Eastern Tribes Promise to Help
Joshua 1:10-18

Back at the camp, Joshua prepared the people to march into the Promised Land.

"Pack plenty of food," he told them. "In a few days we will cross the Jordan River. On the other side is a land of riches, and God has promised to give us this land!"

Then Joshua met with the leaders of the Eastern tribes of Israel. He said to them, "God has given you the land to the east of the Jordan River. Your land is peaceful, and you can settle here right away. But the rest of us still have to fight off the people living in our lands. And since we are one people, we hope you will help. Then God will give us all peace."

The Eastern tribes gave their word to Joshua and promised to help.

JOSHUA

DAY 93
Rahab Helps the Spies
Joshua 2:1-7

Joshua sent two spies into Canaan to the town of Jericho. They met a woman there named Rahab. She loved God, and she let the spies stay in her home. But someone found out about them. "Some Israeli men have come to spy on us," they told the king of Jericho. "They are staying in Rahab's home."

So the king ordered his soldiers to go and arrest the men. The soldiers found Rahab's house and knocked on her front door. But Rahab had been clever and covered the spies up on the roof underneath some leafy plants. Then she went and opened her door.

The soldiers said, "Where are the spies you've been hiding? We have come to arrest them."

"They were here," Rahab replied, "but they left already. If you hurry you may be able to catch them."

So the soldiers went away and searched the road near the Jordan River.

JOSHUA

DAY 94
Rahab Asks a Favor

Joshua 2:8-14

Meanwhile back in Jericho, Rahab told the spies, "The soldiers are gone! You can come out now." Then she told them, "I know that God has given Israel this land. He rules the heaven and earth. Everyone in Jericho has heard how God parted the Red Sea. And everyone knows that God led your people out of Egypt. Now they shake with fear because you are coming. But when the day comes for you to take Jericho, please remember my family. Treat them with the same kindness that I have treated you."

The spies replied, "If you keep quiet, we will do as you have asked. We won't harm your family, and may God punish us if we don't keep our promise."

DAY 95
The Spies Escape
Joshua 2:15-24

Rahab tied a red rope from her upper window. It ran all the way down to the ground below. She told the two spies, "Use this rope to lower yourselves down. You must leave quietly, and then go hide in the hills. The king's soldiers won't find you there. They'll give up and come back to Jericho. Then you'll be safe."

The spies thanked Rahab and began to lower themselves down. But before they did, they turned around and said to her, "When our people take Jericho, leave this red rope hanging in your window. Then we will remember not to harm you or your family inside." Rahab agreed.

The spies left Jericho and hid in the hills for three days. And the soldiers never found them. When the spies returned to the camp, they told Joshua and the people of Israel everything that had happened. "The people of Jericho are frightened," the spies said. "They know the Lord is with us!"

DAY 96
The Sacred Chest Leads the Way
Joshua 3:1-8

Early the next morning, Joshua and the Israelites left their camp and traveled to the Jordan River. They camped by the banks of the water. The leaders went around and gave instructions to the people. "We will march into Canaan and into the city of Jericho," they told them. "The priests will carry the sacred chest, and everyone else will follow behind them." Then Joshua told them, "Keep your eyes open! The Lord is going to do some amazing things for us today." Joshua told the priests to carry the sacred chest into the Jordan River. They obeyed and lifted the sacred chest up on their shoulders.

Then the Lord told Joshua, "Today I will show the people you are their leader! They will know that I am with you, just like I was with Moses."

DAY 97
Israel Crosses the Jordan River
Joshua 3:9-17; 4:10-18

"Listen to what your Lord God will do," Joshua told the people. "God will show you His power. There are tribes on the other side of this river. But the Lord will force them out of the land. Just watch what the Lord is about to do right now! As soon as the priests carry the sacred chest into the water, the water will stop flowing and pile up."

So the priests carried the sacred chest into the water. And just as Joshua said, the water stopped flowing and piled up. The men walked out into the middle of the dry river. Then the people of Israel crossed over to the other side. The people rejoiced!

Israel had finally reached the Promised Land.

DAY 98
A Monument
Joshua 4:1-9

God told Joshua, "Have one man from each tribe find a large rock in the middle of the dry riverbed. Carry the rocks to the place where you will camp tonight. Then set up the rocks as a monument to this day. Someday your children or your grandchildren might come here and stumble upon them. You can tell them the story of how God stopped the river and led His people into the Promised Land."

Joshua obeyed and chose twelve strong men, one from each tribe. They picked out the biggest rocks they could find. Then they carried the rocks to their camping spot.

Joshua had the men build another monument. They put twelve large rocks in the place where the priests had stood in the middle of the dry riverbed. And it's still there today.

DAY 99
The Battle of Jericho
Joshua 6:1-14

The people of Jericho knew the Israelites were coming. They stayed in their houses, shut the windows, and locked the doors. All the while, Israel marched closer to Jericho.

God told Joshua what to do. "March slowly around the city one time every day," he said. "Do this for six days. Carry the sacred chest in front of you, and have the priests hold trumpets. Then, on the seventh day, march seven times around the city. Blow the trumpets and shout! All the walls will fall down, and you can run into the city from every side."

Joshua listened carefully to God's plan. He told the people what God had said. The people agreed, so Joshua shouted, "Let's march!" The priests went in front carrying the sacred chest. Some of them held trumpets. Then the people marched behind them. The walls of Jericho towered above them, but the people trusted the Lord's plan. They marched around once a day for six days.

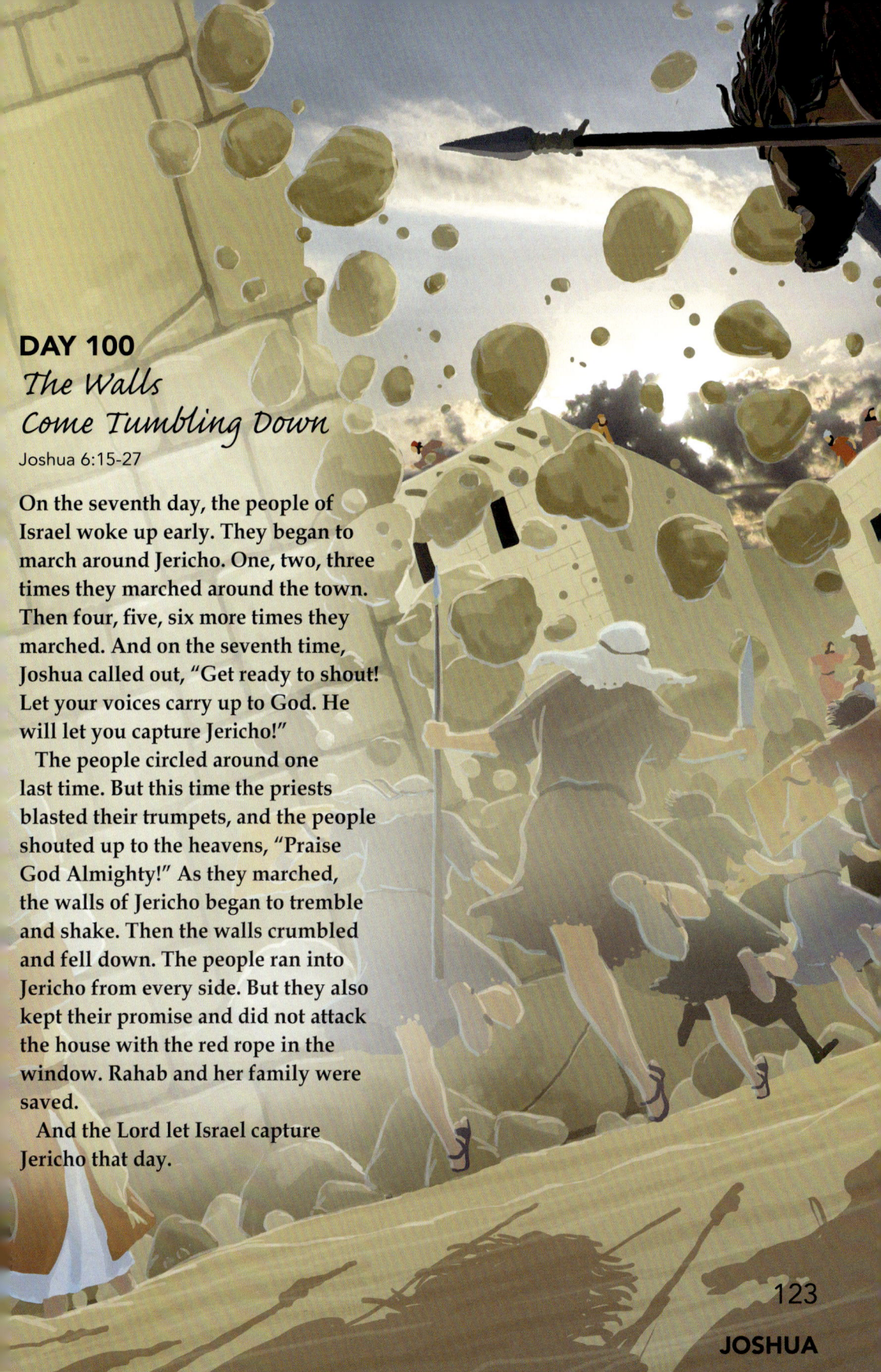

DAY 100
The Walls Come Tumbling Down
Joshua 6:15-27

On the seventh day, the people of Israel woke up early. They began to march around Jericho. One, two, three times they marched around the town. Then four, five, six more times they marched. And on the seventh time, Joshua called out, "Get ready to shout! Let your voices carry up to God. He will let you capture Jericho!"

The people circled around one last time. But this time the priests blasted their trumpets, and the people shouted up to the heavens, "Praise God Almighty!" As they marched, the walls of Jericho began to tremble and shake. Then the walls crumbled and fell down. The people ran into Jericho from every side. But they also kept their promise and did not attack the house with the red rope in the window. Rahab and her family were saved.

And the Lord let Israel capture Jericho that day.

DAY 101
Joshua Commands the Sun to Stand Still
Joshua 10:1-15

The king of Jerusalem heard about Joshua and the battle of Jericho. He was afraid that Israel would capture Jerusalem too. He also got word that Israel had signed a peace treaty with the Gibeonites. The king knew that the people of Gibeon were great warriors.

"What if the Gibeonites help Israel and attack us?" the king wondered.

So he decided to ask the Amorite kings for help. The Amorite kings attacked Gibeon and kept the people as prisoners. The people of Gibeon sent word to Joshua, saying, "Please come and rescue us! We've been attacked! Don't let us down."

Joshua and his army were faithful. They came and fought the Amorites and sent them running in all directions. Then the Lord created a hailstorm that wiped out their enemies.

Joshua saw that the Lord was helping Israel. He prayed, "Lord, make the sun stop in the sky. Make the moon stand still. Do this until we have won over our enemies."

So the sun stood in the sky for a whole day until Israel had won the battle.

DAY 102

"We Will Worship and Obey the Lord"

Joshua 24:14-28

Joshua called the people of Israel together for a meeting. "Worship the Lord," he told them. "He is the reason we have won our battles. Don't forget to obey Him, and be faithful servants. We are in a new land! The people here worship idols and false gods. Are you going to worship their gods? I'm not! My family and I will worship and obey the Lord."

The people answered, "We saw how God brought us out of Egypt. He protected us wherever we went. The Lord is our God, and we will only worship Him."

Joshua told them, "If you turn your back on God, you will be lost. I know that some of you still have idols and statues. You must get rid of them and worship God alone."

Then Joshua set up a large stone under an oak tree. "Do you see this stone?" he asked the people. "This stone will be our witness if you ever turn against God."

The people promised, "We will only worship God." So Joshua helped the people make an agreement with the Lord that day. Then he sent everyone home.

DAY 103
Israel in the Promised Land

Joshua 21:43-45

The Israelites settled in the land that the Lord had promised them. It was rich and beautiful, just like they had been told. Some of Israel's tribes settled in the valleys. Others settled along the sea. But wherever they went, God was always with them. They had good land to grow food, and plenty to eat. Their families grew and grew. Whenever the Israelites had to go to war, the Lord helped them win. He promised many good things for Israel, and He kept his promise every time.

DAY 104
Joshua's Farewell Speech
Joshua 23:1-14

Joshua lived a long time. He was a good leader. While he was alive, Israel lived in peace. Before he died, Joshua called together a meeting with the leaders of Israel.

"The Lord has been good to us," he told them. "You have seen the things He has done and how He has fought for Israel. There are some enemies that still remain in our land. But God is faithful, and He will give this land to you. I have already divided this land between the tribes so that everyone will have something."

Then Joshua said, "I will die soon, just like everyone must. I will not be here to guide you, so remember to obey the word of God. Love the Lord, and remain faithful to your people. Don't be afraid. Any single one of you could defeat a thousand enemy soldiers, because God is on your side! He fights for you, and He keeps His promises."

DAY 105
Judah's Army Defeats Their Enemies

Judges 1:1-15

When Joshua died, the people of Israel had no one to lead them. They were preparing to go to battle with the Canaanites. The people prayed, "Lord, what shall we do? Which tribe should attack our enemies first?"

"Judah," the Lord answered. "I will help them take back the land."

Caleb was the leader of the Judah tribe. He called his soldiers together. Then he told them that the first man to defeat the enemy could marry his daughter named Achsah. The tribe of Judah went into battle with the Canaanites.

Othniel was a brave soldier of Judah. He captured the enemy town and won the battle for Israel. Just as he had promised, Caleb let Othniel marry his daughter.

After the wedding, Achsah told Othniel that he should ask her father for more land. He never did, so she went to see her father herself. As Achsah road up to the house on her donkey, Caleb could tell something was wrong.

"What's bothering you, daughter?" he asked her.

"I need your help," she replied. "The land you have given us is in the

Southern Desert. It's hot and dry there. Please give me some land with springs, so that we can have water."

Caleb gave her a couple of small springs named Higher Springs and Lower Springs.

DAY 106
The Lord Chooses Leaders
Judges 2:16-19

As the years passed, Israel became less and less obedient to God. They forgot about how the Lord led them out of Egypt and into the Promised Land. Now they were even forgetting God. But God had not forgotten them. He decided to put judges in charge of Israel. The judges reminded people of the Lord's almighty power and love. They also helped make decisions for the twelve tribes. They were fighters too. Whenever enemies came and attacked Israel, the judges fought against them. Because the judges were obedient and good, the Lord always helped them win. As long as the judges were alive, the Lord let Israel live in peace.

DAY 107
Rescued by Othniel
Judges 3:7-11

God warned Israel that they would be tricked into worshipping other people's gods. And that's exactly what happened. They bowed down to idols, and they worshipped the gods of their enemies. This made the Lord angry. So He let Israel be ruled by Aram for eight years. They were poor and miserable. They called out to God for help. God loved His people, and He took pity on them.

He chose Othniel to rescue the people. The Lord's Spirit took control of Othniel, and he led Israel into war against the Syrian king. God let Israel beat their enemies. The people rejoiced and they lived in peace for forty more years.

DAY 108
God Chooses Ehud
Judges 3:11-19

After Othniel died, the Israelites disobeyed the Lord again. So He let King Eglon of Moab rule over the Israelites for eighteen years. He made the Israelites pay heavy taxes. The people prayed to God, and He answered their prayer. He forgave the people. This time He chose a man named Ehud to rescue the people from the king.

Ehud was an Israeli from the Benjamin tribe. One day the people sent Ehud to the king with their tax money. But before he left, Ehud hid a sharp dagger under his robes. He went to the king and said, "Your majesty, I have a message to you from God—but it's a secret." So the king sent all the servants out of the room.

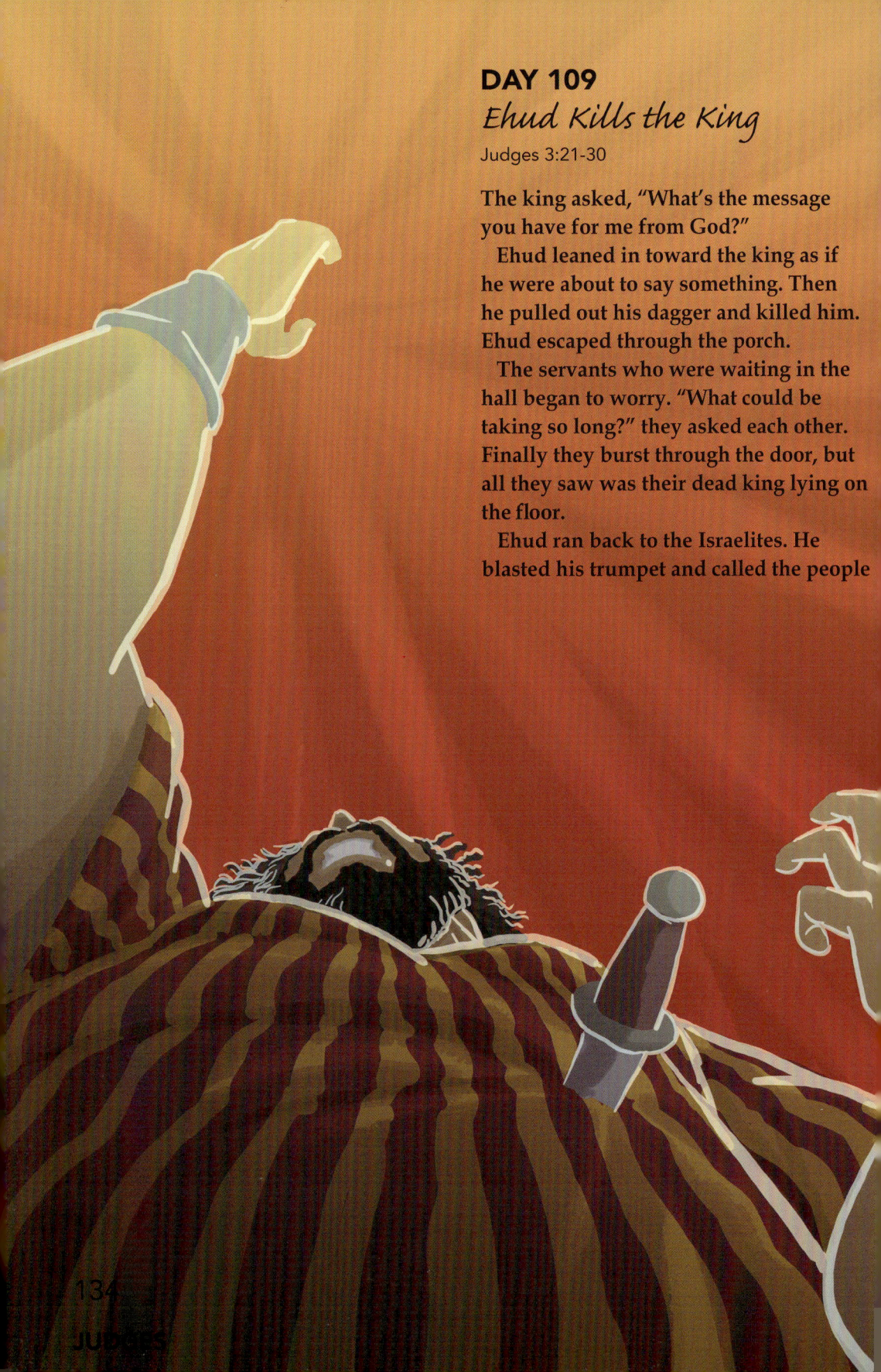

DAY 109
Ehud Kills the King
Judges 3:21-30

The king asked, "What's the message you have for me from God?"

Ehud leaned in toward the king as if he were about to say something. Then he pulled out his dagger and killed him. Ehud escaped through the porch.

The servants who were waiting in the hall began to worry. "What could be taking so long?" they asked each other. Finally they burst through the door, but all they saw was their dead king lying on the floor.

Ehud ran back to the Israelites. He blasted his trumpet and called the people together. They came out of their houses to see what was going on. "Follow me!" Ehud shouted to them. "The Lord will let us fight the Moabites and win!"

So the people followed Ehud down to the Jordan Valley. They fought their enemies and won. The people of Israel lived in peace for another eighty years.

DAY 110
Deborah and Barak
Judges 4:1-10

After Ehud died, the Israelites started to sin again. The Lord let the Canaanite king named Jabin capture Israel. Jabin had a great army. The leader of the army was a man named Siseria. He was tough and cruel to the Israelites. The people prayed for God's help.

At this time, Deborah was a special leader of Israel. Everyday Deborah sat under a palm tree. The people came to her with their problems, and she would help them. The Lord had given her wisdom. She was a prophet of God, and sometimes God spoke to her and told her what to do.

One day Deborah received a message

DEBORAH

from God. She sent for a man named Barak to meet her under the palm tree. She said, "Barak, I have a message to you from God. Gather an army of ten thousand people and lead them to Mount Tabor. The Lord is going to help you defeat the Canaanites. Our enemy Siseria will be there with his army. They may have fancy chariots and weapons, but we will have God on our side."

Barak said, "I will only go if you go too."

"Alright, I'll go," said Deborah. "But don't expect to get any glory. Today the Lord is going to let a woman win against Siseria."

Then Barak and Deborah left to gather the troops.

DAY 111
The Lord Fights for Israel
Judges 4:10-24; 5:31

Deborah and Barak led their army toward Mount Tabor. Siseria got word that Israel was preparing for battle. "Let's go," he called out to his soldiers. "The Israelites think they're going to beat us today!" The soldiers laughed and made fun of Israel as they climbed into their iron chariots.

Meanwhile Deborah told Barak, "The Lord has already gone on ahead to fight for us!" Barak led the troops down the mountain. Siseria and his army were waiting below. During the battle, the Lord fought for Israel. He confused Siseria's army and made them afraid. They began to jump off their chariots and run away. Even Siseria tried to run away, but Barak's army ran after them. The Canaanites no longer had any power over Israel. That day Deborah and Barak sang, "Our Lord we pray that all Your enemies will die like Siseria. But let everyone who loves You shine brightly like the sun at dawn."

Israel lived in peace for about forty years.

DEBORAH

DAY 112
Midian Steals Everything from Israel
Judges 6:1-10

The Israelites could not stop sinning. They began to worship other gods again. So the Lord let the nation of Midian rule Israel for seven years. The Midianites were cruel to them. Whenever the Israelites planted crops, the Midianites came and camped in their fields. Then they would let their cows and sheep graze there until every last piece of grain was eaten. The Midianites stole whatever they could from the people of Israel. It was so bad that some Israelites ran away into the mountains and hid in caves. They cried out to God, "Help us!" So God sent a prophet to tell His people, "I am your God. You were slaves in Egypt, but I rescued you. When your enemies were against you, I helped you get rid of them. But even after all this, you still disobeyed Me."

DAY 113
The Lord Chooses Gideon
Judges 6:11-24

At this time, the Lord sent an angel to the town of Ophrah. The angel sat down under a big oak tree. A young man named Gideon was nearby harvesting wheat.

The angel walked up to Gideon and said, "The Lord is with you. You are a strong warrior."

Gideon replied, "Then why are these awful things happening to us? We hear the stories of how God rescued our ancestors in Egypt. But I think He must have forgotten about us. He hasn't done anything to save us from the Midianites."

This time the Lord spoke, "Don't worry anymore. I am choosing you to save Israel."

"Why choose me?" Gideon asked. "My clan is the weakest among our tribe. And I am no one special."

The Lord answered, "You can rescue Israel because I am going to help you.

You will beat the Midianites just as easily as if they were one man."

"Let me see if You are really the Lord," Gideon said. "Wait here, and I will prepare an offering."

So Gideon killed a young goat and boiled the meat. He placed the meat under a tree with some bread. Then Gideon watched as the angel touched the offering with the tip of His walking stick. The offering set on fire and the smoke rose up to the sky. Gideon was afraid. But the Lord said, "There is nothing to fear."

So Gideon set up an altar for God. He called the altar "The Lord Calms Our Fear."

DAY 114
Gideon Tears Down Baal's Altar
Judges 6:25-31

That night the Lord spoke to Gideon, "Take your father's bull and use it to pull down the altar where the people worship Baal. Then build a new altar in honor of Me."

Gideon found ten servants to help him. But he was afraid that someone would see them. He had them work at night while everyone was asleep.

The next morning the people found that the altar of Baal had been torn down. They saw a new one dedicated to God. They got angry and yelled, "Who did this?"

"Gideon did it," someone said.

The people went to Gideon's house, and his father Joash answered the door.

"Bring out your son!" they yelled. "He has ruined Baal's altar. He must die!"

Joash did not try to hide from the angry mob, and he wasn't afraid of them.

"Are you trying to save Baal?" he asked them. "If Baal is really a god, he can take care of himself. Let him take his own revenge on my son."

DAY 115
Gideon Asks God for a Sign
Judges 6:33-40

The Midianites and many other nations were planning to attack Israel. They crossed the Jordan River and camped in Jezreel Valley.

At that moment, Gideon was filled with the Lord's Spirit. He blew a trumpet and sent messengers out to bring all the Israelite tribes together. They formed an army and prepared to fight.

Gideon was nervous. He prayed, "Lord, I need a sign that You will rescue us. I'll put some wool on the stone floor. If You are with us, make the wool wet with dew, and leave the floor dry."

Gideon got up the next morning. He checked the wool. It was heavy and damp and he squeezed the water out into a bowl. But the floor was dry.

Gideon still wasn't convinced. He prayed again, "Lord, show me one more time that You are with us. This time, let the wool stay dry while the floor is wet."

That night the Lord did just as Gideon asked. The Lord had calmed his fears again.

DAY 116
A Small Army
Judges 7:1-8

The next morning Gideon and his army traveled to a place called Fear Spring. They camped there for the night.

The Lord told Gideon, "Your army is too big. You don't need this many soldiers. I will help you win. Let everyone who is afraid go home." So thousands of men got up and turned around to go home. But there were still ten thousand men left.

The Lord told Gideon, "You need a smaller army. Take the men down to the spring, and I will test them. Some of them will go with you, and some will go home."

So Gideon led his army down to the spring. The Lord said to Gideon, "Watch how the men get a drink of water. Divide the men into two groups: those who lap up the water like a dog and those who kneel to drink."

Three hundred men lapped up the water, and the rest kneeled.

The Lord said, "Take all the men who lapped up water like a dog. The rest can go home."

Gideon was left with an army of three hundred men.

DAY 117
Gideon Spies on the Enemy
Judges 7:9-15

That night the Lord came to Gideon and said, "Get up, it's time to fight! If you are still afraid, then sneak into the enemy camp. Listen to what your enemies are saying, and you won't be scared anymore."

Gideon was afraid. So he and his servant Purah quietly snuck down into the enemy camp. Thousands of enemy soldiers were swarming around the place like locusts. Gideon heard what some of them were saying. One man said, "I dreamed that a loaf of barley bread went tumbling through our camp and knocked over the main tent. The tent flipped over and fell down." The other soldier said, "Your dream must have been about Gideon, the Israeli commander. It means God will let him defeat our army."

When Gideon heard this, he was not afraid anymore. He went back to the Israeli camp and shouted, "Let's go! The Lord is going to let us win."

DAY 118
Trumpets and Torches
Judges 7:16-24

Gideon handed out a trumpet to each of his soldiers. Then he handed out a clay jar with a torch inside. He told them, "Carry your trumpets. And when you hear my signal, blow them as loud as you can. Then smash the clay jars and hold your torches up high. Now, let's go fight for the Lord!"

Gideon and his army marched toward the enemy camp. Then Gideon blew his trumpet signal. All the soldiers picked up their trumpets and blew as loud as they could. Then they shouted, "Fight with your swords for the Lord and for Gideon!" They smashed their clay jars and held up the burning torches.

The Midianites heard the mighty sound and covered their ears. The glow of the torches lit up their frightened faces. They began to tremble and shake.

GIDEON

They picked up their swords, but the Lord made them confused. They began to fight their own people. Some of them tried to run away and cross the Jordan River. But Gideon already had every spring, stream, and river guarded. Not one single enemy could escape.

DAY 119

The Israelites Ask Gideon to Be Their King

Judges 8:22-35

When the battle was over and Israel had won, the people cheered. They flocked around Gideon and praised him.

"You saved us!" they told him. "Be our king. And after you are gone, your son can rule and his son after that!"

But Gideon said, "I won't be your king, and my son won't be king either. Only the Lord is your King. But I will ask one thing of you. Each of you give me a gold earring from all the precious gold you took from the Midianites during the battle."

So the people obeyed. They laid gold rings, jewels, and camel ornaments down at Gideon's feet. He took all of it home and melted it down. Then he made a gold figure. He put the statue in his home town of Ophrah. The people began to worship the statue. Even Gideon was tricked into bowing down in front of it.

But as long as Gideon was alive, the Lord let Israel live in peace.

DAY 120
Abimelech Tries to Be King
Judges 9:1-7

God let Gideon live a long time. He had seventy sons, and one of them was named Abimelech. After Gideon died, Abimelech wanted to be ruler. He gathered his relatives together and told them, "Do you really want all my brothers ruling over you? One man would be better. Let me be king!" So his relatives agreed.

To be sure that he would be the only king, Abimelech decided to kill his brothers. He hired a gang of rough men to do the job. They went to the house of his brothers and killed all of them—except one. Jotham was the youngest brother. He snuck away and hid out in the wilderness. Then he climbed up to the top of Mount Gerezim. Down below, he could see all the people gathering around. They were about to crown Abimelech as their new king. So Jotham yelled down to them, "Listen to my story! And maybe God will listen to you."

DAY 121
Jotham's Curse
Judges 9:8-55

"Once there was a forest," Jotham told the people. "And the trees of the forest wanted a king. They asked the olive tree, but he said, 'Why should I be king just to wave over other trees?' They asked the fig tree, but the fig tree said, 'Why should I stop growing my fruit just to wave over other trees?' They asked the grape vine, but the grape vine said, 'Why should I stop making wine just to wave over other trees?' Finally, they asked the thornbush. The thornbush said, 'I'll be your king. But if you betray me, I'll start a fire that will destroy all the trees.'"

Then Jotham shouted, "My father Gideon was like the thornbush that gave you protection. Is this how you repay him? All of his sons have been killed. If you did right, I hope you are all happy. But if you did wrong, I hope a fire comes and destroys all of you."

Then Jotham ran away and never came back. But his curse came true. Abimelech turned his back on the people and set fire to the city. Many people died, and Abimelech finally died too.

DAY 122
Israel Is Unfaithful Again
Judges 10:6-16

The Lord was tired of Israel's unfaithful ways. He let Ammon rule over Israel for eighteen years. They crushed the Israelites with their power. They would not let them own any land, and they made the Israelites miserable.

The people called out to God, "Please help us! We have sinned against You, but don't turn away from us."

The Lord replied, "I have always saved you from your enemies. But every time I do, you forget Me again. You don't worship Me; you worship other gods. So let them save you when you need help."

"We've done wrong," the people said. "But if we must be punished, we'd rather You do it than the Ammonites. Please rescue us." The people began to worship God again. They threw all their idols away. And they prayed to God for forgiveness.

DAY 123
The Lord Helps Jephthah
Judges 11:1-33

At this time, there lived a man named Jephthath. He was a great warrior. He lived in Gilead, but his brothers kicked him out because he was different from them. They told him, "You don't belong here."

So Jephthath was forced to live in the land of Tob.

The Israelites of Gilead were preparing to fight the Ammonites. But they needed a leader. Then they remembered Jephthath. They begged him, "Please come back to Gilead and help us fight our enemies."

But Jephthath said, "You only want me back because you're in trouble."

So they promised him, "If you come back we will make you the ruler of Gilead."

Jephthath came back and led the army. He sent messengers to the king of Ammon with a message. It read: "You have taken land that belongs to Israel, and I would like to know why." But the king sent a reply saying, "The land belongs to us."

Then the Lord's Spirit took control of Jephthath. He raised an army and attacked the Ammonites. He captured all their towns and defeated their army. Israel rejoiced, and they crowned Jephthath as their new ruler.

DAY 124
Samson Is Born
Judges 13:1-24

Israel lived in peace for a long time. Then they began to disobey God again. So the Philistines ruled over Israel for forty years.

Manoah was a man from the town of Zorah. His wife was not able to have children. But one day an angel came to her and said, "God will give you a son. He will belong to the Lord. Because of this you must never cut his hair."

The woman ran to Manoah and said, "I have seen an angel! He told me that we are going to have a son!"

Manoah prayed to the Lord, "Please let me see the angel too."

When the woman was out in the field, the angel appeared to her again. So she ran back and got her husband, "Come quick," she said. "The angel has returned!"

Manoah got up and ran out to the field. The angel said to him, "Your wife must take good care of herself because she will give birth to a special boy."

Manoah and his wife bowed down and worshiped God. They burnt an offering. Then the angel went up to heaven with the smoke.

Not long after, the woman gave birth to a baby boy. She named him Samson.

DAY 125
Samson Fights a Lion
Judges 14:1-9

One day when Samson was a young man, he took a trip to the town of Timnah. He saw a Philistine woman there. The Lord made Samson fall in love with her.

When he came home he told his parents, "I met a Philistine woman I want to marry."

"A Philistine!" his parents replied. "Why don't you marry a woman of Israel? The Philistines are our enemies."

"No, I want to marry her," Samson said.

So his parents went with him to Timnah. As they were walking, Samson wandered off by himself. He saw a lion. The lion chased him and showed his sharp white teeth. Then the

Lord's Spirit took control of Samson. He tore the lion apart with his bare hands, as if it were a goat. But he didn't tell his parents what happened.

When they arrived, Samson found the Philistine woman. He asked her to marry him. His parents made wedding plans with the bride's family. Then Samson and his parents went home.

On the way, Samson saw the bone-dry skeleton of the lion. A hive of bees were living inside the skull. They had made some honey. Samson scooped up the honey in his hands and ate it as he walked along.

DAY 126
Samson Tells a Riddle
Judges 14:10-19

Samson threw a party and invited thirty men. They would have a big feast every night for seven days. On the first night, Samson said, "Let's play a game. I'll tell you a riddle and you give me the answer. If you get it right, I'll give you all brand new clothes. If you guess wrong, you'll have to give me brand new clothes."

"What's the riddle?" the men asked.

Samson said, "Once so strong and mighty, now so sweet and tasty. What is it?"

The men tried to think of an answer. But they were wrong every time.

Three days went by. So the men went to Samson's bride and said, "If you don't find out the answer to the riddle, we'll kill you and your family."

Samson's bride went to her husband and begged him to tell her the answer. She fell down on the floor and cried. But he refused. She kept nagging him every day. So finally Samson told her, and she told the other men.

On the last night, the men told Samson the answer. "What is stronger than a lion? And what is tastier than honey?" Samson was angry. He knew his wife had told them the answer. That night he went home to his parents; he was too angry to see his wife.

DAY 127
Samson Takes Revenge
Judges 14:20; 15:1-8

Once Samson had calmed down, he went back to Timnah to see his wife. He brought along a young goat as a gift. Samson found her father and said, "I want to go to my wife. Where is she?"

"You can't do that," her father replied. "You were so angry when you left that I thought you had divorced her. She's already married to someone else."

Samson was furious. "This time I really have a reason to hurt some Philistines," he said.

Then Samson went into the fields owned by the Philistines. He caught three hundred foxes and tied them together with rags soaked in oil. Then he lit their tails on fire and let them go. The foxes ran all over, and the fields caught on fire.

When the Philistines saw this, they screamed, "Who did this?"

"It was Samson," someone told them, "He took revenge because his wife married someone else."

The Philistines went to Timnah and burned Samson's wife and her father. But this made Samson even angrier. He went to them and said, "You killed her! Now I'll get even with you!" And he killed each one of them with his sword.

Then Samson left Philistia and hid out in a cave at Etam Rock.

DAY 128
The Philistines Look for Samson
Judges 15:9-20

The Philistines looked everywhere for Samson. They wanted to kill him. So they invaded the land of Judah, ripping homes apart and scouring the fields. But the Philistines couldn't find Samson anywhere.

One day some Israelites stumbled upon Samson at the rock of Etam where he was hiding. "Samson," they told him, "the Philistines are looking for you. And if they find you here, they'll punish us too. We have to turn you in."

Samson knew they were right. "I know you must, and I won't fight against you," he told them. "But I only ask that you don't hurt me yourselves."

They led Samson back to the Philistine camp. When the Philistines saw that Samson had been caught, they cheered. They began to run toward him. But the Lord's Spirit moved inside Samson. He snapped the ropes off around his wrist as easily as if it had been burnt cloth. Then he picked up a donkey bone and killed a thousand Philistine men with it. The Lord gave Samson all his power. He went back to his people, and he ruled Israel for twenty years.

DAY 129
Samson and Delilah
Judges 16:4-15

Samson fell in love with a woman named Delilah. One day a bunch of Philistines went to Delilah and said, "How would you like eleven hundred pieces of silver? If you find out what makes Samson so strong, we'll pay you."

The next time Delilah saw Samson, she asked, "What makes you so strong?"

"Tie me up with seven bowstrings," Samson replied. "Then I'll be just as weak as anyone else."

When Samson was asleep she tied him up. "The Philistines are attacking!"

she yelled. He woke up and snapped the bowstrings as easily as if they were string near a flame.

"Samson! You lied to me. What is it that makes you so strong?" Delilah said.

"Okay, use ropes that have never been used," said Samson. "Then I'll be weak."

When he was asleep, Delilah tied him with new ropes.

"The Philistines are attacking!" she yelled. But Samson snapped the ropes off as if they were thread.

"Stop making me look like a fool," Delilah said. "Tell me the truth."

"Weave my braided hair on a loom," Samson told her. "Nail the loom to a wall and you'll see how weak I become."

When Samson was asleep she weaved his hair on a loom and nailed it to the wall. "The Philistines are attacking!" she yelled. Samson jumped up and all his hair came loose from the loom nailed to the wall.

So Delilah said, "Samson, I don't think you love me. You have lied to me three times!"

DAY 130
Delilah Tricks Samson
Judges 16:17-22

Samson told Delilah the truth. "The Lord makes me strong," he said. "My hair has never been cut. As long as my hair is uncut, I will always be strong."

So Delilah went to the Philistines and said, "I know what makes Samson strong! Come to my house tonight while he is asleep."

The Philistines paid Delilah the money they had promised her. Then they came to her house after Samson had fallen asleep. He was laying his head in Delilah's lap. She told the Philistines to come and shave off his hair. After they had done this, they tied Samson up with ropes.

Then Delilah yelled, "Samson, the Philistines are attacking!" Samson jumped up and tried to break loose from the ropes, but all his strength was gone. The Philistines arrested him and poked out his eyes so that he was blind. Then they put shackles on him and forced him to be a slave. Samson was miserable. But little by little, his hair began to grow again.

DAY 131
Samson Pulls Down a Temple
Judges 16:23-30

One day the Philistine rulers were having a party in the temple. They were eating and drinking and having a good time. Someone shouted, "Bring out Samson; he's always a good laugh!"

A guard went and brought Samson out to the main room. Samson asked the guard, "Please lead me in between the two pillars so I can rest against them."

The guard led him toward the two pillars. Samson stood between them while the Philistines laughed and made jokes about him. "Where's all your strength now?" they teased him. Samson prayed to God, "Make me strong one last time. Let me have my revenge on these Philistines for poking out my eyes."

Then Samson stretched out his arms and pressed against the two pillars. They began to tremble and shake. "Now let me die with the Philistines!" Samson prayed. God answered his prayer. He pushed with all his might, and the pillars crumbled. The roof caved in and crushed the Philistines.

DAY 132
Ruth Is Loyal to Naomi
Ruth 1:1-19

Once there was a woman named Naomi. Her husband died, but she had two sons that she loved very much. They grew up and married good women. Ten years later both of Naomi's sons died. Naomi was heartbroken. But her daughter-in-laws stayed with her because she had no family left. They were named Orpah and Ruth.

At that time, there was a famine in the land. The three women were starving. So Naomi and her daughter-in-laws went to the land of Judah to search for food. On the way, Naomi said to her daughter-in-laws, "Why don't you go back to your own mothers? You've been with me long enough." But the women would not go.

"We want to be with you," they said.

"But what good am I to you?" Naomi asked them. "I have no more sons to give you."

So Orpah went back to her family, but Ruth stayed with Naomi. Ruth told Naomi, "You are my family, and I will not leave you alone. Where you go, I will go. Your people will be my people. And your God will be my God."

Naomi squeezed Ruth's hand. Then they traveled on until they reached the town of Bethlehem. Naomi lived there once long ago. All her old friends and family still lived there. When they saw her, they said, "Naomi is back! And she has brought her daughter-in-law!"

DAY 133
Ruth Meets Boaz
Ruth 2:1-23

Ruth told Naomi, "Why don't you rest. I'll go see if I can find us some food."

So Ruth walked out into the fields where the men were working. The field was owned by a man named Boaz. He was one of Naomi's relatives. He was a rich and important man, but he was also kind and gentle. When he saw Ruth wandering in his fields, he asked his workers who she was.

"That's Naomi's daughter-in-law," they answered. "She has never left Naomi's side. She wants to gather the leftovers from our field."

So Boaz walked over to Ruth and smiled. "You're welcome to pick up whatever is leftover in my field," he told her. "I told the men not to bother you. And be sure to drink from the water jar whenever you're thirsty."

Ruth bowed down and asked, "Why are you being so kind to me?"

"Because you have been good to my relative Naomi," he said. "I have heard how you left your home and your family. You are very brave. I pray the Lord will reward you."

So Ruth worked in the fields all day. When she returned to Naomi, her back was aching and her arms were sore. But she had food.

"Daughter, you picked all of this from Boaz's field?" Naomi exclaimed. "May the Lord bless him!"

Boaz let Ruth pick the wheat and barley in his fields until the harvest was over.

DAY 134
Ruth and Boaz Get Married
Ruth 3:1-18; 4:1-17

One day Naomi said to Ruth, "You're still young, and Boaz has been so good to us. Why don't you go to Boaz's bed and lie down at his feet. Then he will see that you would like to be his wife."

So Ruth picked out her nicest clothes and put on some perfume. Then she went down to the place where Boaz ate and drank his food. Ruth secretly watched him until he had gone to bed. Then she lifted the corner of the blanket near his feet and lay down. Boaz didn't wake up until the middle of the night. He felt someone moving near his feet. "Who's there?" he asked.

"It's Ruth," she answered. "Boaz, I came here to see if you would take me as your wife."

Boaz was old, but his eyes still twinkled. He smiled and said, "Ruth, you are such a lovely woman. Any young man would marry you. But you have asked me, and that shows you are loyal to your family."

Boaz married Ruth and the whole town gave them their blessing. Ruth became pregnant with a son. She named him Obed. Naomi was a very proud grandma.

She would spend hours bouncing the baby on her lap. The townspeople began to call him "Naomi's Boy."

When Obed grew up, he had a son named Jesse. And Jesse's son was David—the king of Israel. So Naomi became the great-grandmother of a king!

DAY 135

Hannah Asks the Lord for a Child
1 Samuel 1:1-17

Hannah was a woman of God. She had a husband named Elkanah. But he also had another wife named Peninnah. She had many children, but Hannah had none. Hannah wanted a child more than anything in the world. Elkanah didn't mind. He loved Hannah more than Peninnah. She was kind and beautiful, and she loved the Lord with her whole heart.

One day Elkanah took a trip with his family to worship the Lord at Shiloh. He sacrificed an animal to God. Then he gave his wives and children some of the meat. Because he loved Hannah the most, he always gave her the biggest piece. Peninnah was jealous. So she teased Hannah, saying, "Children are such a joy. It's too bad the Lord won't give you any."

Hannah began to cry, and she couldn't eat her food. So she went to the holy temple and prayed, "Lord, you have given me so much. But I am so sad. Please let me have a son. I promise he will be yours until the day he dies."

Eli was the priest of the temple, and he heard Hannah's prayer. Her lips were moving, but no words were coming out. Her prayer was deep inside her heart.

Eli walked up to Hannah and put his hand on her shoulder. "Go home now," he told her. "I am sure that God will answer your prayer!"

DAY 136
Samuel Is Born
1 Samuel 1:19-28; 2:18-21

God answered Hannah's prayer. She gave birth to a son, and she named him Samuel. When Samuel was just a toddler, Hannah brought him to the temple at Shiloh. She found Eli the priest and told him, "A few years ago I stood here and prayed for a son. You told me that the Lord would answer my prayer, and He did!"

Samuel peeked out behind his mother's skirt and looked up shyly at Eli. Then Hannah said, "I am giving him over to you so that he can grow up in the Lord's house."

Eli agreed to keep Samuel with him at Shiloh. He was like a father toward Samuel, and he taught him about the Lord. Once a year, Samuel's mother would come to visit. She always brought Samuel new clothes to wear. Eli knew how much Hannah loved her son. He blessed Hannah and told her, "Samuel was born to answer your prayers. You did the right thing by giving him to God. But I pray that the Lord will bless you with more children!"

God was good to Hannah. He gave her three more sons and two daughters.

DAY 137
God Calls Samuel
1 Samuel 2:12; 3:2-18

Eli the priest had two sons. But his sons didn't care about the ministry of God. So Samuel became Eli's closest companion. One night after they both had gone to bed, Samuel heard someone call his name.

He ran to Eli's room and said, "Here I am."

But Eli said, "I didn't call for you. Go back to bed."

So Samuel went back and tried to go to sleep. But again a voice called, "Samuel!"

Samuel went to Eli again, "Here I am. I heard you call me."

"No son," said Eli. "I didn't call you. Go back to bed."

Once Samuel had lain down, a voice called to him a third time, "Samuel!"

Samuel went to Eli's a third time, "Here I am. I heard you call me."

By this time Eli realized what was happening. He told Samuel, "When you hear the voice call you again, say, 'Here I am, Lord. I am listening?'"

Samuel went back to bed. And the Lord called, "Samuel!"

Then Samuel said, "Here I am, Lord. I am listening."

And the Lord said, "I have warned Eli that his sons were sinning. But he has not listened to Me. Now I have no choice but to punish him and his family for their sins."

The next morning Eli asked Samuel what the Lord had told him. Samuel was frightened that Eli would be angry. But he told Eli everything. Eli was sad, but he said, "He is the Lord. He will do what is right."

DAY 138
The Philistines Capture the Sacred Chest
1 Samuel 4:1-11

The Lord was with Samuel as he grew older. He was a prophet of God, and everyone in Israel respected him.

At this time the Philistines were attacking Israel. They went around burning down homes and killing families. "Why isn't God with us?" the elders asked each other. "Let's get the sacred chest at Shiloh. Maybe then God will let us win."

When they brought the sacred chest back into Israel's camp, the people cheered so loudly that the ground shook. Back at the Philistine camp, they could feel the ground rumble. "Why are they cheering?" the Philistines wondered. Then someone told them about the sacred chest. "We are doomed!" the Philistines said. "That's the same sacred chest that led the Israelites out of Egypt. We must fight like warriors!"

The Philistines fought with all their might. And Israel lost the battle. They no longer had enough soldiers to guard the sacred chest. So the Philistines stole it and took it back to their camp.

DAY 139
The Philistines Return the Sacred Chest
1 Samuel 5:1-12; 6:10-13

The Philistines put the sacred chest next to a statue of a god they worshiped called Dagon. But the next morning they found Dagon's statue face down on the floor.

"Who has done this?" they asked each other. But no one knew. So they put the statue back up again and forgot about it.

The next morning they went to the temple and found the statue smashed on the ground in front of the sacred chest. Then God sent a rash down on the Philistines. Their skin was covered in sores that itched miserably. "The Lord of the Israelites has done this," the people cried, "because we have stolen the sacred chest."

They sent the chest to the land of Gath. But the people of Gath were infected with sores too. "Send it to the land of Ekron!" the people said. But the people in Ekron said, "No, we don't want it either." So they put the sacred chest on a cart led by two cows. "If it goes toward Israel," they said, "then we'll know this was the Lord's doing."

The Israelites were working in the fields when they saw the sacred chest coming towards them on a cart. They ran toward the cart like happy children, laughing and singing all the way. They knew that the Lord was with them.

SAMUEL

DAY 140
Samuel Leads Israel
1 Samuel 7:3-13

Samuel saw that the people began to have faith in God again. He gathered them together and said, "If you really want to trust in God with all your hearts, get rid of your idols. The Lord will save you from the Philistines, but you must trust in Him."

Then Samuel called a meeting at a place called Mizpah. The people of Israel came there to worship the Lord and ask forgiveness for their sins. But the Philistines had sent soldiers to attack Mizpah. When the Israelites found out, they were afraid.

Samuel stood up in front of the people and said, "Trust in God! Why did you stop praying just because your enemies are coming?"

So the people prayed while Samuel gave a burnt offering to the Lord. Then the Philistines stormed in on Mizpah with their swords. But the Lord sent such a loud rumble of thunder that the Philistines panicked and ran away. The Israelites chased after them, and the Lord made them win. Then Samuel set up a monument. He said, "This will be called 'Help Monument,' because the Lord has helped us today."

DAY 141
The People of Israel Want a King
1 Samuel 8–10:1-2

Israel was not like other nations because the people of Israel did not have a king. God was their king. But the people of Israel began to complain and say, "We want a king just like all the other nations!" Samuel was God's prophet in Israel. When Samuel heard this, he felt sad. He knew there was no greater king than God, and yet this was still not good enough for the people. They wanted another king. He prayed about it. God answered Samuel and said, "Do everything your people ask. In time they will learn there is only one true king who will never disappoint them."

The next day, a young man named Saul was wandering around looking for his lost donkeys. God said to Samuel, "This is the man whom I choose to rule over Israel." Samuel went over to Saul and said, "Do not worry about your donkeys. Everything in Israel now belongs to you!" Then Samuel poured olive oil on Saul's head and told him what God had said. Saul was surprised. "But I'm from the smallest tribe," Saul said, "and the least important clan in Israel. Why am I to be king?"

Samuel smiled and answered, "God has chosen you."

DAY 142
Saul Becomes King
1 Samuel 10:17-25

Samuel brought all the people together to meet the king God had chosen for them. The crowd began to whisper and gossip. "Who would God choose?" they wondered. Samuel called out above the crowd, "God has chosen Saul!"

The people grew quiet and waited

for Saul to come forward. But he did not come. Then God said, "He is hiding behind the baggage." Saul stood up from where he had been hiding. He was shy in front of so many people who were turning to look at him. But the crowd began to shout and chant, "Hooray! Long live Saul!" Then Samuel said, "There is no one like Saul among all of God's people. You have asked for a king, and your God has given him to you." The crowd cheered with joy and praise! They kept on celebrating late into the day. Finally Samuel sent them all home, and Saul went to bed that night feeling very good about himself.

DAY 143
Jonathan Attacks the Philistines
1 Samuel 14:3-16

Saul was a strong ruler of Israel. He built up a brave army of soldiers who were always ready to fight. Saul's own sons were also soldiers in his army. Saul's eldest son Jonathan was a particularly brave and spirited soldier. He was eager to fight the neighboring Philistine enemies. Jonathan told the servant who carried his weapons that it would be best to attack the Philistines when they least

expected—if only Saul would give the go-ahead. "God will surely let us win!" said Jonathan confidently. "We are his people!"

Finally Jonathan could wait no longer. He and his servant slipped out of their camp that evening and sneaked over to the other side of the valley. As the two soldiers were approaching the enemy camp, the Philistines caught sight of them. "Look at those two soldiers of Israel," they joked. "They've finally crawled out of the holes they've been hiding in." The Philistine soldiers ran down to meet them, but Jonathan and his servant killed them before they even had a chance to fight back. The rest of the Philistine army got word that they had been attacked. They panicked and ran in all directions.

DAY 144
Saul and His Men Join the Battle
1 Samuel 14:16-24

Back at the camp of the Israelites, the two runaway soldiers had been spotted from the lookout tower. Saul had his officers do a name call. He found out that it was his own son Jonathan and Jonathan's servant who were missing.

Saul called for his holy priest. He trembled and asked the priest, "What shall we do? Two of my soldiers have gone to fight the Philistines. One of them is my son! They can't possibly win against so many enemies!" The priest began to pray with Saul, but Saul was impatient. He decided to send out his entire army to help the two soldiers.

God was with Saul and his army. He allowed Saul to finish the fight with triumph over their enemies.

DAY 145
Saul Disobeys God
1 Samuel 15:10-35

Saul was proud of his victory; he was already busy building a monument so that everyone would remember the glorious day when the Israelites beat the Philistines.

God's prophet Samuel was walking across the empty battlefield when he heard the bleating of sheep and the mooing of cattle. He ran back to Saul and asked him, "Why have you saved the sheep and cattle of our enemy?"

Saul replied, "We have won our battle! I have saved them to sacrifice to God in thanks."

Then Samuel became angry. He said, "God does not want your sacrifices. He wants you to obey Him. He told you to destroy everything belonging to our enemy, even the sheep and cattle! Why did you choose to listen to some of the things God said and not others?"

God was disappointed in Saul. He knew the time was coming for a new king of Israel—one that would obey Him with a pure heart.

DAY 146

Jesse's Sons

1 Samuel 16:1-7

God told Samuel he would find the new king for Israel in the town of Bethlehem. God told him, "Find a man named Jesse. Bring along an animal to sacrifice for Me together with Jesse and his sons. Jesse's sons will gather around you. One of his sons will be the king I have chosen."

Samuel obeyed God and went to Bethlehem. After he arrived, Samuel found Jesse and his sons, and he invited them to sacrifice an animal with him. Samuel couldn't help but notice Jesse's oldest son, Eliab. He has to be the one God has chosen. Samuel thought, "He is so handsome and tall!" But God told Samuel, "I judge people by what is in their hearts and not what they look like."

DAVID

DAY 147
David, God's New King
1 Samuel 16:8-13

Each of Jesse's sons appeared before Samuel. Samuel waited patiently for God to speak, but God had not chosen any of them. Samuel was a little bit worried. He finally asked Jesse, "Do you have any more sons?"

"Yes. There is David," said Jesse.

Samuel had Jesse send for David. After a moment, there was David—smiling softly and holding his shepherd's stick. He had just come from the field where he had been caring for the sheep. David was the youngest and the smallest among all of his brothers, but he had a sparkle in his eye. At last God spoke, "David is the one who will be King of Israel!" Samuel poured oil on David's head and blessed him.

DAY 148
David Sings for Saul
1 Samuel 16:14-23

Saul was still the king of Israel, but God's Spirit had left him. At night Saul often awoke with horrible nightmares. During the day he wrestled with bad thoughts. Because God was no longer with Saul, he had been taken over by an evil spirit that would not give him peace.

One day when Saul was feeling particularly bad, Saul's servants sent for a musician to come and play and calm him down. David was still a young man, but he played the harp very well. Saul's servants heard good things about David so they hired him to play the harp for Saul. When David plucked the strings of his instrument, a peaceful melody filled the air. His music seemed to come from heaven above. Saul immediately relaxed, and the bad spirits left him. Saul loved David's company, and David enjoyed playing the harp for Saul. David was thankful he had the gift of music to help his king. He spent many afternoons playing music for Saul.

DAY 149
Goliath the Giant
1 Samuel 17:3-16

The Philistines were planning an attack on the people of Israel. King Saul commanded all his best men to prepare for battle. They pulled on their shiny armor, carried their spears, and walked toward the battlefield with confidence.

Then they saw Goliath.

Goliath was the hero of the Philistine army. He was huge! He towered over the other men like a fierce giant. His legs were as thick as tree trunks, and his arms bulged with muscles. Goliath laughed and snorted at the army of Israel. When he spoke, his words sounded like a beastly roar. "I am the best soldier of our army!" Goliath shouted. "Can one among you kill me? If so, the Philistines will be your slaves. But if I kill him, the people of Israel will be our slaves!" Saul and his men were terrified. Even the bravest among the soldiers of Israel began to shake in their shoes with fright. "Who could possibly beat someone like Goliath?" they wondered.

DAVID

DAY 150
David's Response to Goliath's Insults
1 Samuel 17:17-27

The Israelite army could do nothing more than wait—hoping someone would be brave enough to fight Goliath. Meanwhile Goliath was yelling insults from across the field. "You are cowards!" he taunted. "Where is your God to help you?"

King Saul started to worry. He decided to offer a reward to any soldier who could fight and kill Goliath. "The man who does this will get to marry my daughter!" Saul announced. "He will be treated like royalty and have the finest things in the land." But even with these tempting rewards, no one dared to stand up to such a frightening enemy. Saul was getting desperate.

All the while, young David had been running around delivering food for the soldiers. He had not heard what was going on. He innocently asked what all the fuss was about—why was everyone sitting around with such gloomy faces? The soldiers told David about Goliath and what he had said. David turned beet red with anger. "Who does Goliath think he is?" he said. "He is trying to fight the army of God!" Then David dashed off to find Saul.

DAY 151
David Meets Goliath
1 Samuel 17:34-40

David went up to Saul and said, "I have killed lions and bears when they have dared to take my sheep. Now let me fight Goliath who has dared to laugh at God's people." But Saul was not so sure about this. Still, he admired David and gave him his armor and sword. David put on the heavy chain mail and the iron helmet. But he was uncomfortable. "I can't move with this stuff on," he said. David threw off the armor and picked up his shepherd's stick. Then he picked up some rocks. With his sling in his hand, he went straight toward Goliath.

DAY 152
David Kills Goliath
1 Samuel 17:41-51

Goliath howled with laughter when he saw David. He said, "Do you think I am a dog? Are you going to come after me with a stick?"

But David answered bravely, "You have come with a sword and a dagger. I have come with God Almighty on my side." Then David put a rock in his sling and hit Goliath right in the forehead. Goliath wobbled and swayed with dizziness. Then his eyes rolled to the back of his head, and he fell down onto the ground with a thud. David had killed him, and Israel was saved!

DAY 153
King Saul Is Jealous
1 Samuel 18:6-16

The army of Israel returned home to celebrate their victory. Everyone danced and played their harps and tambourines. Women sang out, "Saul has killed a thousand enemies, but David has killed ten thousand!"

Saul heard all the praise people were giving David. He was jealous. "Why is David getting all the praise and glory?" he wondered. "I am the king!"

From that day on, Saul began to despise David.

David came to play the harp for Saul the next afternoon. But David noticed that he did not look friendly, and he was holding a sharp sword in his hand. Before David could think twice, Saul had already hurled the sword in David's direction. But David was quick and dodged the sword just in time! Then David ran out of the king's palace and did not return.

Saul had another plan. He decided to send David out as the leading soldier in all of Israel's battles. He hoped David would be killed this way. So David fought, but he never came to any harm because God was with him. David won all of his battles, and the people loved him even more for his strength and bravery.

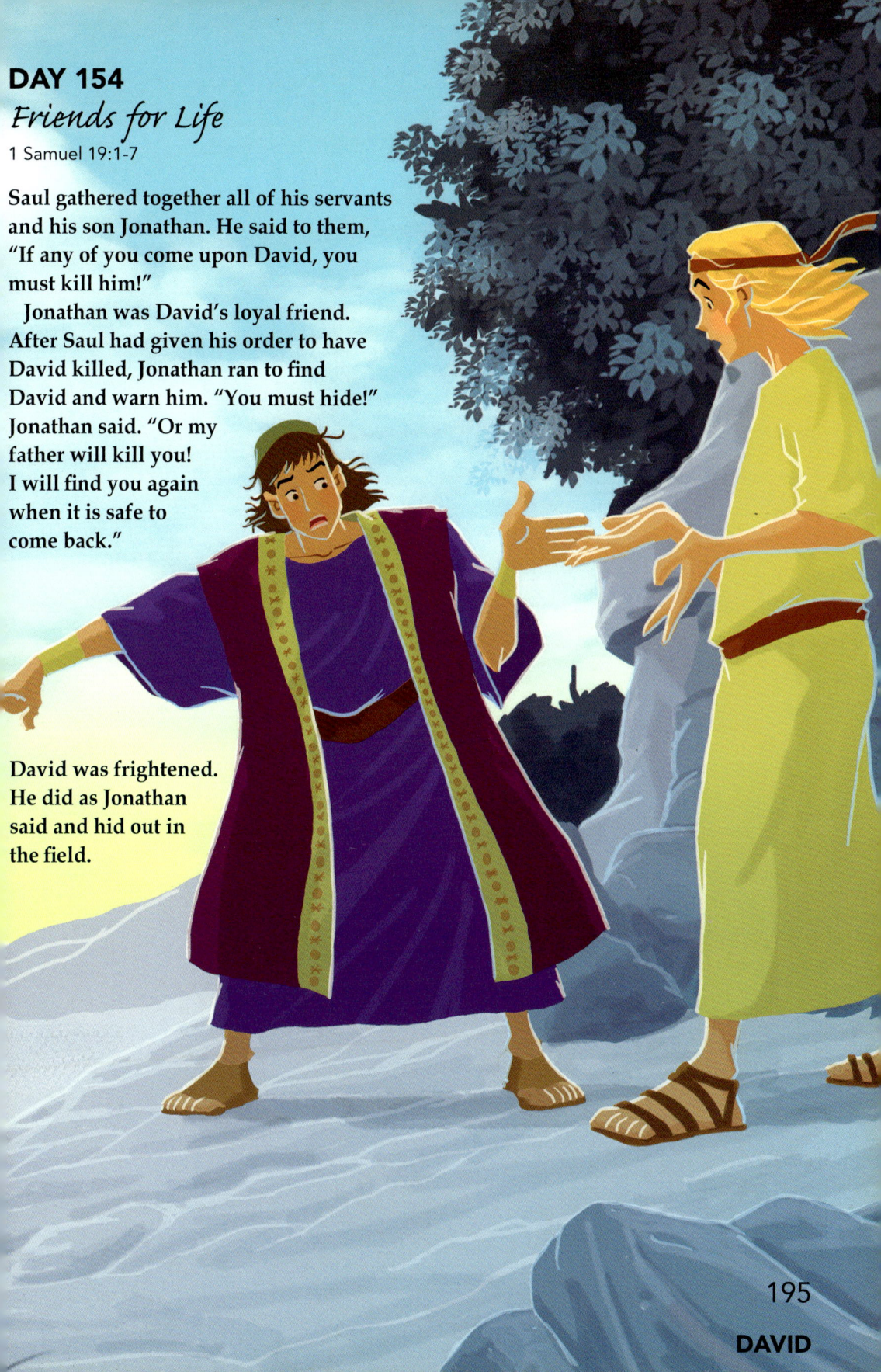

DAY 154
Friends for Life
1 Samuel 19:1-7

Saul gathered together all of his servants and his son Jonathan. He said to them, "If any of you come upon David, you must kill him!"

Jonathan was David's loyal friend. After Saul had given his order to have David killed, Jonathan ran to find David and warn him. "You must hide!" Jonathan said. "Or my father will kill you! I will find you again when it is safe to come back."

David was frightened. He did as Jonathan said and hid out in the field.

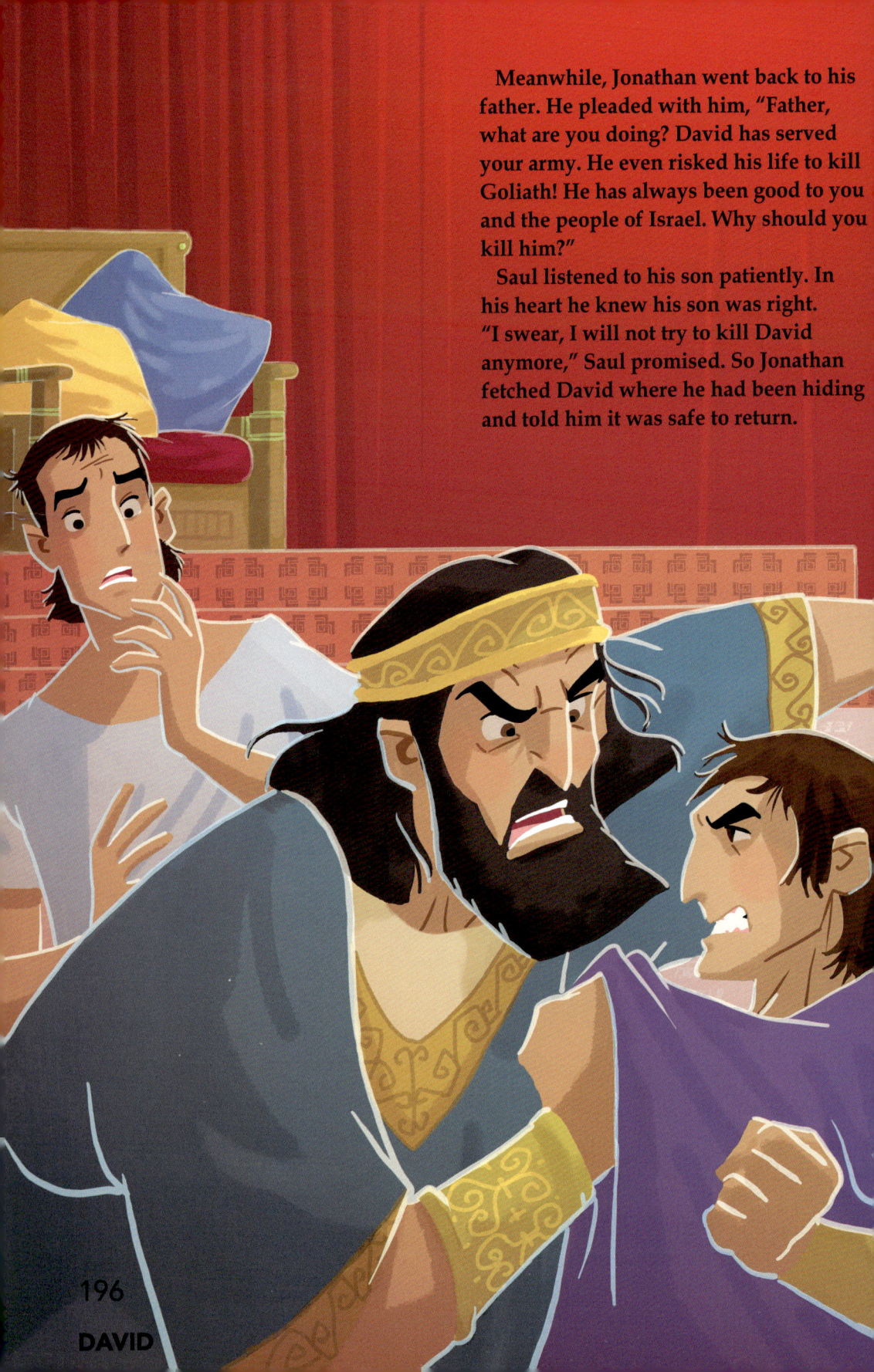

Meanwhile, Jonathan went back to his father. He pleaded with him, "Father, what are you doing? David has served your army. He even risked his life to kill Goliath! He has always been good to you and the people of Israel. Why should you kill him?"

Saul listened to his son patiently. In his heart he knew his son was right. "I swear, I will not try to kill David anymore," Saul promised. So Jonathan fetched David where he had been hiding and told him it was safe to return.

DAY 155
Jonathan's Plan
1 Samuel 19:9-20:24

Saul did not keep his promise very long. David returned to the palace to play the harp for Saul just like he used to. Saul could not control the evil spirits inside him, and he threw a sword at David again. David ducked out of the way and escaped.

Jonathan found David and told him, "Here is what we will do. Go hide. I will come back and shoot three arrows near where you are hiding. If I tell my servant boy, 'Pick up the arrows on the side of you!' those words mean it is safe to return. If I tell my servant boy, 'The arrow is farther away—run!' It means it is not safe and you must never return." David agreed with the plan and went off into hiding.

DAY 156
Jonathan Saves David's Life
1 Samuel 20:27-41

The next day Saul noticed that David was gone. Jonathan told his father, "I told David he could go to Bethlehem today. That is why he is gone." Saul was furious. He grabbed Jonathan by the arm and shouted, "What? You let David go? He deserves to die! When he comes back I will kill him!"

Later Jonathan hurried out to meet David. He shot an arrow and called out to the servant boy who was with him, "The arrow is farther away—run!" So the servant boy ran off after the arrow. David came out to meet Jonathan. They both knew David had to leave or be killed. The friends wept and hugged each other good-bye. Then Jonathan went back to the palace, and David went off to live a life wandering in the hills and the deserts.

DAY 157
Ahimelech Helps David
1 Samuel 21:1-9

The first place David fled to was the town of Nob. He needed food and supplies.

David went to the door of a priest by the name of Ahimelech. The priest opened the door looking suspiciously out at David. "Who are you with? Why are you alone?" the priest asked. He thought David might be a robber or a thief. David knew that the priest would not help him unless he had a good reason. So David told him, "I am on a soldier's mission for king Saul, but I am not supposed to speak about it. Do you have any bread you can spare?"

"The only bread I have is the sacred bread," the priest answered. Then he motioned for David to come inside. David assured him, "God is with me on my mission."

The priest piled five loaves of bread in David's arms.

Then David asked, "Do you have a spear or a sword? I had to leave before I could grab my weapons." The priest left the room and came back with something wrapped in cloth. "This was Goliath's sword," he said as he handed it to David. "You killed him, so you should have it." David took the sword. He smiled as he remembered the day he, as a boy, killed Goliath. "Thank you, priest!" David said. Then he left the house and ran off into the night.

DAY 158
Jonathan Encourages David
1 Samuel 23:14-18

David lived a wanderer's life, but he was not alone. With him were a group of men who were his friends and followers.

Saul was constantly searching for David. He often sent out soldiers to try and hunt him down. But God protected David and his men from harm. They had to move from place to place almost every night to keep from being caught. It was a hard, weary life. They had to watch out for wolves and other wild animals, and they often went hungry.

One day Jonathan went out to find his friend David whom he missed. When he finally found him, he put his hand on his friend's shoulder and said, "I know it must be hard to be without a home, but my father Saul will never get his hands on you. You are going to be king of Israel someday! Even my father knows it's true. When that day comes I will be your most faithful servant." David and Jonathan vowed always to be loyal friends. Then Jonathan went home again.

DAY 159
Alone in a Cave
1 Samuel 24:2-19

Back at the palace, Saul had decided to take three thousand of his best men out to capture David once and for all. He led his soldiers through the wilderness on horseback.

One night while they were camped near some desert rocks, Saul had to relieve himself. He stepped inside a dark cave for some privacy. He didn't realize that it was the same cave David and his men were living in! David and his men saw Saul, but they stayed quiet so as not to let Saul know they were there in the darkness. The men whispered, "David! Here is our chance to kill Saul!" But David whispered back to them, "No—do not hurt him." Instead David cut off a piece of Saul's robe secretly in the dark.

After Saul left the cave, David called out to him, "Your majesty!" Then he waved the cloth wildly in the air saying, "I could have killed you in that cave. But I did not because you are my God's chosen king. I don't want to harm you. So why do you want to harm me?" Saul was stunned. He called back, "David, you have spared my life. You are a better man than I am. May God reward you!"

DAVID

DAY 160
Nabal Rejects David
1 Samuel 25:2-13

David was now free to wander the hills without fear of Saul and his army. David and his men often roamed the land where shepherds would tend to their flocks. David was kind to the shepherds; he always offered protection for their sheep whenever they were in danger.

One day, David and his men were hungry and they had no food to eat. David sent ten of his men with a message to a man named Nabal. Nabal was a wealthy landowner in charge of many flocks in the town of Carmel. The message David sent said: "Friend, we have never done any harm to your shepherds or sheep. Please be kind in return and share some of your food with us." But Nabal was gruff and mean. He told David's messengers, "Why should I give my food to a ragged, no-good runaway like David?" So David's messengers came back and told David what Nabal had said. David felt insulted, and he clenched his fists in anger. He told his men, "Get your swords. We'll show Nabal and his family a thing or two!"

The men started off with their weapons toward Carmel.

DAY 161
Abigail Meets David
1 Samuel 25:14-31

Abigail was Nabal's wife. She had heard that her husband had not been kind to David. She was sorry, but she was also worried that David would take his revenge out on Nabal and their family. She left at once to apologize and offer David the food he had asked for. Abigail walked out into the desert where she heard that David was living. Behind her were several donkeys carrying heavy sacks on their backs. The sacks were overflowing with wine, meat, raisins, figs, and all kinds of good things to eat and drink.

When Abigail saw David she fell down on her knees. "My husband is foolish," she cried out. "He does not realize that God has promised to make you the ruler of Israel! Please forgive him and do not harm us. You have never killed innocent people before because you are good, and God is with you." Then Abigail opened up the sacks of food and passed them around to the men.

DAY 162
Nabal Dies
David Marries Abigail
1 Samuel 25:32-42

After David heard what Abigail had to say, he smiled. "God must have sent you here today just for me," David told her.

"I was about to do a bad thing and attack innocent people. You should be praised. You have reminded me that God has greater plans for me than taking revenge on my enemies. Abigail, go home now. Don't worry. We will not harm you or your husband!" So Abigail thanked David and went home.

When she got home, Abigail found her husband Nabal stuffing his mouth full of food, laughing and drinking, and acting foolish. Abigail waited until the morning when her husband was sober. Then she told Nabal that David had planned to attack him until she had gone to make peace. Nabal was so surprised that he had a heart attack. Then ten days later, he died. David heard the news and remarked to his friends, "I did not have to kill Nabal. Nabal killed himself with his own foolish behavior."

Then David sent a message to Abigail asking her to marry him. Abigail rode out to the desert and accepted his proposal. They were married right there in the desert with God's blessing.

DAY 163
David Rescues His Soldiers' Families
1 Samuel 30:1-18

Enemy tribes were attacking towns all over Israel. David got word of this. He took his men and went out to see what was going on. When David and his men came to their old homes and villages, they found them burned. People were nowhere to be seen. David's men stood dumbfounded, and then they cried with sorrow over their lost families. David prayed to God.

God told David, "Go after the Amalekites who have taken your families! Catch up with them. There is still time to save your people!" David comforted his men and told them, "Let us go do something to save our families before it is too late!" They caught up with the enemies who were busy throwing a big party for their victory over the Israelites. They did not notice David and his men coming closer to them. Just before sunrise, David gave the orders to attack the Amalekites.

God was with David and his men, and they won the battle. Then they found their family members who had been taken as prisoners, and they rescued them.

DAY 164
Saul and Jonathan Die
1 Samuel 31:1-6

While David had been fighting the Amalekites, Saul was busy fighting the Philistines on Mt. Gilboa in Israel's desert. The battle was brutal and violent. Almost all of Saul's soldiers were killed. Those who were left ran away from the Philistine army in fear for their lives. Saul watched as all three of his sons were killed, even Jonathan, David's loyal friend.

Finally Saul saw that it was hopeless. He said to his servant, "Kill me with your sword! Otherwise the Philistines will take me and be mean to me. Then they will kill me." But the servant could not bear to kill his king. So Saul stuck his sword into his own stomach and fell on it. The servant was full of grief to see his king die, so he killed himself in exactly the same manner.

It was a dark and dreary day for the Israelite army. Saul's days of being king had finally come to an end. The rule of a new king was about to begin.

DAY 165
David Is Crowned
2 Samuel 5:1-10; 1 Chronicles 14:8-17

The news spread quickly to the Philistines that David had been crowned king of Israel. They sent out a huge army to capture David. David prayed to God just as he always had done. God answered David's prayer. When David marched out to meet the Philistines, he and his army won the battle. The people of Israel loved David for his strength and bravery. They showered him with praises, but David did not accept the glory. Instead he said, "I have won only because of God! He broke through my enemies like a mighty flood!"

Jerusalem became a splendid city, and David made sure that God was at the center of its majesty.

DAY 166
David Dances for God
1 Chronicles 15:1–16:6

David invited the people of Israel to come to Jerusalem for a big celebration. The Ark of God, a heavy chest that held the Ten Commandments, was going to be carried into town. David had a tent made especially for the ark until a proper temple could be built for it.

The people sang and clapped and danced down the street as four men carried the Ark of God on their shoulders. David knew it was a joyous occasion because the Word of God was with him and his people. Cymbals clanged together and horns blew in happy celebration. David danced along with his people and praised God.

Meanwhile, one of David's wives, Michal, was looking down from an upper window with a sour look on her face. "David!" she shouted, "How can you leap and dance like such a fool? You are a king now!" David only smiled up at her and replied, "I dance because God is my King, and I am happy. No one can be a fool when they are dancing for God!"

DAY 167
David Has Uriah Killed
2 Samuel 11:2-17

One day David went up to the roof of his palace. From there he had a wonderful view of Jerusalem. As he was looking out into the distance, he spotted a beautiful woman taking a bath in the moonlight. He asked his servant, "Who is that woman?"

"Her name is Bathsheba. She is the wife of one of your soldiers, Uriah," the servant answered.

David sent for Bathsheba. He fell in love with her. He was selfish and wanted her for his wife even though she was someone else's wife.

Bathsheba became pregnant with David's child. When David heard the news, he sent for Uriah. He talked about the army in a man-to-man way with Uriah, but David did not say anything about Bathsheba and the baby on the way. When David sent Uriah home, Uriah did not go to Bathsheba. Instead, he slept right out on the street in front of the palace! He did this because he was a faithful soldier, and he wanted to show his loyalty to King David.

But David wanted to find a way to get rid of Uriah. He ordered Uriah to fight on the front lines of the next big battle. In the battle, Uriah was wounded and killed just as David had planned.

Now David was free to marry Bathsheba. But God was not pleased.

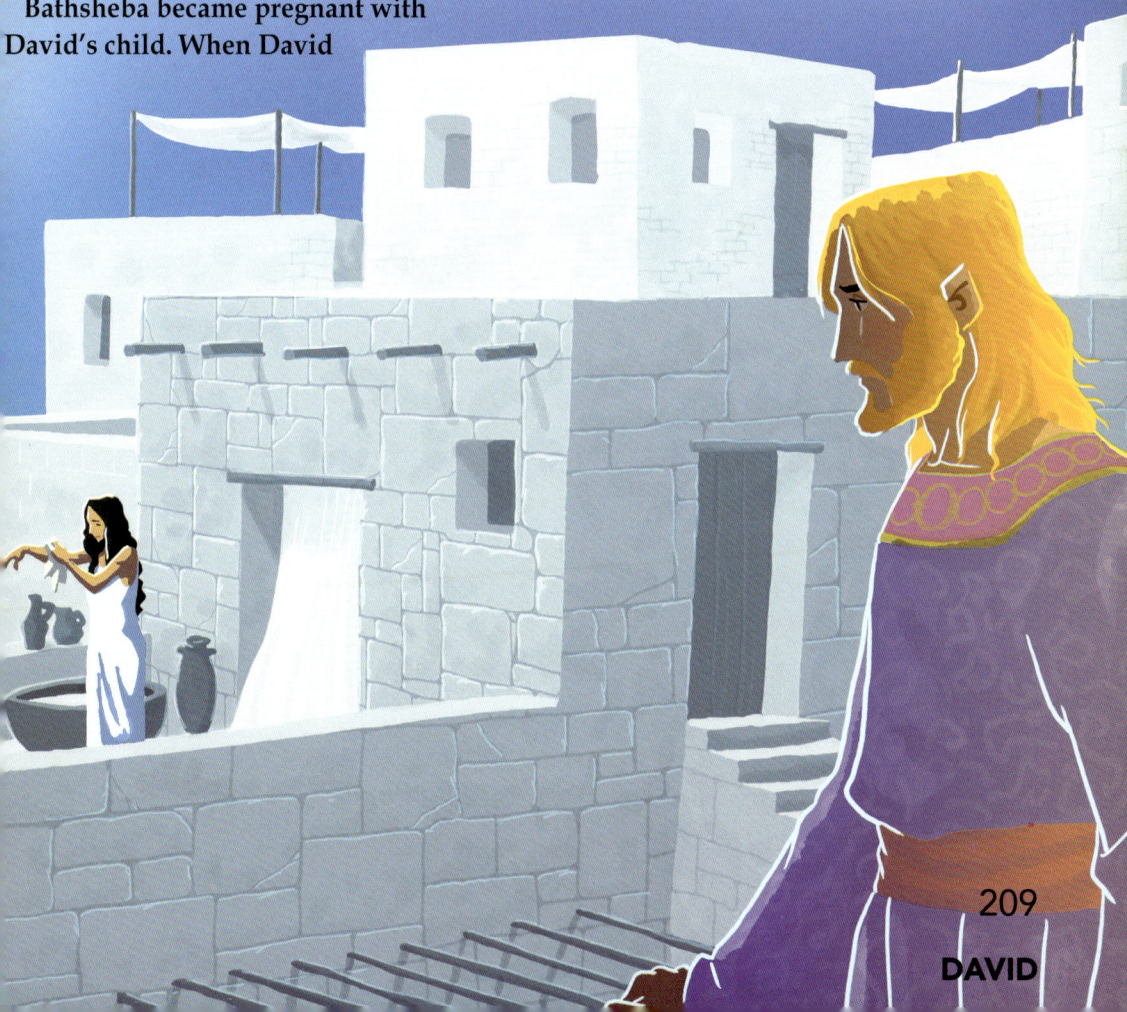

DAVID

DAY 168
A Broken King
2 Samuel 12:1-14

God saw what David had done. He was angry. He sent a man named Nathan to tell David a story. "Listen to my story," said Nathan to David, "and tell me what you think."

"Once there were two men. One was rich with lots of sheep and cattle. The other was poor. He had only one little lamb. The lamb was precious to him. He even let the lamb eat from his plate, drink from his cup, and sleep in his lap! One day the rich man had a visitor. He did not want to waste any of his own animals, so he stole the poor man's lamb and served it to his visitor for supper."

After Nathan had finished, David said, "The rich man behaved selfishly. He took the one thing that was important to the poor man. He should be punished!"

"You are that rich man!" Nathan cried out in response. "You had Uriah killed because you wanted what he had—his wife, Bathsheba!"

David knew that Nathan was right. He hung his head in shame.

"God has already forgiven you," said Nathan, "but because of this your newborn son will die."

DAVID

DAY 169
Solomon's Wish
2 Samuel 12:15-24; 1 Kings 2:10-11; 3:5-15

Just as Nathan had said, David's baby boy died. When Bathsheba gave birth to another child, they named him Solomon. Solomon became king after David died. He was loved by all the people just like his father was.

One night God came to Solomon in a dream and said, "What do you want? Ask and I will give it to you."

Solomon answered, "I am supposed to rule over Your chosen people, yet there are so many of them! Please give me wisdom so that I can be a good king for this great nation of Yours."

God was pleased. He said, "Solomon, you could have asked for a long life, or countless jewels, or revenge on your enemies. Instead you have asked for something that will help your people. You have asked for wisdom. I will make you wiser than anyone who has ever lived. I will also give you great wealth and a long life because you have pleased Me."

Then Solomon woke up. He remembered what God had said, and he felt happy inside. Solomon had a big feast that day to celebrate God's words.

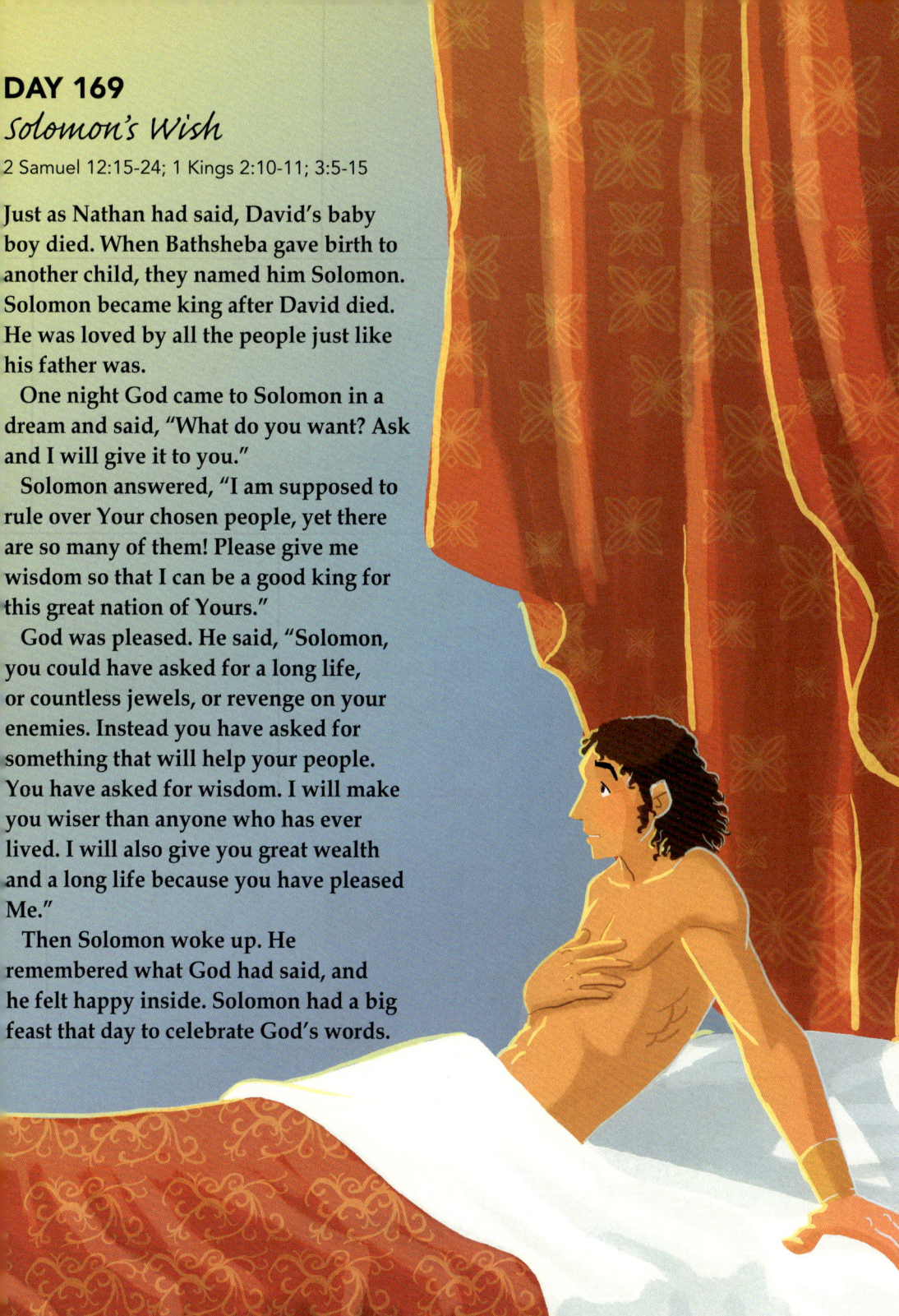

DAY 170
Solomon's Wise Decision
1 Kings 3:16-28

Solomon grew wise indeed. He took care of many decisions at the palace.

One day two women came to him with a big problem that no one could solve.

One of the women cried out to Solomon, "Help me! This woman and I live in the same house, and we both had babies. While this woman was asleep, she rolled on top of her baby and it died. While I was asleep she took my baby and traded it for her dead baby. When I woke up, I saw the baby's face, and I knew he was not mine. She has taken my baby!"

The other woman yelled, "It's not true! This baby is mine!"

Solomon knew the solution.

"Someone bring me a sword," David said. "We will split the baby right down the middle. That way both of you can have half of him."

One of the women screamed and sobbed, "No! I love the dear little babe! Give it to this other woman if you must—just don't kill him!"

Solomon knew that only the true mother of the baby would make such a tearful scene, and so he gave the baby back to her.

DAY 171
Solomon Builds a Temple to the Lord
1 Kings 5:1-6:38

Hiram was a neighboring king that ruled over the land of Tyre. He had been one of King David's good friends. Solomon knew this, so he sent Hiram a message.

He wrote: "My father King David had always wanted to build a temple where God would be worshipped. But every time my father began his plans, enemies attacked the area, making it impossible for my father to begin. Now there is peace. I would like to use your workers to cut down the cedar and pine trees and finally build the temple. You were one of my father's most loyal friends. Will you help me?"

King Hiram was delighted to hear that Solomon was going to fulfill his father's dream of building a temple for God. He wrote back, "God has given David a wise son. Of course I will help you by giving you all the cedar and pine logs you need."

So after seven years of hard work, God's holy temple was built. God told Solomon, "Obey My words, and I will keep the promise I made to your father. I will live among My people in the temple you have built for Me."

DAY 172
The Queen of Sheba Visits Solomon
1 Kings 4:29-33; 10:1-7

God had blessed Solomon with many things—abundant harvests, blooming gardens, and great wealth. People in far-off lands heard about Solomon's magnificent city. They heard of Solomon's knowledge about everything from plants and trees to reptiles and fish. Yet not only was Solomon wise, he was also a poet who could create beautiful songs.

The queen of Sheba wanted to see this great man for herself. She traveled a long way to Jerusalem and finally arrived at the palace. Tables were overloaded with fruit and good things to eat. The cups and plates and utensils were all made out of gold. Servants were dressed in richly colored uniforms made of expensive fabric. But the queen wanted to meet Solomon. She wondered, "Was he really as wise as people said?"

Solomon greeted her kindly. Then the queen of Sheba asked Solomon every difficult question she could think of. Solomon answered each one with ease. He had no trouble at all coming up with wise answers to each question she asked him.

"I have heard all about your wealth and wisdom," said the queen, "but I could not believe it until now. I am convinced. Solomon, you are more wise and magnificent than anyone I have ever met. May God bless you!"

SOLOMON

DAY 173
Elijah in the Wilderness
1 Kings 16:32-33; 17:1-7

After Solomon died, Israel was ruled by king after king. But it was King Ahab who angered God more than any of the others. He disobeyed God by worshiping idols and setting up an altar to Baal. Elijah was a prophet. He went to King Ahab and told him, "I serve the Lord God. And the Lord has sent me to tell you that it won't rain until I say so. For the next few years, there won't even be dew on the ground." Then God told Elijah to go and hide near Cherith Creek east of the Jordan River. "You can drink from the creek," the Lord told him. "And I will send the ravens to bring you food."

So Elijah obeyed the Lord and lived in the wilderness. He drank the water from the brook. And every morning and evening, ravens came to Elijah bringing him bread and meat. But because the Lord had stopped the rain, the creek soon dried up, and Elijah had nothing to drink.

DAY 174
Elijah Helps a Widow
1 Kings 17:8-16

Elijah was thirsty. The Lord told Elijah, "Go to the town of Zarephath. There's a widow living there. She will give you what you need." So Elijah walked until he came to the town gates. He saw a

widow gathering sticks for a fire. "Would you give me a drink of water?" he asked her. And so the widow brought him some water.

Then he asked her, "Is there a piece of bread I might have too?"

The widow answered, "I don't have any bread. I only have some flour and some olive oil. I was going home to build a fire to cook what I have left. After that my son and I will starve."

Elijah told her, "Don't worry. Go home and cook what you have for you and your son. But first make a small cake for me. Then you will see how God provides. He will fill up your jar of flour and your bottle of olive oil. And He will keep them filled until He sends rain again." So the widow went home and did what Elijah told her. She made a small cake and brought it to Elijah. Then she cooked the rest for her and her son. When she went back to the kitchen, she saw that her jar of flour and her bottle of olive oil had been filled up again! She invited Elijah to stay with her, and they never ran out of food.

DAY 175
A Contest
1 Kings 18:16-24

God told Elijah to go to King Ahab and tell him that the Lord would send rain. When King Ahab heard that Elijah was coming, he ran out to meet him. "You troublemaker!" he yelled. "Look at all the suffering you've caused Israel!"

But Elijah told him, "You are the troublemaker. You have disobeyed God and worshipped Baal. Let's sacrifice two bulls. You can sacrifice your bull to Baal. I'll sacrifice my bull to the Lord God. But we won't light them on fire. Instead we will pray. Let the true God answer our prayer by lighting the bull on fire."

DAY 176
The True God
1 Kings 18:25-39

So King Ahab prepared two bulls and put them on two altars. King Ahab brought out his prophets. They danced around the bull. "Answer us, Baal!" they prayed. But nothing happened all morning. "Pray louder—" Elijah teased

them, "maybe he's daydreaming. Or maybe he's taking a nap, and you have to wake him up."

Then Elijah went over to his altar. "Lord, please answer me," Elijah prayed. "Let these people know that You are God. Then they will give their hearts back to You." King Ahab and all his prophets watched as Elijah's altar lit up in flames. Even the pebbles on the ground were scorched and burnt. King Ahab and his men bowed down and said, "The Lord is God!"

Elijah jumped up and told his servant, "Go warn King Ahab to hurry home. Otherwise the rain will stop him."

Then the wind began to whistle through the trees. The cloud that seemed so small filled up the whole sky and turned it black. Rain poured down and flooded the ground. Elijah wrapped his coat around him and ran as fast as he could. He made it to Jezreel faster than the king, even though the king had his chariot.

DAY 177
The Raincloud
1 Kings 18:41-46

Elijah told King Ahab, "Go get some rest. Have a drink and eat some food. The Lord is going to send rain." So King Ahab headed back to Jezreel in his chariot.

But Elijah climbed to the top of Mount Carmel. He crouched on the ground and sunk his head between his knees. Then he said to his servant, "Go and look toward the sea." The servant looked but he didn't see anything. So Elijah told him to go and look again. The servant gazed out as far as he could. But there was nothing.

Then, on the seventh time, the servant told Elijah, "I see a cloud. But it's no bigger than a fist."

DAY 178
Elijah Says Good-bye
2 Kings 2:1-12

Elijah gained many followers. One of his most important helpers was Elisha.

When it was time for Elijah to go be with the Lord, Elisha followed him to the Jordan River to say good-bye. Fifty other prophets came and followed behind them.

Then Elijah took off his coat and struck the water with it. The Jordan River split apart and made a path. Elijah and Elisha walked across to the other side. Then Elijah asked him, "What can I do for you before the Lord takes me away?"

Elisha answered, "Please give me twice as much of your power. I want to lead the people like you did."

Elijah said, "That's not an easy thing to give. But if you see me as the Lord takes me away, then you'll get it."

Elijah and Elisha went on talking until they saw a flaming chariot driven by beautiful horses coming toward them. Elisha looked on in wonder as a strong wind blew Elijah away with the chariot up toward heaven. "The Lord has taken my master away!" Elisha cried. He tore his clothes and wept because he was sad to lose his friend.

DAY 179
Elisha Can Perform Miracles
2 Kings 2:13-18

Elisha found Elijah's coat still lying on the ground near the river bank. He picked it up and struck the Jordan River with it. "Will the Lord's Spirit be in me as it was in Elijah?" Elisha asked aloud. And suddenly the river parted and made a path to the other side. Elisha walked across and met the prophets who were waiting for him on the other side. They bowed down at his feet. "You have Elijah's power," they told him. "But let us go search for Elijah. Maybe the Lord just carried him off to the mountains or into a valley."

"No," Elisha said. "You won't find him."

But the fifty prophets were stubborn. They begged Elisha to let them go look for Elijah. And soon Elisha was embarrassed to say no one more time. So he let them go. The men searched for three days but found no sign of Elijah. They went back to Jericho where Elisha was staying. "We didn't find him," they said.

"I told you that you wouldn't find him," Elisha replied.

DAY 180
The Bottomless Jar of Olive Oil
2 Kings 4:1-7

One of the Lord's fifty prophets died. His wife went to Elisha in tears. "My husband loved the Lord," she told him. "But he owed a man some money before he died. Now that man has come to take my two sons away as slaves."

Elisha said, "I'll do my best to help you. What do you have left in your house?"

"All I have is a little bottle of oil," she said.

"Go quickly and ask your neighbors for all their empty jars. Then go home and fill the jars with the oil you have left. Set each jar aside, and keep filling."

So the woman collected as many jars as she could. Her sons helped her, and then they began to fill the jars with oil. The oil did not stop flowing. They filled jar after jar after jar. "Give me another," the woman told her sons.

"But mother," they said, "we have used them all."

So the woman went back to Elisha. "What do I do now?" she asked him.

"Go sell all your bottles of olive oil. And you can give the man what you owe him. You and your sons can live on whatever is left. You don't have to worry anymore."

DAY 181
Jonah Runs from the Lord
Jonah 1:1-6

One day the Lord came to a man named Jonah. He said, "Go to the city of Nineveh. The people there keep sinning. Tell the people about the Lord their God so they may turn their hearts back to Me."

But Jonah didn't go. He ran away instead. He went to the seaside town of Joppa. Then he got on a ship for Spain. He thought that he could hide from God by going far away. The Lord saw Jonah and punished him by sending a great storm on the sea. The sailors were frightened. They began to throw out the cargo to make the ship lighter. But it was no use, the ship was about to be broken to pieces. All the people on board began to pray to their own gods—except Jonah. Jonah went below deck and fell asleep.

DAY 182
Jonah Is Thrown into the Sea
Jonah 1:7-16

The captain shook Jonah by the shoulders. "How can you sleep at a time like this? Start praying!" he shouted. Meanwhile the sailors wanted to know who caused such an awful storm. They decided it was Jonah. "Look what you've done!" they yelled at him.

Jonah said, "Yes, I caused this storm. Throw me into the water, and it will calm down."

The sailors tried everything they could to keep from drowning. They rowed with all their might to get out of the crashing waves. But the storm only got worse. They prayed to their gods, "Don't be angry with us for killing this man." Then they threw Jonah overboard into the wild waves. But at that moment the sea calmed down.

DAY 183
Jonah and the Big Fish
Jonah 1:17-2:10

Jonah was adrift in the ocean. He could not swim. He began to sink down into the deep, past underwater mountains and all kinds of sea creatures. Then out of the dark, a gigantic fish swam toward Jonah. The Lord had sent it to swallow him. The fish opened its huge, wide mouth and gulped Jonah down to its belly. Jonah was alive inside the big fish for three days and three nights.

From inside the fish's belly, Jonah prayed, "Lord God, You sent me down to the darkest part of the ocean. The seaweed wrapped around my head, and the waters swallowed me. I thought You would end my life. But in the very lowest of places, You heard my prayer. You saved my life. I praise You because You have the power to save those who turn their backs on You."

God heard Jonah's prayer. So He made the big fish spit Jonah up onto dry land.

DAY 184
Jonah Warns the People
Jonah 3:1-10

The Lord came a second time to Jonah. He said, "Now go to Nineveh and tell the people that I have seen their sins." So Jonah obeyed and went to Nineveh. The city was big. It took Jonah three days to walk through it. He shouted in the streets, "The Lord is angry with your city. In forty days it will crumble."

The people believed Jonah. They stopped eating to show the Lord their obedience. They dressed in sackcloth. And when the king heard Jonah's message, he took off his fancy robes and dressed in sackcloth too. He sat in the dust and told the people, "Do not eat or drink. Dress in sackcloth and put them on your animals too. Then pray to the Lord God with your whole heart. Maybe He will see how sorry we are and show mercy."

God heard the prayers of the people. They begged for forgiveness and promised to stop sinning. So the Lord showed His love and did not destroy the city as He planned.

DAY 185
Jonah Gets Angry
Jonah 4:1-6

But there was one person who was not happy that Nineveh had been saved. Jonah was annoyed. "Lord, I knew this would happen," he prayed. "That's why I ran away and got on that ship. You are a kind and loving God. You don't punish people; You forgive them instead. So why was I sent here? Just let me die. I would be better off dead."

The Lord replied, "Why are you angry?"

But Jonah didn't answer. He walked through the gate of the city and found a place to sit. Then he built a shelter around him. He waited to see if God would destroy Nineveh. The Lord made a vine grow up and shade Jonah from the hot sun. Then Jonah fell asleep.

DAY 186
God Shows Mercy
Jonah 4:7-11

The next morning Jonah saw that the vine had dried up. The Lord sent a worm to eat its leaves. Jonah was upset. He felt the hot sun beating down on him, and he began to feel faint. "I wish I were dead," he moaned.

"Do you have the right to be angry about a vine?" the Lord asked Jonah.

"Yes," Jonah grumbled. "And I'm angry enough to die."

The Lord replied, "You are angry with a vine. But you didn't create the vine. And you didn't care for the vine. What about the city of Nineveh? I created the people, and I cared for them. Don't they deserve My concern?"

DAY 187
Jerusalem Is Destroyed
2 Chronicles 36:11-21

Zedekiah was a king of Judah. He ruled over the city of Jerusalem for eleven years. But he didn't care about serving the Lord. He did whatever he wanted to do, and not what God wanted. Even when God's prophets warned him, his heart was hardened, and he didn't listen. One day King Nebuchadnezzar of Babylonia asked Zedekiah to promise in God's name he would be loyal. Zedekiah would not do it.

Because the king was unfaithful, the people of Jerusalem began to be unfaithful too. They did not care about the temple of the Lord. But God didn't want to hurt the people. So He sent prophets out to tell them about their sins. The people just laughed at these prophets and called them names. So the Lord punished the land of Judah. He sent King Nebuchadnezzar and his army to attack the whole country. They broke down the walls of Jerusalem. They tore down the buildings. And they took the people back to Babylonia to be their slaves.

Judah was an empty desert. You could not hear the sound of a dog barking or a child laughing anywhere. The Lord let it stay that way for seventy years.

DAY 188
Daniel and His Friends
Daniel 1:3-7

King Nebuchadnezzar did not keep all of the Israelites as slaves. He ordered his chief official to pick some of them to come and work in his palace. "Make sure they are healthy and smart and handsome," he told him. "I only want the very best working for me." Then he said, "They must be turned into Babylonians. Don't let them speak Hebrew. Teach them our language instead. And make sure they read all our books. After three years of training, they can work for me."

So the king's official went to the Israelites. He tested their strength and their smarts. When he had finally picked out the best ones, he brought them back to the king's palace. The king refused to let them keep their Jewish names. He gave them each a Babylonian name instead. Daniel was one of the young men chosen. But they changed his name to Belteshazzar. Daniel's three friends were also chosen. They were renamed Shadrach, Meshach, and Abednego.

DANIEL

DAY 189
The King's Diet
Daniel 1:8-14

The king let Daniel and his friends eat the royal food and wine served at the palace. But no matter how delicious it smelled, Daniel would not eat it. He only wanted the food that God approved. The official was friendly to Daniel. But he told him, "You must eat or else the king will notice you're too skinny. He'll have me killed for it." But Daniel still refused.

That night Daniel went to the guard in charge of him and his three friends. He told him, "Give us only vegetables and water for the next ten days. On the last day see how we look compared with the other men who have been feasting on the king's food."

DAY 190
A Test of Faith
Daniel 1:15-21

The guard did as Daniel asked. But on the tenth day, Daniel and his friends were stronger and healthier looking than any of the other men. So the guard let them continue to eat only vegetables and water. They never became weak. Instead they grew stronger and more intelligent. They read every book in the palace and knew many things. Daniel could even tell the meaning of dreams. The king thought, "They're so wise they make my magicians and advisors look like fools!"

The king gave Daniel and his three friends high positions in the royal court.

DAY 191
Nebuchadnezzar's Dream
Daniel 2:1-13

King Nebuchadnezzar began to wake up with horrible nightmares. For several nights he dreamed the same thing. Sweat poured from his forehead, and he was afraid to shut his eyes. He went to his best magicians and some of his wise men. "I am very upset about my dream," he told them. "I don't know what it means."

"Tell us what it was about," they said, "and maybe we can tell you the meaning."

But the king said, "Aren't you magicians and wise men? You should be able to tell me what I dreamt and its meaning. If you don't I'll chop you into pieces and tear your houses down. But if you do, then I'll reward you."

Once more they replied, "We'll tell you what it means if you tell us the dream."

"No," the king said angrily. "You only want me to tell you the dream so you have time to make something up. Now tell me what I dreamt."

"That's impossible," they cried. "No one could know that except for gods. And we are not gods." The king became furious. He gave orders for every wise man in Babylonia to be put to death. Daniel and his three friends were included.

DANIEL

DAY 192
God Reveals the Dream to Daniel
Daniel 2:19-48

That night the Lord revealed the king's dream to Daniel. Then he prayed, "Praise to You, God, for You reveal mysteries." The next day Daniel went to the official in charge of rounding up the wise men and killing them. "Stop!" he shouted. "I know the king's dream, and I know its meaning." So the official rushed Daniel to the king.

"Your majesty," said Daniel, "no man, no matter how wise, could tell you what your dream meant. Only God knows. But last night He made your dream known to me. You looked up and you saw a terrifying statue standing over you. The statue's head was of gold, its chest and arms of silver, its belly and thighs of bronze, its legs of iron, and its feet of both iron and clay. Then you watched a stone being cut away from a mountain. The stone fell on the statue's feet, and the whole thing was crushed and blown away. That was your dream.

Now I will tell you what your dream meant. You are the statue's head made of gold. After you are gone, another kingdom will rule. Then, a kingdom of bronze will rule—and then a kingdom of iron. Lastly, a kingdom divided will rule, just like the feet were a mixture of iron and clay."

The king was amazed. He told Daniel, "Your God gave you the power to understand my dream. Now I know that your God is the true Lord."

So the king made Daniel governor of Babylon.

235
DANIEL

DAY 193
Three Brave Men

Daniel 3:1-18

King Nebuchadnezzar had a statue made like the one in his dream. It was ninety feet tall and made of gold. Then he had a ceremony to dedicate the statue. Many people came and when they had all gathered, an official told them, "When you hear the horns blast and the harps sound and the flutes play, then bow down and worship the statue. Whoever does not will be thrown into the fiery furnace."

So when the music began, all the people fell on their knees. But Shadrach, Meshach, and Abednego would not bow down.

"Your majesty," the people yelled. "Look at those Jews—they refuse to listen to you. They aren't worshiping your statue as you have ordered."

King Nebuchadnezzar was furious and sent for Shadrach, Meshach, and Abednego. "Why aren't you bowing down to my statue?" he asked them.

The three men replied, "Your majesty, we are not afraid. We worship God, and He will save us from the furnace. But even if He does not save us, we still won't bow down to anyone but Him."

DAY 194
The Blazing Furnace
Daniel 3:19-29

"Heat the furnaces," King Nebuchadnezzar ordered. "And make them seven times hotter than usual." He was furious at Shadrach, Meshach, and Abednego for disobeying his order. The three men were tied up with ropes. Then the king's soldiers led them over to the furnace. They opened the door and the flames licked the soldiers and killed some of them. The three men were pushed into the fire.

"I only ordered three men to be burned, right?" the king suddenly shouted.

"Yes, your majesty," his men answered.

"So why are there four men walking around in the flames? They aren't even tied up. And the fourth one looks like a god."

"Come out, come out," the king shouted. "Shadrach, Meshach, and Abednego, you are servants of the true God!"

The three men stepped out of the furnace. They had not been burned. Not a single hair on their heads had been singed. Their clothes weren't blackened. And they didn't even smell a bit like smoke.

"Praise the God of Shadrach, Meshach, and Abednego," the king said. "He sent an angel to rescue these brave men. They chose to die rather than disobey their Lord. From this day forward no one is allowed to speak a single bad word against the God they worship."

DANIEL

DAY 195
King Belshazzar's Banquet
Daniel 5:1-6

King Belshazzar ruled over Babylon after his father Nebuchadnezzar died. One evening he threw a party at his palace. He had a feast prepared and set a long, beautiful table. He ordered only the best gold and silver cups to be used. So they took the cups from the temple in Jerusalem. All of the king's highest officials were invited. They ate and drank and praised their idols made of gold, silver, bronze, iron, wood, and stone.

While they were busy having a good time, a hand was writing on the wall of the palace. The king suddenly looked up and saw the hand. He turned as white as a ghost, and his knees began to knock together because he was so frightened.

DAY 196
King Belshazzar' Sends for Daniel
Daniel 5:7-12

"What does this say?" the king asked his advisors, pointing to the writing. "Whoever can read this will be the third most powerful man in Babylon. He can wear purple robes and a gold chain and live like royalty."

The king's highest officials studied the writing but they were stumped. They couldn't understand a word of it. The queen came in and heard the men talking. She told her husband, "Don't look so scared. There is one man who can solve riddles and explain dreams. Don't you remember Daniel? Bring him in here, and he'll solve the mystery for you."

DAY 197
Daniel Is Brought In
Daniel 5:13-24

Daniel was brought before the king.

"I hear that you have the ability to interpret dreams," the king said to him. "If you can read me the writing on the wall and tell me what it means, I will make you very rich."

"Your majesty," Daniel replied, "I will tell you what the writing means. But keep all your jewels and fancy robes. I don't want them. I saw how rich your father was, but his heart was hard, and his mind was like an animal. He had power over a whole kingdom, but because he did not obey God, he lost everything."

239

DANIEL

"Now I'm afraid you are following in his footsteps, your majesty. You are using the cups from God's temple to drink wine with your friends. You're bowing down to idols and statues. That's why God has sent this hand to write on the wall."

DAY 198
Daniel Reads the Writing
Daniel 5:25-31

"The words written here," continued Daniel, "mean numbered, weighed, and divided. And these words mean that God has numbered your days as king. He has weighed your time in power and you fall short. He is also going to divide your kingdom between the Medes and the Persians."

So the king sent Daniel away, keeping his promise to make him the third most powerful man in Babylon. But that night the king was killed by Darius the Mede.

DAY 199
King Darius's Law
Daniel 6:1-10

Darius divided his kingdom and put leaders in charge of each part. After he discovered how wise Daniel was, he made him head of all the other leaders. The others were jealous of Daniel. They tried to find something wrong with him. But Daniel was an honest man, and he always did excellent work. "Maybe we can trick Daniel into getting in trouble," they schemed.

They went to Darius and said, "Why don't you make a law that for the next thirty days no one can pray to anyone but you."

So King Darius agreed and put the law in writing.

Daniel heard about the law. But he went home that night and prayed to God just like he had always done. Just outside his door there were spies. They saw Daniel praying and ran back to the king. "Your majesty," they cried, "Daniel hasn't listened to you. He's in his room praying to God."

DAY 200
Daniel in the Lions' Den
Daniel 6:11-28

King Darius liked Daniel, and he didn't want to hurt him. But at last he said, "I can't take back what I have put in the law." So Daniel was taken away and thrown into a pit full of hungry lions. They rolled a stone over the pit and left him to die.

That night Darius couldn't sleep. He kept thinking about Daniel in the lions'

den. As soon as the sun came up, Darius went back to the pit to see what happened. He rolled away the stone. "Daniel, has your God saved you?" he yelled into the darkness.

"Yes, your majesty," Daniel answered. "God sent an angel to keep the lions from hurting me. He knew I was innocent." So the king had Daniel taken out of the pit. He didn't even have a scratch on him. God had protected him because of his faithfulness.

Darius ordered all the men who had plotted against Daniel to be thrown into the pit. The lions crushed them before they even touched the bottom.

DAY 201
The Proud King
Esther 1:1-8

Xerxes was King of Persia. He ruled over many people, and he had a grand palace in the capital city of Susa. One day he decided to give a big celebration to show off all his wealth. He invited his officials and officers. The dinner was such a success that the king decided to make the festivities last one hundred and eighty days. After that, the king gave a seven-day banquet. He invited everyone from the city of Susa to come no matter who they were.

The king opened up his palace gardens and had tables laid out full of delicious food. The cups were made of gold, and each one had a different pattern. The garden was decorated with colorful blue and white curtains that swooped between the tall columns. The floors were made of marble and adorned in jewels. There were couches made of gold and silver. And everyone who came was very impressed. When the royal wine was brought out, the king said to the people, "Drink as much as you want!"

DAY 202
Queen Vashti Disobeys
Esther 1:10-21

The king and his guests were in a good mood from all the wine. By the seventh day they did nothing but laugh and joke around. "Bring out my wife," the king said to his servants. "Let's see how beautiful and rich she looks with the royal crown on her head."

The servants went to Queen Vashti and told her what her husband had said. But Queen Vashti didn't want to go. So she stayed in her room. The servants went back and told the king. He pounded his fists on the table in anger. He was embarrassed that his wife had refused him in front of all his guests.

"Your majesty," the officials told the king, "her behavior is terrible. She is insulting you and every other husband in the kingdom. You should make a law against that kind of behavior. Then search the kingdom for the prettiest woman, and you can make her the new queen."

The king liked this idea. He immediately wrote up a law that said all wives must obey their husbands. Then his guests went home, and the king went to bed and fell into a deep sleep. Everyone was exhausted from eating and drinking so much.

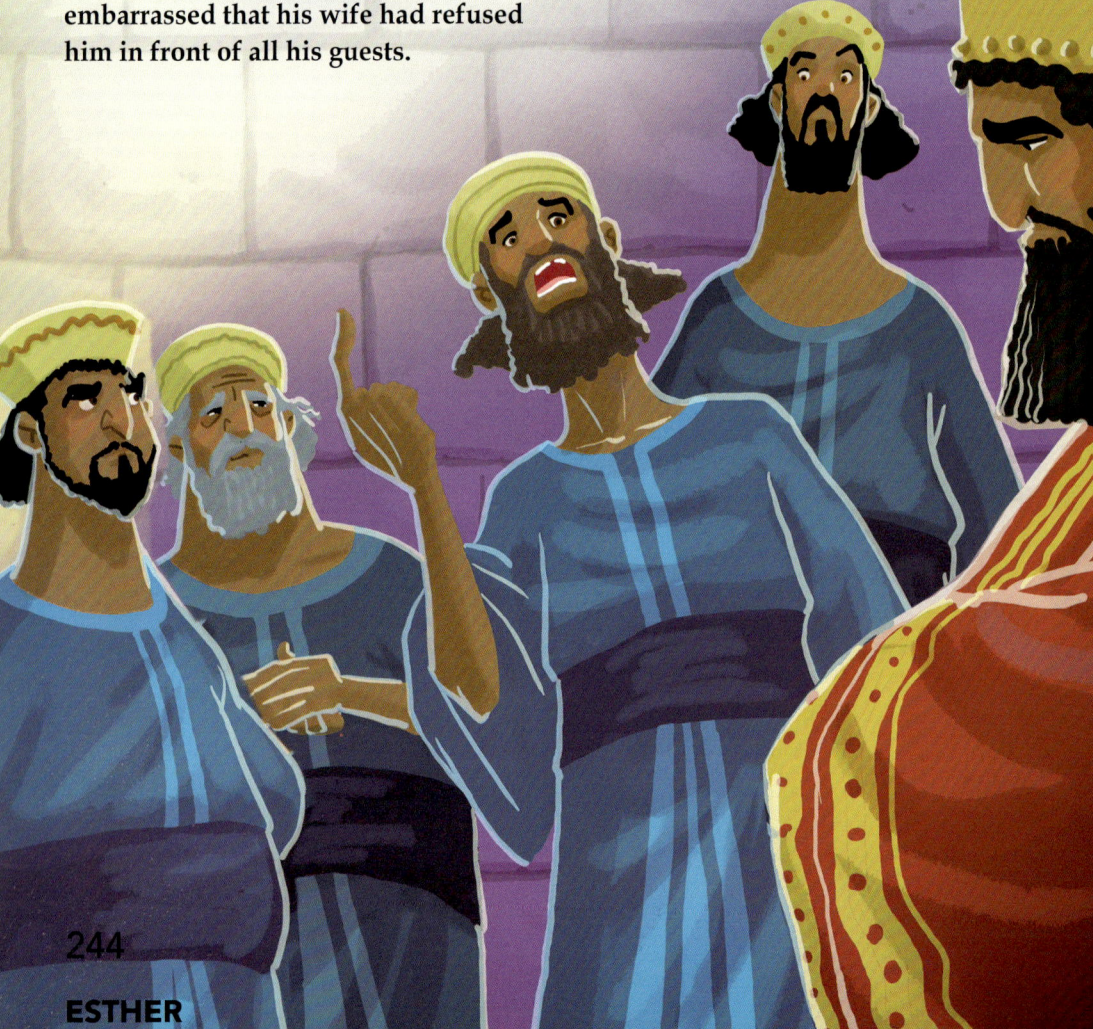

DAY 203
Esther Becomes Queen
Esther 2:1-17

King Xerxes began his search for a new queen. He had his officials round up the most beautiful young women in the kingdom. Esther was one of them. Esther was a Hebrew woman who had been raised by her cousin Mordecai because she didn't have any parents.

When Esther arrived at the palace, the king chose her along with his other favorites to stay with him for a whole year. They were flooded with gifts of expensive perfumes and scented oils. They each had a room with their own maids. And every day they had a beauty treatment to make them look even more beautiful.

During this time Mordecai would sneak into the courtyard and make sure Esther was okay. Then he would remind her not to tell anyone, especially the king, that she was a Hebrew.

When it was Esther's turn to meet privately with the king, she was so charming and gracious that he fell in love with her. Her beauty outshone the others. "I have found my new bride," he told all his officials. Then he put the crown on her head and made Esther queen.

DAY 204
Haman's Order
Esther 2:19–3:15

After Esther had become queen, her cousin Mordecai was made a palace official. But the king gave the highest position in his palace to a man named Haman. Everyone was ordered to kneel down to Haman. But when Mordecai's turn came to kneel, he would not do it. "Why aren't you kneeling down like you were told?" the other officials asked him.

"Because I am a Hebrew," Mordecai said. "And I don't kneel to anyone but God."

Haman was furious. He couldn't believe that someone had dishonored him. When he found out that it was because Mordecai was Jewish, he came up with a plan.

Haman went to the king and said, "The Jews in your kingdom are different from everybody else. They won't follow the king's laws or obey the rules. We can't put up with it anymore; let's kill them all."

"You have my permission," replied the king. "Do whatever you want."

So Haman sent out an announcement to everyone in the kingdom that read: "All Jewish men and women and their children are to be killed."

The news traveled from one ear into another. No one could believe it. "Why would the king order such a horrible thing?" the people wondered. Everyone started to panic.

DAY 205
Esther Has a Plan
Esther 4:8–5:9

Mordecai heard about Haman's order to kill the Jews. He tore up his clothes and went through Susa wailing and crying. But as soon as he saw Esther's servant in the city square, he told him, "Quick, tell Esther that her people are going to be murdered! Tell her to beg the king to save the Jews."

Esther got Mordecai's message that same day. But she sent one right back, saying, "No one is allowed to see the king without being invited. And it's been thirty days since he has asked for me."

Mordecai wrote back, "Esther, you are a Jew, and you will be killed too. If you don't speak up now, we will all be dead soon. And maybe God made you queen so that you could save your people at a time like this."

Esther knew that Mordecai was right. She decided to go to the king uninvited, even if it meant she must die. She put on her royal robes and made sure she looked her best. Then she opened the door to the court where the king sat on his throne.

"My darling," the king said happily surprised, "what brings you here? Whatever it is, just ask. I promise to give it to you."

"Come to the dinner I have prepared tonight," Esther answered. "And bring Haman with you."

So the king agreed and sent his servants to tell Haman too.

DAY 206
Esther Saves Her People
Esther 7:1-6

That night Esther dined with the king and Haman. They ate and drank together. And finally as they were finishing their meal, the king said, "Esther, what can I do for you? You have pleased me so much that I would give you half my kingdom if you asked."

Esther knew this was the moment.

"Your majesty," she said, "if you love me, then I ask you to do one thing for me. Save my people. There is an order going around the kingdom that all Jews must die."

"Who would dare order such a thing?" the king asked.

"Haman," Esther said. "He is the cruel-hearted one who is out to get us."

Haman looked back and forth between the king and queen. But his face was pale, and his eyes were full of fear.

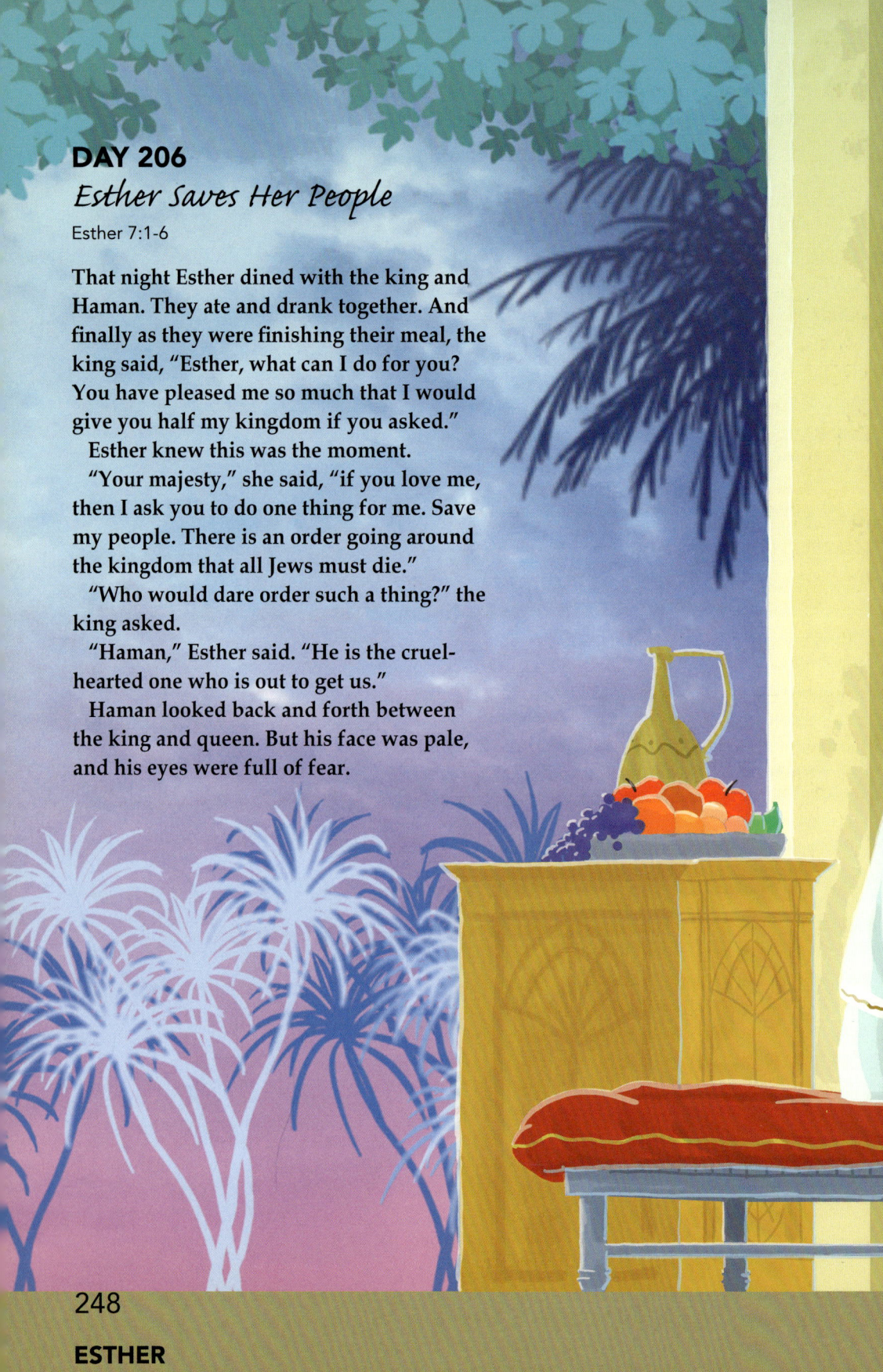

ESTHER

DAY 207
Haman Is Punished
Esther 7:7-8:2

The king was so angry he could barely even look at Haman. So he stormed off from the table and left his wine. Haman knew that it was no use to chase after him. He stayed and pleaded with Esther for his life. He dropped to his knees on the ground in front of her. But just then the king came back in the room. "Look at you!" the king shouted. "Now you are even bullying my wife right here in my own palace!"

"Your majesty, that's not all," one of the king's servants said. "Have you heard about the tower he built? He was going to let Mordecai hang from it." So the king gave an order for Haman to be hung on the tower instead. Then the king gave Esther everything that once belonged to Haman. He also made Mordecai one of his highest officials. He put Haman's ring on Mordecai's finger and gave him Haman's house and all of his land.

DAY 208
A Time to Celebrate
Esther 8:3-17; 9:1-28

King Xerxes said to Esther and Mordecai, "Now you can change the law. Seal it with my ring so that it can never be changed. Save your people!"

So the law was rewritten that no Jew was to be hurt. Secretaries wrote the new law down and messengers rode out as fast as they could, spreading the announcement. All the Jewish people of the kingdom had big parties and celebrated.

All the Jews united together. And no matter who tried to hurt them, the Lord was with them. They fought against their enemies and everyone became afraid of their power.

Mordecai wrote about the wonderful way things worked out. Then he sent letters to the Jews and told them, "This month is a time when our tears turned into smiles and celebration. Have parties and share your food with friends and family, as well as the poor. Never forget how the Lord has been good to you."

DAY 209
An Angel Visits Zechariah
Luke 1:5-25

Zechariah was a priest from Judea. His wife was Elizabeth. They were both growing old, and the Lord had not given them any children.

One day Zechariah was in the temple when he heard a voice say, "Don't be afraid!" Zechariah looked up and saw an angel standing by the altar. "Your wife is going to have a son. He will be a special person. God is going to use his life to help people see the truth. Your son will also make parents more loving toward their children. Name him John."

Zechariah did not know what to think. "How can this be true? My wife and I are much too old to have any children," he said to the angel.

"I am the angel Gabriel, and I speak the truth. I know you don't believe me. But just wait and you'll see the wonderful blessing God has in store for you."

Zechariah didn't know what to think. He went home to his wife Elizabeth and told her about the angel. Elizabeth had no doubt that God would keep His promise. "The Lord has done this for me," she said to herself. "I will finally get to be a mother."

254

JESUS' BIRTH

DAY 210
An Angel Visits Mary
Luke 1:26-38

Then Gabriel went to the town of Nazareth. He had a message for a young woman named Mary. "Greetings," he told her, "you are truly blessed!" But Mary was frightened. She didn't know what the angel was talking about. "Don't be afraid. The Lord is with you," the angel said. "He has sent me to tell you that you will give birth to a son. He will be called the Son of God. And God will make him a king, just like his ancestor David. But His kingdom will never end."

"How can I have a child?" Mary asked him. "I'm not married."

The angel answered, "The Holy Spirit will give you your child. That's why He will be called the Son of God. Even your relative Elizabeth is going to have a child. She thought she was too old. Nothing is impossible for God!"

"I am God's servant," Mary said. "I will do whatever He wants." Then the angel Gabriel left her.

JESUS' BIRTH

DAY 211
Mary and Elizabeth
Luke 1:39-45

Mary was excited. She ran all the way to Judea to find her relative Elizabeth.

"I have heard the news! The Lord is blessing you with a baby," Mary told her. "And the angel of the Lord has told me I will have a son too. He will be the Son of God, and His name will be Jesus."

Elizabeth felt her baby kick inside of her.

"My baby is moving—he's rejoicing!" Elizabeth said. "He knows that God has blessed you and your son. You have been given a gift greater than any other woman."

Mary beamed with happiness. Elizabeth saw that Mary trusted in the Lord completely. "The Lord has blessed you because you believed that He will keep His promise. He knows that your faith is strong. I am thrilled that you have come to tell me this great news."

DAY 212
Joseph's Dream
Matthew 1:18-24

Mary was engaged to a carpenter named Joseph. He was a good man, and she loved him very much. But after the angel had told her about Jesus, she wasn't sure if they should marry each other anymore. She talked it over with him, and they decided to call off the wedding. Joseph didn't want her to be unfaithful in the eyes of God.

That night while Joseph was in bed, an angel came and spoke to him. "Joseph," the angel said, "it's true that Mary's baby will be the Son of God. But don't call off your wedding. Marry her and raise the child together. His name will be Jesus, and He will save people from their sins."

Joseph woke up and felt joy in his heart. He remembered his dream and told Mary. They married each other with God's blessing.

JESUS' BIRTH

DAY 213
Jesus Is Born
Luke 2:1-7

The Emperor of Rome had made a rule that everyone must list their families in record books. People had to register from their hometown. So Joseph left Nazareth and went to Bethlehem, the hometown of his ancestor King David. Mary came with him, and she was almost ready to have her baby.

By the time they arrived, it was dark, and they were tired. They went to the inn, but there was no room. So Joseph and Mary had to stay in a barn. It was a cozy place with animals and soft hay. That night Mary gave birth to Jesus. She wrapped Him in cloths so He wouldn't be cold. Then she made a little bed of hay and laid Jesus down on it. Mary and Joseph admired him as he fell asleep. He was a beautiful child.

DAY 214
The Shepherds
Luke 2:8-20

That night some shepherds were out in the fields with their sheep. Suddenly the angel of the Lord came and showered them with light. They were frightened and hid their faces. "Don't be afraid," the angel said. "I have brought good news. Today in King David's town, a little baby has been born. He is Christ the Lord. Go and praise Him. You'll find Him asleep on a bed of hay." Then the angel of the Lord was joined by other angels all singing praises to God. "Peace on earth," they said. "Praise God in heaven!" Then they left and went back up to God.

The shepherds were left alone in the dark night. But the light still twinkled in their eyes. "Let's go and see what the angel was talking about," they said to each other.

They went to Bethlehem and found Jesus asleep on the hay. "The angel said He is Christ the Lord," the shepherds told Mary. Then they bowed down and worshipped the child. Mary listened to the shepherds and stored up their words like treasures in her heart. Then the shepherds left, but the whole way home they kept praising the Lord.

DAY 215
King Herod Hears about Jesus
Matthew 2:1-6

The good news of Jesus' birth spread into distant lands. Three wise men from the east traveled a long way to see him. They didn't know where he was so they went to King Herod in Jerusalem. "Where can we find the child they call the king of the Jews?" they asked. "We are following His star and have come to worship Him."

King Herod had never heard of Jesus before. But he started to worry. "So they call him a king," he said to himself. "I thought I was the king."

Then he called in his priests and holy men. "Where will the Messiah be born?" he asked them. "Your majesty," they answered, "the prophets wrote that He would be born in Bethlehem. They say that He will be a leader of Israel and lead the people like a shepherd to His flock."

DAY 216
The Three Wise Men
Matthew 2:7-12

King Herod sent for the three wise men. He told them, "Go to Bethlehem. Search for the child, and when you find Him, come back and tell me. I want to go and worship Him too."

The wise men agreed and left for Bethlehem. They followed the bright star until it stopped over the place where Jesus lived with Mary and Joseph. "Now we've finally arrived," the wise men said. They were glad because they had been traveling a long time.

When the wise men saw Jesus, they knelt down and laid gifts at his feet. They had brought gold, frankincense, and myrrh from their country in the east. They adored Jesus and showered Him with their praises.

That night while the three wise men were asleep, a voice spoke to them in their dreams. The voice told them not to go back to King Herod. So the three wise men returned home by a different road.

JESUS' BIRTH

DAY 217
Jesus of Nazareth
Matthew 2:13-23; Luke 2:40

King Herod waited for the wise men to come back and tell him where Jesus lived. But they never came. He thought they were tricking him. Herod was jealous of Jesus and all the attention He was getting. He did not want Jesus to grow up and become a king. So he gave an order to kill the baby boys of Bethlehem.

That night an angel came to Joseph in a dream. "Get up!" the angel said. "Take the child and His mother to Egypt. King Herod is looking for Jesus. He wants to kill Him!" Joseph immediately jumped out of bed and woke up Mary. They loaded their donkey with the things they owned and left for Egypt.

Some time later an angel came to Joseph again in a dream. "It's safe to return to Israel," the angel told him. "King Herod has died, and there is no more danger." The angel told Joseph to go to the town of Nazareth. So Joseph and Mary raised Jesus in that town, and He grew up healthy and happy. Even though He was just a young boy, He was already very wise.

JESUS' CHILDHOOD

DAY 218
Jesus in the Temple
Luke 2:41-52

Mary and Joseph went to Jerusalem every year for Passover. When Jesus was twelve, they made the trip again. After the celebration was over, Mary and Joseph got ready to go back to Nazareth. They thought Jesus was with some friends. But His friends said, "No, we haven't seen Him." So Mary started to panic. "Oh no, we've lost Him!" she cried. They began to search all over Jerusalem.

Three days later they found Jesus in the temple. He was talking with the teachers and asking them questions. Everyone in the temple was awestruck by His wisdom.

"Son," Mary cried out when she saw Him, "why did you scare us like this? We've been looking for You everywhere!"

Jesus replied, "Why did you have to look? Didn't you know that I would be in My Father's house?" Then He went with His parents back to Nazareth. Mary kept thinking about what Jesus said. She was so proud of Him, and God was too. Now whenever Jesus wasn't home, Mary knew exactly where to find Him.

DAY 219
John the Baptist

John 1:19-28

Just as the angel had promised, Zechariah's son John grew up to be a wise leader. He used water to baptize people, so they called him John the Baptist. The leaders of Jerusalem were curious about John. They wanted to know who he really was.

"Are you the Messiah?" they asked him.

John shook his head. "No, I'm not the Messiah," he said.

"Are you Elijah then?" they asked him.

"No," John answered. "I'm not Elijah."

"Maybe you're the prophet?" they asked him.

"No," John answered. "I'm not the prophet."

"Well then who are you?" they asked. "We need an answer."

So John repeated the words of the prophet Isaiah, "I am only someone shouting in the desert, 'Make way for the Lord!'"

So the leaders of Jerusalem left. But then some Pharisees came to see John. They found him knee-deep in the Jordan River. He was baptizing some people.

"Why are you doing that? Are you the Messiah?" they asked him.

John replied, "I use water to baptize people. But why are you troubling yourself over me? There is Someone here greater than I am. I'm not even good enough to untie His sandals."

264

JOHN THE BAPTIST

DAY 220
John Speaks About Jesus
John 1:29-34

The next day Jesus came to visit John. People had gathered around to listen to John speak. But when John saw Jesus coming toward him, he stopped talking.

Then he turned to the people and said, "This is the man I told you about when I said, 'He is greater than I am, because He was alive before I was born.' I may baptize you. But I baptize you so that you will know Him. He is the one who takes away your sins. He is the Lamb of God."

Then John said, "I have known Jesus all my life. He is my relative. But I didn't always realize who Jesus was. God gave me a job to do. He sent me to baptize people with water. Then he told me, 'There is another man who will baptize with the Holy Spirit.' And I was there and saw with my own two eyes when it happened. God's Spirit came down like a dove from heaven and stayed with Jesus. He is the one that can baptize you with life-giving water."

DAY 221
Jesus Is Baptized
Matthew 3:1-17

Many years later John went to live in the wilderness. He only wore clothes made of camel hair. And he ate whatever he could find, like wild honey, berries, and even grasshoppers. He spoke to whomever he met about the kingdom of heaven. So people started to travel from far away to come and listen to him. "Turn back to God," he told the people. "The kingdom of heaven is coming!" Then the people told John their sins, and he baptized them in the river.

One day Jesus went to go visit John. He told John that He wanted to be baptized too. John said, "Jesus, You should be the one baptizing me!" But Jesus answered, "God wants you to baptize Me. And we should do exactly what God wants us to do. That's why I've come." So John baptized Jesus in the Jordan River. As He lifted His head from the water, Jesus saw the sky open up. Then the Spirit of God came down from heaven.

"This is My own Son," the voice of God said. "And I am pleased with Him."

JESUS' EARLY MINISTRY

DAY 222

The Devil Tempts Jesus

Luke 4:1-15

Jesus was being led by the Holy Spirit. One day the Spirit led Him into the desert. Jesus lived in the desert for forty days and forty nights. He didn't eat anything because He was busy listening to God. The devil was there too. He tried to trick Jesus into disobeying God.

One day Jesus was beginning to feel hunger pangs in his belly. "Jesus, You're the Son of God," the devil told Him. "Just ask Your Father to turn this stone into a delicious loaf of bread. Think of how good it will taste!"

But Jesus answered, "No one can live on food alone."

Then the devil took Jesus to a high place. He showed Him many nations. "You can be the ruler over everything. All You have to do is worship me," the devil told Him.

But Jesus answered, "I only worship God."

So the devil took Jesus to the temple in Jerusalem. "Climb up on the roof," the devil told Him. "Then jump off and see if the angels catch You."

But Jesus answered, "It's not right to test God."

After His time in the desert, Jesus went back home to Galilee. He had passed all the devil's tests and stayed true to God.

DAY 223
Jesus Calls His First Disciples
Matthew 4:18-22

While Jesus was walking along the shore of Lake Galilee, He saw two brothers. One was Simon, also known as Peter, and the other was Andrew. They were fishermen, and they were casting their net into the lake.

Jesus said to them, "Come with Me! I will teach you how to bring in people instead of fish." Right then the two brothers dropped their nets and went with Him.

Jesus walked on until he saw James and John, the sons of Zebedee. They were in a boat with their father, mending their nets. Jesus asked them to come with Him too. Right away they left the boat and their father and went with Jesus.

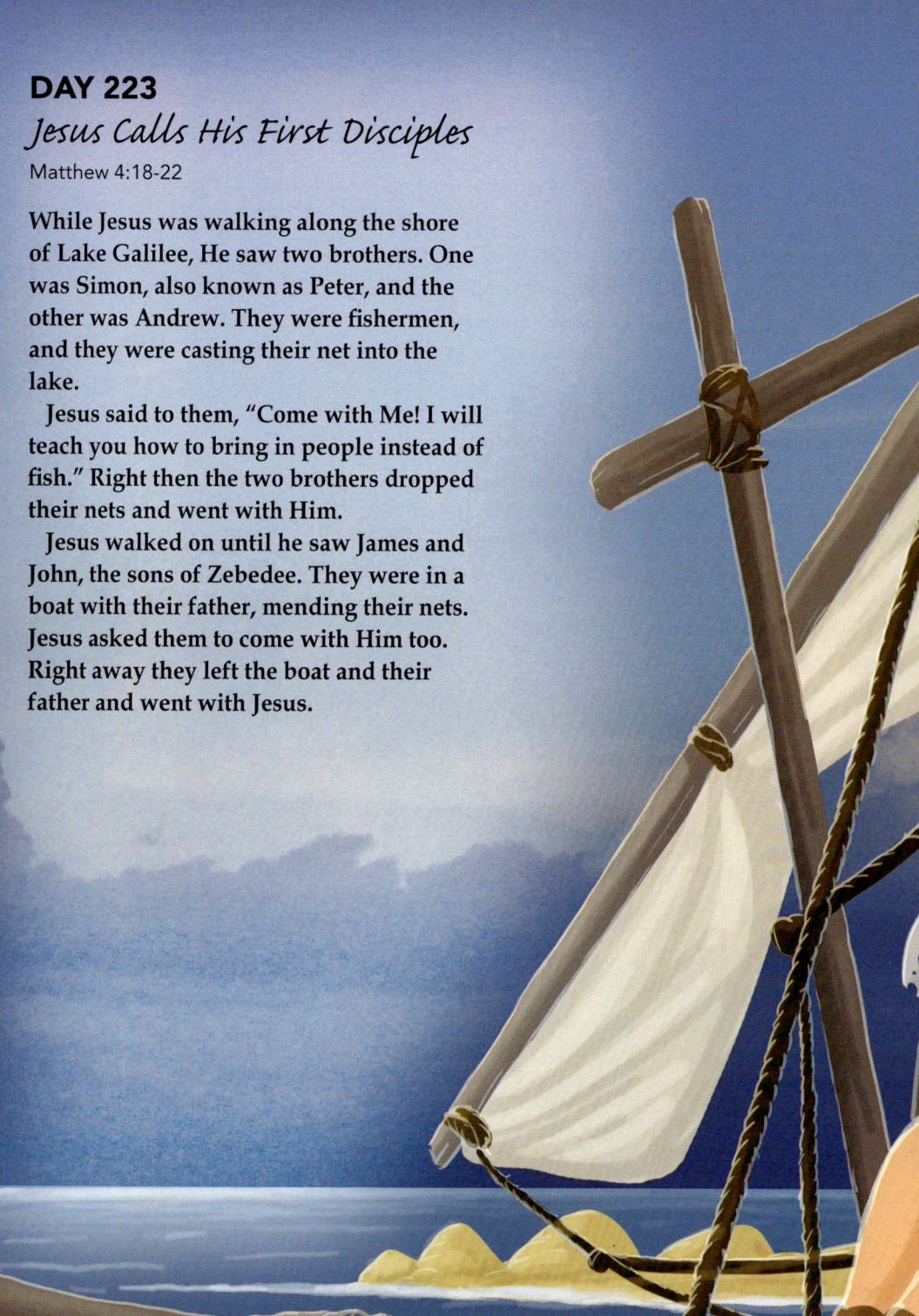

JESUS' EARLY MINISTRY

DAY 224
Fishers of Men
Luke 5:1-11

Jesus was standing by a lake teaching a group of people. Two fishermen's boats were tied up near the water. Jesus got into the boat that belonged to Simon. He told Simon to row a little way from the shore. Then Jesus taught from the boat while the people sat on the shore.

When He was finished, He told Simon to row further out into the lake. Simon obeyed. "Now drop your nets and catch some fish," Jesus said.

"Master," Simon replied, "we've been out fishing all night. There was not a single fish to be caught. But I will do it anyway."

Simon threw the nets overboard, and they filled up with hundreds of fish. They were so heavy that they began to rip. "We need help!" Simon called to the other fishermen. So James and John rowed the other boat out and helped them haul in the nets. Just as soon as they had finished, the boats began to sink. There were too many fish! When

Simon saw all the fish, he knew that Jesus was God's Son. He fell on his knees before Jesus. "Lord, don't come near me. I'm just a sinner." Jesus told Simon, "Don't be afraid! From now on you will be a fisherman of people instead of fish."

When the men reached the shore, they left everything to be Jesus' disciples.

DAY 225
Jesus Turns Water into Wine
John 2:1-11

Jesus went to a wedding in Galilee with His disciples. His mother Mary was also there. Later on in the evening, the wine ran out. So Mary went to Jesus and said, "There's no more wine." But Jesus told His mother, "My time has not come yet. Trust in Me. I know what to do."

There were six big jars at the feast. They were all empty, so Jesus told the servants to fill them with water. Then He told them, "Give a drink to the man who is in charge of the feast." The servants obeyed.

As the man took a sip from the cup, he realized the water had turned into wine. He didn't know that Jesus had done this miracle. He called to the groom and said, "What a surprise! Most people offer the best wine first and the cheap wine last. But you have saved the best for last."

The disciples smiled to one another. They knew that Jesus had performed a miracle. Their faith in Him grew.

JESUS' EARLY MINISTRY

DAY 226
Jesus Visits the Temple
John 2:13-22

Jesus made a trip to Jerusalem. When He arrived He wanted to go to the temple. But as He walked inside He saw something that shocked Him. People were buying and selling animals with one another. Some people were bargaining for cows and sheep. Others were showing off their doves. Money tables were set up everywhere, and men were counting the coins to see how much they had made.

Jesus could hardly believe His eyes. He started to flip the money tables over and all the coins scattered on the ground. "My Father's house is not a marketplace!" Jesus told them. Then He chased the people out the door. "This is a house of prayer."

When all the people had left, Jesus was left alone. But the Jewish leaders came to speak to Him. "Who are you to be angry?" they asked Him. "Show us a miracle so we know who You are. Then we will trust that You did the right thing."

So Jesus said, "All right. If you destroy the temple, I will rebuild it in three days."

"That's impossible," the Jewish leaders replied. "It took us forty-six years to build this temple."

But they didn't realize what Jesus meant. The real temple Jesus was talking about was His own body. When Jesus rose from the tomb after three days, His disciples remembered His words. He had rebuilt the temple just like He promised.

DAY 227
Jesus and Nicodemus
John 3:1-6, 16-17

Nicodemus was a Jewish leader and a Pharisee. One night he decided to go and visit Jesus. "I know that You've been sent by God," he said to Jesus. "You could not work miracles unless God was with You."

Jesus replied, "I'll tell You the truth. No one can see God's kingdom until he is born again."

Nicodemus was confused. "But how can someone who's grown up be born again?" he asked Jesus.

"Your mother is the only one that can give birth to your body. But God gives birth through the Holy Spirit. When you ask the Holy Spirit to come into you, then you are born again as a child of God. The kingdom of heaven is yours."

JESUS' EARLY MINISTRY

JESUS' EARLY MINISTRY

Then Jesus told Nicodemus, "God loved the people of the world so much that he gave His only Son. Whoever believes in Him will have eternal life. They'll never die. God didn't send His Son to judge people. He sent His Son to save them! The light has come into the world. When people do evil, they hide from the light so they won't be seen. When people do good, they come into the light. They want to be with God."

DAY 228
The Water of Life
John 4:4-26

Jesus was traveling with His disciples through Samaria. They came upon the same field that Jacob had given his son Joseph long ago. Even Jacob's well was still there. Jesus was tired so he sat down for a rest while His disciples went out to find food.

Just then a Samaritan woman came to fetch water from the well. "Would you give Me a drink?" Jesus asked her.

"But You are a Jew," she answered, "and I am a Samaritan. How can You ask me? Jews and Samaritans aren't even supposed to talk to one another."

Jesus told her, "If you knew who I was, then you might be the one asking Me for a drink. I give the water of life to those who thirst."

"Sir," the woman said, "if You give life-giving water, then where's the bucket You use to fetch it with?"

Jesus answered, "My water is not from a well. Whoever drinks that water will only get thirsty again. The water I give is eternal life. You'll never need another drink again."

But the woman just shrugged. "When the one they call Christ comes, I will listen to Him. I'm sure He can explain all these things to us," she said.

"Here I am," Jesus told her. "I am speaking to you now."

DAY 229
The Samaritans Believe
John 4:27-42

When the disciples came back, they found Jesus by the well. He was still talking to the Samaritan woman. She then dropped her water jar and started back toward town to tell all the people about Jesus.

The disciples told Jesus, "We've found food. Eat something, Jesus."

Jesus said, "I already have food. It's a kind you know nothing about."

The disciples looked at one another. "Did someone bring You food?" they asked.

"No," Jesus explained. "My food is to do what God wants. He sent Me here for a purpose. The farmer works hard in his field, and other people reap the reward. I am like the farmer. I will do God's work so that you may benefit from it."

When the people from Samaria heard about Jesus from the woman at the well, they ran to see Him. Jesus loved to talk with people, so He stayed in Samaria for two days. He told the people that He had come to save their sins. He told them about the right way to follow the Lord and gain the kingdom of heaven. The Samaritans put their faith in Him. They told the woman from the well, "We

275

JESUS' EARLY MINISTRY

know Jesus is the Savior of the world. And it's not because you told us so, but because we have listened to Him for ourselves."

DAY 230
Jesus Heals an Official's Son
John 4:43-54

Every day Jesus' followers grew. He had many people who believed in him. Some of them had seen Him perform miracles. Others only had to listen to Jesus, and they knew He was the Son of God. After Jesus had been traveling a long time, He went back to Galilee. The people there welcomed Him.

While He was there, Jesus visited the town where He had turned water into wine. A man heard that Jesus was in that town. So He walked a long way to come and find Him. And when he did, he dropped on his knees. "Jesus," he begged, "Please save my son. He's very sick, and he will die soon."

But Jesus told him, "You won't have faith unless you see miracles and wonders!"

"Please help me," the man kept begging, "before it's too late."

So Jesus told him, "Go back home. Your son will live."

The man believed Jesus. He thanked Him and started to go home again. The next day he was nearing his house when he saw his servants come up the road. "You'll never believe it," they said to him. "Your son's fever left at seven o'clock yesterday. He will live!" But the man had never doubted Jesus. He knew He would keep His promise. It was at exactly one o'clock the day before that Jesus had made His promise. "Praise the Lord," the man exclaimed. "He does amazing things!"

JESUS' EARLY MINISTRY

DAY 231
The Power of the Son
John 5:19-30

Jesus told the people, "The Son can do nothing without the Father. And because the Father loves His Son, He gives Him the power to do miracles. But the Father can do even greater things. Just as the Father can give life, the Son can give life too.

"The Father is pleased when His Son is honored. So when you hear My message, have faith in Me. Follow Me, and you will never need to worry about death. You will already have eternal life!"

"The time has come to hear the voice of the Son of God. Those who listen to His voice will be given eternity! Reach out to one another and do good things. Listen to My words and follow them. But remember that I don't say these things on My own. The Father sent Me, and I obey Him. He has taught Me how to judge with fairness."

DAY 232
Witnesses for Jesus
John 5:31-47

Jesus said, "There are many people who have told you about Me. John the Baptist told you that the Father sent Me. And you enjoyed listening to him. He was like a lamp that shed light for you. You have also enjoyed listening to the words of the old prophets. Moses wrote about me. But if you truly believed Moses, then you would believe in Me too.

"Still there is someone more important than John who speaks for Me. And there is someone more important than Moses sending you a message. Why do you listen to their voice but not to the voice of Him whom they spoke about? The Father sent Me, and He also speaks for Me. But you don't hear His voice because you don't have faith in His Son.

"I don't care about human praise. I am not speaking to you to please Myself. Many of you like to be praised and admired by your friends. But I have not come here for that. I want the praise that only God can give. Have faith in Me, and you will also win God's praise."

JESUS' EARLY MINISTRY

DAY 233
Jesus Heals a Crippled Man
Luke 5:17-26

One day Jesus was teaching a group of people who had come from all over Israel to hear Him speak. The crowd gathered into one room, and soon there was no place left to stand or sit. A crippled man had come also. Some men were carrying him on a mat because he couldn't walk. But there were too many people, so the crippled man could not see Jesus.

Then the men carrying him had an idea. They took the crippled man up to the roof. Then they removed a couple of tiles and lowered the man down through the ceiling.

Jesus saw how faithful the crippled man was. He said to him, "My friend, all your sins are forgiven."

The Pharisees heard Jesus and became angry. "Who does He think He is?" they said to each other. "Only God can forgive sins."

So Jesus told them, "The Son of Man has been sent by God to forgive the sins of the world. So why do you say these things?" Then Jesus turned to the crippled man and smiled. "You have shown Me your faith. Pick up your mat and walk home!" The man started to stand up. His crippled legs had been healed, and he could walk! All the people in the room were amazed. "We have seen a miracle today!" they said to one another. Then they praised God and said, "We believe."

DAY 234
Jesus Will Return to the Father
John 7:32-36

Jesus was becoming very popular. Everyone was talking about the

incredible miracles He performed. Those who believed in Him were His followers. But some people didn't like Jesus. Some of the Pharisees thought Jesus was gaining too much power. So they went to the temple police and said, "It's time we arrest Jesus—He's causing too much trouble."

Jesus knew what was going to happen to Him. He said to his followers, "I will only be with you for a little while longer. Then I must return to My Father. When I do, you will try to look for Me. But I'm going somewhere that you cannot follow."

"Where's He going?" His followers asked each other. "Why can't we go too? Maybe He's going on a trip to a country faraway. Or maybe He's going to Greece to teach the people about God. Why did He say we wouldn't be able to find Him?"

But none of them understood what Jesus meant.

JESUS' EARLY MINISTRY

DAY 235
Nicodemus Defends Jesus
John 7:42-52

The temple police were sent to arrest Jesus. But He hadn't done anything wrong. So instead of arresting Him, they just listened to Him speak. They were very impressed by everything He said. Later on when they came back to the Pharisees, they said, "Jesus isn't a criminal. No one has ever spoken like He does."

"You've been fooled," the Pharisees replied. "None of us believe a word he says." So the Pharisees and the police began to argue. Everyone had a different opinion about who Jesus was. And everyone had a different opinion about what to do with Him.

Nicodemus was one of the men among the council. He stood up for Jesus. "Listen to all of you fighting," he said. "How can we make a decision before we know what Jesus has done wrong? Doesn't Jesus have a right to speak up for Himself?"

The Pharisees laughed at Nicodemus. "You must be from Galilee," they teased him. "Why

are you standing up for a man from that place? Nothing good can come from Galilee. And especially not a prophet—that's what the Scriptures say."

DAY 236
Levi and the Dinner Guests
Mark 2:13-17

As Jesus was going along, He saw a man named Levi. Levi was sitting at the booth where people pay their taxes. "Come with Me!" Jesus said to him. So Levi left his post and went with Jesus.

That night Levi invited Jesus over for dinner. Jesus' disciples also came and so did some of the Pharisees. But when the Pharisees learned that Levi was a tax collector, they got angry. "Why does Jesus choose to eat with a tax collector? Doesn't He know that they're sinners?" Jesus heard what they said. So He asked them, "Have you ever seen a healthy person visit a doctor? Only sick people need a doctor. I have not come to save the good people; I have come to save the sinners."

DAY 237
Mary and Martha
Luke 10:38-42

Jesus was traveling with His disciples. They were weary and tired from the journey. When they came to the village of Bethany, they stopped to rest.

Martha and Mary were two sisters who lived in Bethany. They welcomed Jesus and His disciples to stay in their home. Martha had heard about Jesus, and she knew He was a special guest. She began to worry and fuss about the way her house looked.

"What if Jesus thought it looked shabby?" she worried. So Martha rushed around, dusting and sweeping and cooking and cleaning.

Martha's sister had also heard of Jesus. She was so excited to see Him that she sat right down on the floor in front of Him. As Jesus spoke, Mary listened to every word He said. Martha was annoyed by this. "I'm doing all the work," she told Jesus. "Mary is doing none. Don't You think that's unfair?"

Jesus answered, "Martha, you are so upset! But only one thing is necessary. Mary has chosen what is best. She has chosen to listen to My words."

JESUS' TEACHING

285

JESUS' TEACHING

DAY 238
Planting Seeds
Mark 4:1-8

While Jesus was teaching by the Sea of Galilee, a big crowd gathered who had come to hear Him speak. There were so many people that Jesus had to teach from a boat on the lake while the crowd stood on the shore. He told them this story, saying, "A farmer went out to scatter his seeds. Some seeds fell between the rocks. They sprouted, but died quickly because there was not enough deep soil to grow strong roots. Some seeds fell among the thornbushes. These were choked by the prickles. But a few of the farmer's seeds fell on good ground. These seeds turned into a great harvest, one hundred times the size of what had been planted."

DAY 239
Jesus Explains the Story
Mark 4:10-20

"It is the same with God's people!" Jesus said. "Some do not hear what I say, and the message does not grow within them. But the ones who hear My words will be rewarded."

Then a disciple called out, "Jesus, why do You always tell stories?"

So Jesus explained, "Many people hear, but they don't really hear. Many people see, but they don't really see. I tell stories so that your eyes, ears, and hearts will understand God's message!"

DAY 240
Wheat and Weeds
Matthew 13:24-30, 36-39

Jesus told this story next.

He said, "Once, a farmer scattered his seeds in a field. After he left, an enemy came and scattered weeds in that same field. The plants began to grow, and the weed grew right along with the plants. The servants of the farmer ran to him and said, 'Sir, why are there weeds growing among your grain?' The farmer replied, 'An enemy must have done this. Leave the weeds alone until harvest time. Otherwise you may pull up the wheat when you are trying to pull out the weeds. When the time is right, we will separate the two and throw the weeds away.'"

Jesus explained, "The farmer's good seeds are like the people who hear My message and take it to heart," Jesus said. "But the weeds are like the people who do not listen. Someday God will bring judgment to His people. God will separate them, just like the farmer separated the weeds from his wheat."

DAY 241
God's Kingdom Like a Seed
Mark 4:26-32

"Even while the farmer is asleep," Jesus said, "the seeds he scattered keep growing from the soil that nurtures them. Take a look at a mustard seed! It's the smallest of the seeds. But when it is fully grown, it is huge. Even the birds build nests in its big, leafy branches!"

DAY 242
God's Kingdom Like a Yeast
Matthew 13:33

"Now think of a woman making bread," Jesus continued. "How would the dough turn into bread without the yeast that makes it rise? The yeast is important even though it is small."

JESUS' TEACHING

DAY 243
The Greatest in Heaven
Matthew 18:1-5

Then the disciples asked Jesus, "Who will be the greatest in God's kingdom?" Jesus looked around and saw a child peeking out from behind the people in the crowd. Then He called the child over and pulled him gently into His arms.

"I promise you this," said Jesus to the disciples, "if you don't change and become like this child, you will never get into the kingdom of heaven. A child accepts God with a pure and humble heart. If you do this, you will be the greatest in God's kingdom. When you welcome one of these children, you welcome Me."

DAY 244
The Lost Sheep
Matthew 18:10-14

"Don't be cruel to any of these little ones! Their angels are with My God in heaven."

"Now let Me ask you this," Jesus said. "What would you do if you had a hundred sheep and one was lost? Wouldn't you leave the others to find the lost one? I am sure that finding the one lost sheep would make you happier than having all the rest that were not lost. That is how it is with My Father in heaven. He doesn't want any of these little ones to be lost."

DAY 245
Let the Children Come to Me
Mark 10:13-16

Many parents brought their children to Jesus hoping He would bless them. The children crowded around Jesus and began to play with Him. But Jesus' disciples tried to keep them from coming near Jesus.

"Step back," they instructed the children. "Jesus doesn't want to be bothered."

But Jesus cried out, "Let the children come to Me! Don't stop them. These children belong to the kingdom of God. None of you can enter God's kingdom unless you accept it the way a child does. Learn from them!"

Then Jesus opened his arms and the little children ran giggling and smiling,

wrapping their arms around Jesus' neck. Jesus placed His hands on them and blessed each one. He told them, "Every one of you is welcome into My Father's kingdom."

DAY 246
The Good Shepherd
John 10:11-18

Jesus said, "I am the good shepherd and you are my flock. The shepherd will give up His life for His sheep. But hired workers don't own the sheep, so they do not care about them. When a wolf comes, they run off and leave the sheep to be taken and eaten. But each little sheep is important to Me. If one is lost, I will search high and low until that sheep is found! I love My sheep, and they love Me just as the Father loves Me, and I love the Father. I bring all My sheep together into one flock and watch over them. I will gladly give up My life for My sheep. No one takes my life from me. I give it up willingly! I have the power to give up My life and the power to receive it back again just as My Father commanded me to do."

JESUS' TEACHING

DAY 247
The Lost Sheep and the Lost Coin
Luke 15:1-10

Jesus was talking and eating with a small group of people when some sinners came up and began to listen to His words. Jesus welcomed them. But the scribes and the Pharisees began to point and stare. "Look at Jesus," they scowled. "He is eating with a bunch of sinners!" Jesus heard them say these things. He turned and faced them.

"Imagine," Jesus said, "that you are a shepherd, and you have lost one of your sheep. Won't you leave the ninety-nine others behind and find the lost one? When you find the sheep, you will be so glad that you will carry it home on your shoulders. Then you will say to your friends, 'Let's celebrate! I've found the one that was lost.'"

"There is more happiness for my Father in heaven if one sinner turns to God than ninety-nine good people who did not need to. And what about a woman who loses one coin in a stack of ten coins? Won't she light a lamp, sweep the floor, and look carefully until she has found it? My Father in heaven will celebrate when one of these sinners who sit with Me turn to Him."

DAY 248
The Loving Father
Luke 15:11-19

Jesus told another story of a man who had two sons:

The man loved them both and wanted to see them do well. He planned to divide his property and money between them. The younger son said, "Father, please give me my share. I want to go out in the world and become successful." He took off and traveled to a faraway country. He spent all his money on silly things. Before he knew it, he reached into his pocket, and there was not one coin left. Desperate for money, the younger son got a job working for a pig farmer. His clothes turned ragged and dirty. His stomach was always growling with hunger. He would've been happy to eat the slop from the trough of the pigs. But at last he thought, "This is foolish! My father treats his servants better than this! I will go to him and ask his forgiveness. Perhaps he will accept me, and I will offer to work for him."

So the son started on the long journey home again back to his father's house.

JESUS' TEACHING

DAY 249
Forgiven
Luke 15:20-24

The father spotted his youngest son walking toward home. He ran out to meet him and showered him in hugs and kisses. He called to his servants, "Bring out our finest clothes! Prepare a big feast! Put a shiny ring on my son's finger! He was lost, and now he is found!" The older son was out in the field working. He ran back to the house to see what had happened.

DAY 250
The Jealous Brother
Luke 15:25-32

"What's going on?" the older brother asked.

"Your brother is back!" the servants replied.

The older brother became angry. He ran to his father and said, "I have been working like a slave for you. I have obeyed you. I have always done

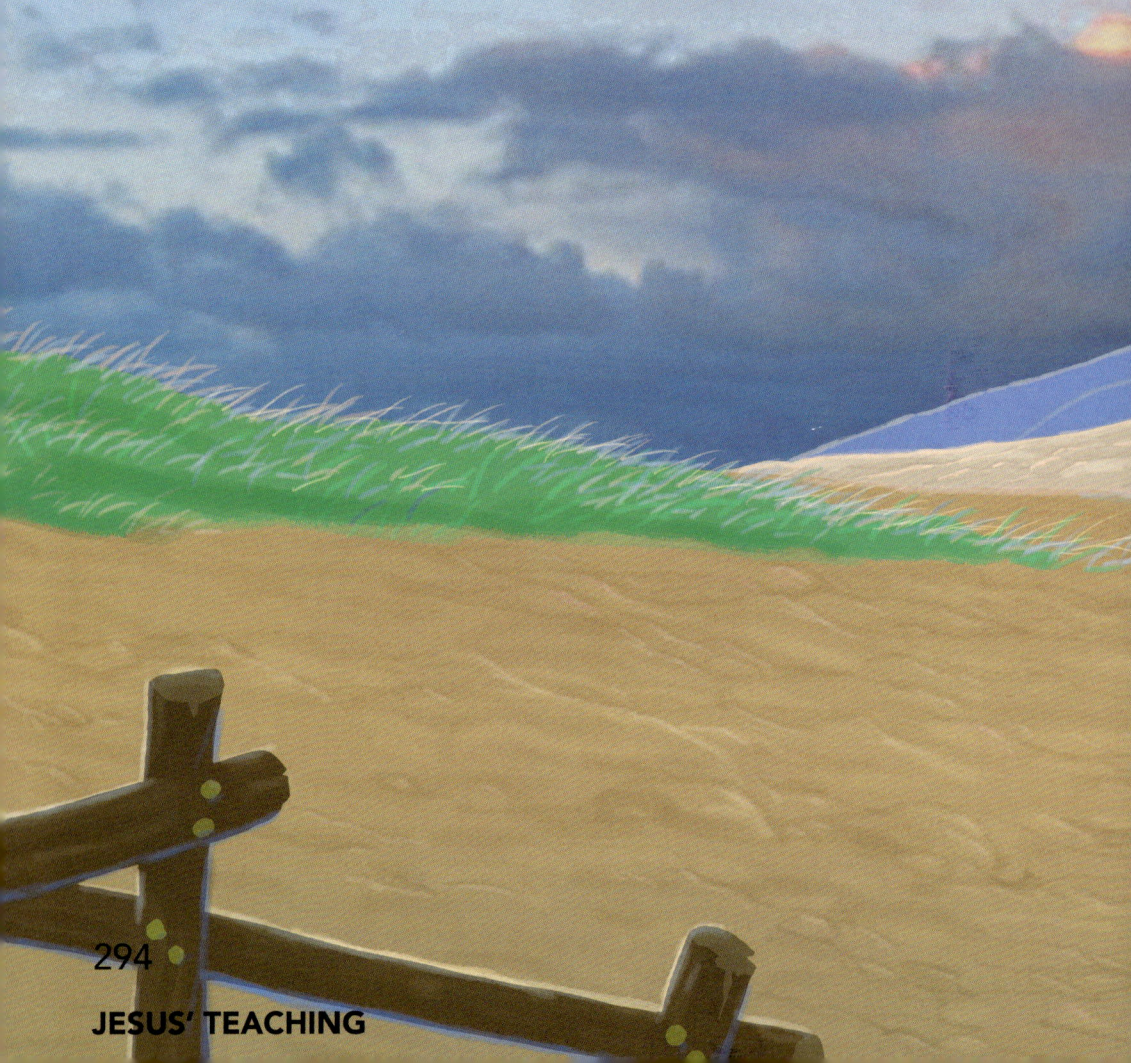

everything you asked me to. But my brother runs away, spends all your money, and disobeys you. Why are you treating him like a prince?" His father answered, "Son, you always did right and obeyed me. You were never lost, but your brother was lost. Be happy and celebrate with me. He has come back to us!"

295

JESUS' TEACHING

DAY 251
God Shows Mercy
Luke 18:9-14

One day, Jesus came upon some people who were acting proud and self-righteous. He walked over to them and told them the story of two men who went into a temple to pray. One was a Pharisee and the other was a tax collector. The Pharisee prayed, "Thank You for making me good. I am not greedy or dishonest. I am faithful in marriage, and I have always given part of my money to You." But the tax collector stayed in the far corner of the temple. He did not think he was good enough to even look up toward heaven. He hung his head and prayed, "God, have pity on me! I am such a sinner."

"Whom do you think God was pleased with more?" Jesus asked. "The man who bragged about how good he was or the man who admitted to his sins? Remember, if you hold yourself high above others, you will be put down. But if you are humble and admit your sins, you will be honored."

DAY 252
A Second Chance
John 8:1-11

Early one morning Jesus went to the temple where he usually went to teach. People were crowding around to hear his lesson. Suddenly a group of angry men burst through the door. They were holding a woman roughly by the arm. "Teacher!" they shouted. "This woman has been caught sleeping with a man who was not her husband. This woman should be stoned for her sins! What do You say?" They asked Jesus this question because they wanted to test Him. Would He say yes or no? But Jesus said neither. Instead He looked around at the crowd that had gathered and said, "Let the person who has never sinned throw the first stone." The men were speechless. They looked around at one another but no one volunteered to throw the first stone because they all had sinned. One by one the men walked away until only Jesus and the woman were left. "Isn't there anyone left to accuse you?" Jesus asked the woman. The woman shook her head. "Then I will not accuse you either," Jesus said. "You are forgiven, but sin no more!"

JESUS' TEACHING

JESUS' TEACHING

DAY 253
An Act of Love
Luke 7:36-39

A Pharisee named Simon invited Jesus to have dinner with him. There was a woman who had heard that Jesus was at Simon's house. She was a sinner, and everyone in the village looked down on her. The woman loved Jesus. She went to Simon's house and brought an expensive bottle of perfume. When the woman saw Jesus, she fell down on the floor near His feet, and she began to cry tears of love. Her tears fell on Jesus' feet, and she began to wash and dry them with her hair. Next the woman poured her expensive perfume on Jesus' feet; then she covered them with her kisses.

Simon had been watching all of this. He felt confused and angry. "If Jesus were really a prophet of God," Simon thought, "He would know what kind of a sinner this woman was."

DAY 254
Love and Forgiveness
Luke 7:41-50

Jesus knew what Simon was thinking. He said, "Simon, I'd like to tell you a story. Two people owed money to a lender.

JESUS' TEACHING

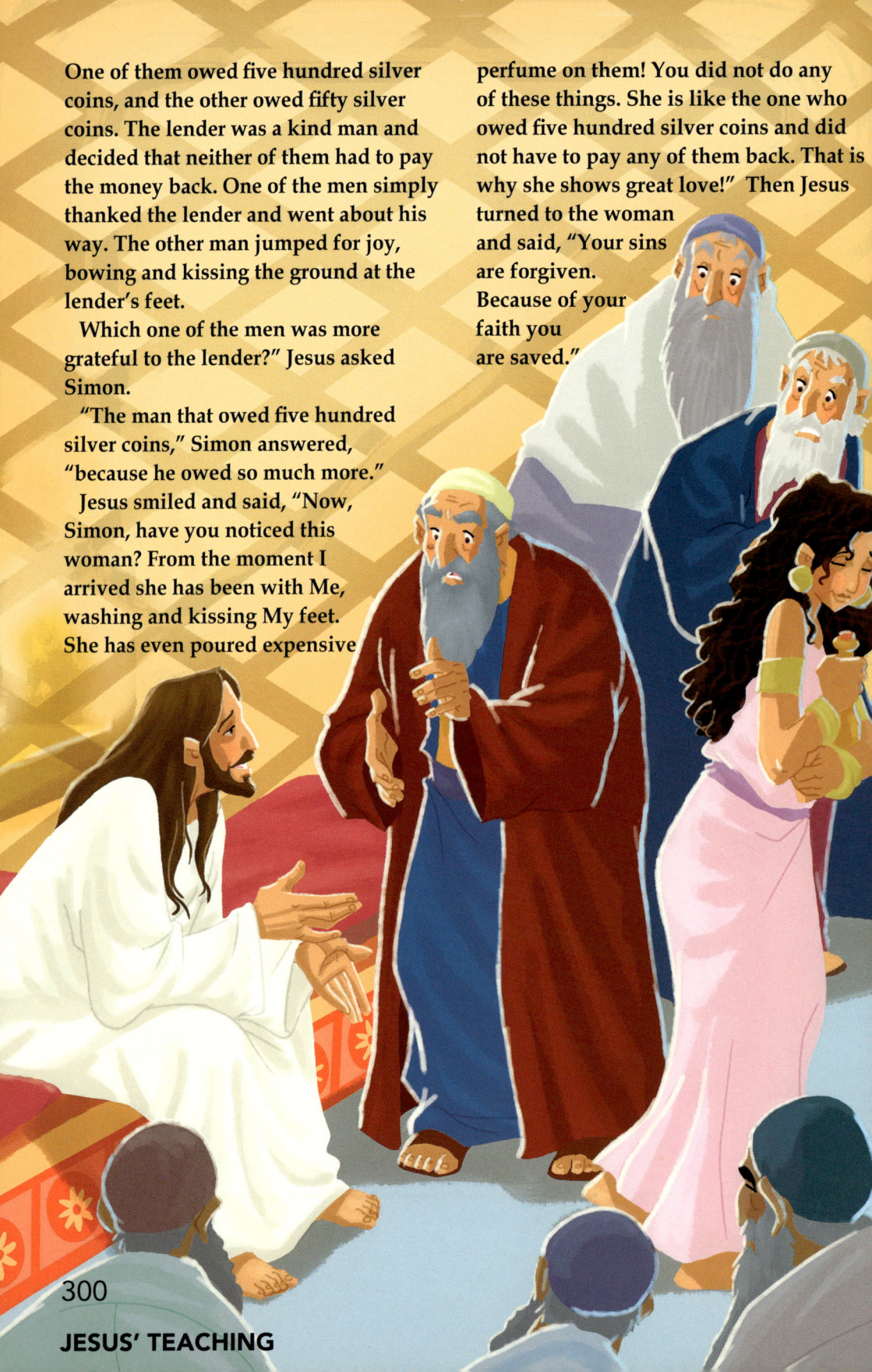

One of them owed five hundred silver coins, and the other owed fifty silver coins. The lender was a kind man and decided that neither of them had to pay the money back. One of the men simply thanked the lender and went about his way. The other man jumped for joy, bowing and kissing the ground at the lender's feet.

Which one of the men was more grateful to the lender?" Jesus asked Simon.

"The man that owed five hundred silver coins," Simon answered, "because he owed so much more."

Jesus smiled and said, "Now, Simon, have you noticed this woman? From the moment I arrived she has been with Me, washing and kissing My feet. She has even poured expensive perfume on them! You did not do any of these things. She is like the one who owed five hundred silver coins and did not have to pay any of them back. That is why she shows great love!" Then Jesus turned to the woman and said, "Your sins are forgiven. Because of your faith you are saved."

JESUS' TEACHING

DAY 255
Who Gave the Most?
Mark 12:41-44

Jesus was sitting in the temple near the offering box. He was watching people put in their gifts to God. The rich people put in handfuls of money. The coins clinked and clanked as they fell into the box. The rich people looked proud that they could give so much. Then an old widow went up to the box. She put in the only two coins she had.

Jesus told His disciples to gather around. Then He said, "This poor widow has put in more than all the others." The disciples shook their heads and said, "She has only put in a couple of coins!"

Jesus nodded. Then He said, "You see, the many coins of the rich do not mean much. They are like loose change in their pockets. But the few coins of the poor are as valuable as gold. They have given the little bit they have up to God."

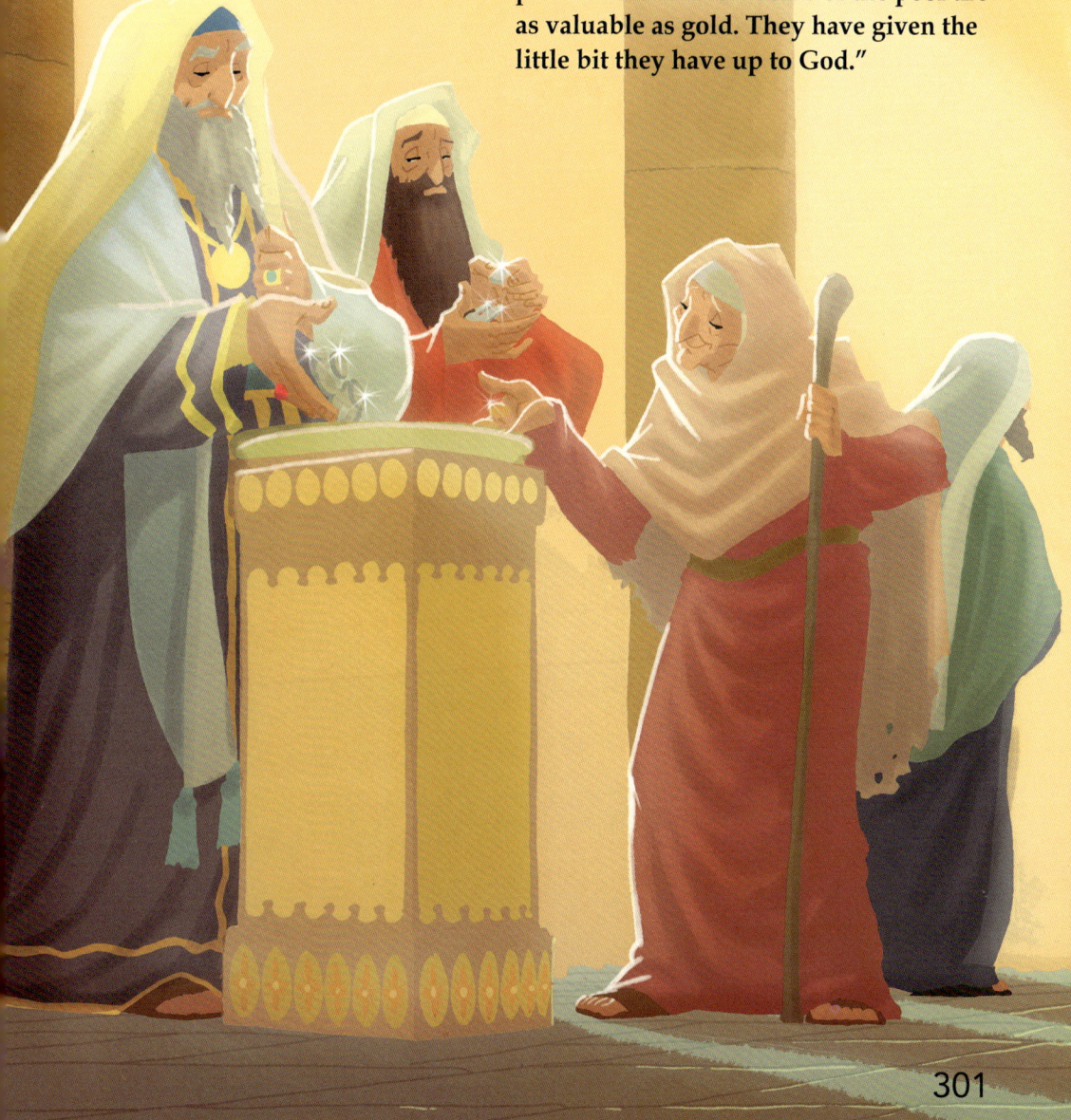

JESUS' TEACHING

DAY 256
Do Not Worry
Matthew 6:19-30

Jesus was speaking to a large crowd that had gathered outside one morning.

He said, "All the things you have here on earth are of little worth. A moth can come and chew your clothes. Rust can ruin your favorite cups and plates. Thieves can come and steal your money. Don't store up these things that can be taken from you. Treasures in heaven cannot be taken from you. Put your heart in God alone! You cannot love riches and God at the same time. Have faith that God will take care of you. He will give you everything you need."

"Look at the birds in the sky. Aren't they cheerful and happy? They don't work all the time, and yet God takes care of them! Look at the wildflowers. They don't worry about clothes, yet even Solomon didn't look as fine and colorful as they do! God takes care of everything that grows, even if it only lives for a day. If He does that for the birds and the flowers, He will certainly do more for His people."

JESUS' TEACHING

DAY 257
I Am with You
Matthew 18:15-20

Jesus said, "If someone sins against you, go and speak with that person. But do it just between the two of you. If that person listens, you have won back a child of God. If that person refuses to listen, take along one or two others and speak with that person again. If the person still does not hear what you say, go to the church. I promise you that whenever you pray with others and your hearts are one, My Father in heaven will answer your prayer. And whenever two or three of you come together in My name, I am there with you."

DAY 258
True Happiness
Matthew 5:1-12

Jesus went up on a mountain and spoke to His disciples.

"My friends," Jesus said, "God blesses those who look to Him for help. They belong to the kingdom of heaven! God blesses those who feel sad and hopeless. He will comfort them! God blesses those who are humble. They belong to God!

JESUS' TEACHING

God blesses those who obey Him. They will be given what they ask for! God blesses those who are forgiving and show mercy to others. They will be treated with forgiveness and mercy! God blesses those whose hearts are pure. They will see Him! God blesses those who make peace. They will be called His children! God blesses those who are treated badly for doing what is right. They belong to God's kingdom! Be happy! Feel excited and joyful today! For those who do what is right by God will have a big reward in the kingdom of heaven."

JESUS' TEACHING

DAY 259
Being Salt and Light
Matthew 5:13-16

Jesus said to His friends, "You are the salt of the earth. What would salt be like if it didn't taste salty? You might as well throw it out and walk over it. You, too, will be useless unless you do as you should. Forgive the people that do you wrong. Love each other. Share what you have with others."

Then Jesus said, "You are the shining light that illuminates the world. No one would light a lamp and put it under a clay pot, would they? All the light would be hidden and of no use to anyone. A lamp is placed on a lampstand where it can give light to everything in the house. Let your light shine bright. Share your light with others. They will see the good you do, and they will do good themselves."

DAY 260
The House on the Rock
Matthew 7:24-29

Jesus said, "Anyone who hears and obeys these teachings of Mine is like the wise man who built his house on solid rock. Rain poured down, rivers flooded, and winds beat against that house. Why did it stay standing? Because it was built on firm ground! Obey My teachings, and they will be a solid rock for you. Even when people hurt you or treat you badly, you will stand strong with God.

"Anyone who hears My teachings and still disobeys will be like the foolish man who built a house on sand. Rain poured down, rivers flooded, and winds beat against that house. It crumbled right to the ground. The foolish man did not keep My teachings as a solid foundation. But if he had kept My words close to his heart, there would be no storm strong enough to destroy him. God would keep him safe from all harm!"

JESUS' TEACHING

DAY 261
The Narrow Gate
Matthew 7:7-14

Jesus told His friends, "If you ask, you will receive. If you search, you will find. If you knock, the door will be opened for you. Everyone who asks will receive. Everyone who searches will find. And the door will be opened for everyone who knocks. Would any of you give your child a stone, if the child asked for bread? Would any of you give your child a snake if the child asked for a fish? Bad people know how to give good gifts to their children. But your Father in heaven is even more willing to give good things to those who ask.

"I tell you, treat others as you want them to treat you.

"Go in through the narrow gate. The gate to destruction is wide, and the road that leads there is easy to follow. A lot of people go through that gate. But the gate to life is very narrow. The road that leads there is so hard to follow that only a few people find it."

DAY 262
Following Jesus
Mark 10:23-31

Jesus said to his disciples, "It is easier for a camel to go through the eye of a needle than it is for a rich person to get into God's kingdom."

Jesus' disciples were amazed. "But how can anyone ever be saved?" they cried.

"With God, all things are possible," Jesus answered.

Peter said, "We left everything to follow You, Jesus!"

Jesus turned to him and said, "Anyone who gives up his home or his family or the things he owns for me will be rewarded. It is not easy to follow My words. You may be mistreated. You may feel lonely and scared. But in the world to come you will be rewarded with eternal life! Many who are last here on earth will be first in heaven. And many who are first now will later be last."

DAY 263
The Rich Young Man
Matthew 19:16-22

A rich man came to Jesus and asked, "Teacher, what good things must I do to get into heaven?" Jesus answered, "Only God is truly good. If you want to enter into heaven, obey God's words."

Then the man asked, "Which words should I obey?" Jesus answered, "The commandments: Do not murder. Be faithful in marriage. Do not steal. Do not tell lies. Respect your parents. And love others as you do yourself!"

The man nodded. "Yes, Jesus. I have obeyed all of these rules," he said, "What else should I do?" Jesus replied, "If you want to do more, go beyond simply obeying the rules. Sell the things you own and give to those who do not have anything. Love other people with your whole heart. Forgive the people that hurt you. That way you will truly honor God! Then come and be My follower, and you will be on the right path."

JESUS' TEACHING

DAY 264
Eternal Life
Luke 10:25-28

An expert in the Old Testament came forward and asked Jesus a tricky question to see what He would say. "Teacher," he asked, "what must I do to have eternal life?"

Jesus answered, "What is written in the Old Testament? What do the Scriptures say?"

The man answered, "The Scriptures say, 'Love the Lord your God with all your heart, soul, strength, and mind.' They also say, 'Love your neighbor as you love yourself.'"

Jesus said, "That's right. Do this, and you will have eternal life."

DAY 265
The Good Samaritan
Luke 10:29-37

The man wasn't quite satisfied with Jesus' answer. "But Jesus," he asked, "who is my neighbor?"

Jesus told him, "Let Me answer your question with a story: A traveling man was walking along a deserted road. Robbers came by and attacked him. They stole everything he had and left him lying in a pitiful heap in the middle of the road. Then they ran off. A priest was traveling down the road and came upon the man. He crossed over to the other side and kept on walking. Next, a temple helper came upon the man. He also crossed to the other side of the road and kept on walking. Finally, a Samaritan came by. When he saw the man, he ran to help him. He treated his wounds with oil and put him on his donkey. Then he took him to an inn and told the innkeeper, 'Please care for the man, and I will pay you however much it costs.'

"Now," Jesus continued, "which of these three men would you say acted as a neighbor?"

The man who had asked the question stood up and said, "The Samaritan who showed pity."

Jesus answered, "Yes! Now go and do the same."

JESUS' TEACHING

DAY 266
The Rich Man and Lazarus
Luke 16:19-31

Jesus told another story about a rich man. The man had expensive clothes, a big house, and all the food he could ask for. One day a beggar named Lazarus came to the man's house asking for the crumbs off of the rich man's table. But the rich man didn't even want to look at Lazarus because he was dirty and sick. The rich man let his dogs sniff Lazarus and lick his wounds. A few days later, both men died. Lazarus went to heaven, but the rich man did not. The rich man cried, "Give me a little water. I am so thirsty!" Abraham in heaven answered, "When you lived on earth, you had everything, and yet you did not have pity on Lazarus who had nothing."

The rich man cried out again, "Then

JESUS' TEACHING

warn my brothers who are still alive, so that they don't have to join me here in this horrible place!" Abraham answered, "Moses and all the prophets have already done that. Your brothers should listen to the words that have already been spoken."

"So," Jesus explained, "do not be like the selfish rich man. He realized his lesson only after it was too late. Be like Lazarus—a man of a pure heart. Although he had nothing on earth, he gained the kingdom of heaven."

JESUS' TEACHING

DAY 267
A Rich Fool
Luke 12:13-21

A young man in the crowd stood up and called to Jesus, "Teacher, tell my brother to be fair and give my share of what our father has left us!"

Jesus answered, "If I did that, it would not help you. What you own will not make your life any better than it is. Think of the farmer who produced a harvest so big that he had to build several new barns just to hold the grain. But the farmer died that very night. What good was all his wealth then?" Then Jesus said to the young man, "Don't be so concerned about what you have and what you don't have. Let God's love be what you hope to possess. Then there will be no end to your wealth!"

DAY 268
Be Ready for the Master
Luke 12:32-40

Jesus also told them, "Don't be afraid, My friends, for your Father has given you the kingdom. Sell what you have and give the money to the poor. Save up your riches in heaven, where no thief can take them. Your heart will always be where your riches are.

Be ready for whatever comes. Have your lamps lit, like servants who are waiting for their master to come home from a wedding feast. When he comes and knocks at midnight, they will open the door for him at once. Happy are those servants whose master finds them awake and ready when he returns! I tell you, He will take off his coat, have them sit down, and will wait on them. And you, too, must be ready, because the Son of Man will come at an hour when He is not expected."

DAY 269
Faithful Servants
Luke 12: 41-48

Peter asked, "Lord, is this parable only for us, or does it apply to everyone?"
 Jesus answered, "Who is the faithful and wise servant? He is the one that his master will put in charge of his household. How happy that servant is if his master finds him doing this when he comes home! I tell you, the master will put that servant in charge of everything he owns. But if that servant says to himself, 'My master is taking a long time to come back,' and if he begins to beat the other servants, and eats and drinks, then the master will come back suddenly at a time he does not expect and punish him together with the unfaithful servants. A lot will be expected from those whom have been given a lot."

JESUS' TEACHING

DAY 270
The Great Banquet
Luke 14:12-24

Jesus had been invited to a dinner party by an important Pharisee. Many rich, well-to-do people were there. One among them said, "The greatest blessing of all is to be at the banquet in God's kingdom!"

Jesus told them of a man who had a banquet full of delicious food prepared. He invited his guests. But the guests kept coming up with reasons why they could not come. One said, "I must tend to the land I've just bought!" Another said, "I'm busy trying out my new oxen." Another said, "I have just gotten married and I cannot come." The master was upset. He told his servant, "Go as fast as you can to every street and alley in town. Bring anyone who is poor or crippled or blind. Let them come to my party!" After the servant did this, there was still room left at the banquet table. So the man said to the servant, "Now go to town and invite everybody you see. But if you see any of the people who rejected my invitation, do not invite them."

Then Jesus turned to the host of the dinner party and said, "Here today you have invited many of your rich friends and neighbors. But I have told you this story to show you that God blesses those who invite the poor, the crippled, and the blind. They cannot pay you back. But God will reward you in heaven."

317

JESUS' TEACHING

DAY 271
The Five Careless Bridesmaids
Matthew 25:1-13

Jesus told this story about preparing for God's kingdom:

Once there was going to be a big wedding party. Ten girls took oil lamps to light the darkness while they waited for the groom to come. Five of the girls were wise and brought extra oil. Five of the girls were foolish and did not. The girls waited and waited. Soon they became drowsy and fell asleep.

Then someone shouted, "The groom is here! Let's go inside!" The doors of the wedding hall were opened. The five girls who did not have extra oil cried out, "We are out of oil! Share some with us." But the other five answered, "You must go buy your own." By the time the five girls came back with their oil, the doors had been shut, and they could not get in.

"My friends," Jesus said, "do not be like the five girls who were not prepared. The doors of heaven will not be open to you unless you are ready for God at any moment."

DAY 272

Warning About Trouble

Matthew 24:3-14

Later, when Jesus sat on the Mount of Olives, the disciples came to Him in private. "Tell us when all this will happen," they asked, "and what will happen immediately before Your return and the end of the world."

Jesus answered, "Be aware, and do not let anyone fool you. Many will come to speak for Me and say, 'I can save you!' and they will fool many people. You are going to hear about wars and rumors of war, but don't be afraid. Such things must happen, but that's not the end. Countries will fight each other, nations will attack one another. There will be famines and earthquakes everywhere. But this is just the beginning.

Then you will be arrested and punished, and even killed. Everyone will hate you because of Me. Many will give up and betray and hate each other. Many false prophets will come and fool many people. Evil will spread, and people will stop loving each other. But if you stay faithful to the end, you will be safe. When the good news about God's kingdom has been preached to all the nations, the end will come."

JESUS' TEACHING

DAY 273
The Forgiving King
Matthew 18:21-27

Peter asked Jesus, "Say my brother keeps doing wrong to me. How many times must I forgive him? Is seven times enough?"

Jesus answered, "No, if he keeps doing wrong to you, you must keep forgiving him. This is what God's kingdom is all about." Then Jesus told this story:

JESUS' TEACHING

One day there lived a king who was collecting money that his officials owed him. An official came in who owed the king sixty million silver coins. But the official had no money. The king ordered him to be sold as a slave, along with his wife and children and all he owned, in order to pay back what he owed him.

"Please, your majesty," the official begged, "have pity on me, and I will pay you back in time!"

The king had a kind heart and decided to let his official go. He even told him that he no longer had to pay his debt."

DAY 274
The Unforgiving Servant
Matthew 18:28-35

Jesus continued His story:

As the official was walking out feeling happy at his good fortune, he saw a man who owed him one hundred silver coins. The official grabbed him by the throat and shouted, "Pay back the money you owe me!"

The man was frightened. He said, "Have pity on me, and I will pay you back!" But the official showed no pity and had the man thrown in jail.

When the king heard about this, he sent for the official. "You owed me money, and I showed mercy on you," said the king. "Why didn't you show mercy on another?" So the king had the official thrown in jail until he paid what he owed.

Then Jesus said, "My friends, My Father in heaven will show mercy on you, just like the king showed mercy on his official. He expects you to do the same with those around you. Forgive others with all your heart as My Father has forgiven you."

DAY 275
The Ten Servants
Luke 19:11-17

The crowd was still listening to Jesus as He was getting close to Jerusalem. Many of them thought that God's kingdom would soon appear, so Jesus told them this story:

There once was a prince who was on his way to a far-off land to be crowned king. Before he left, he gave some money to each of his three servants. He told them, "Use this money to make more money. When I return, I will see how you did." After the king returned from his journey, he called in his first servant. The servant exclaimed, "Look! I have earned ten times the amount of money you gave me." The king said, "Wonderful! You have done what I asked. I will give you ten cities to rule over as a reward."

JESUS' TEACHING

DAY 276
A Job Well Done
Luke 19:18-26

Jesus continued the story:

Next, the second servant came in. He said, "I have earned five times as much." The king nodded his head in approval. "That is good," he said, "I will give you five cities to rule over."

The third servant came in, looking a little nervous. "I have not made any money," he said. "I was afraid of you, so I just kept the money safe in my handkerchief."

The king was angry. He ordered the money to be given to the man who earned ten times as much. The king's officials were standing nearby and they cried out, "But he already has plenty!" The king replied, "Those who do what I say will be given more. Those who are fearful and do nothing will be given nothing."

"It is the same with your Father in heaven," Jesus explained. "Those who use their lives for his sake shall be given more. Those who do not, will be given nothing in return."

DAY 277
A Man with a Crippled Hand
Mark 3:1-6

On Sunday Jesus went into the temple to worship. The Pharisees whispered to each other, "Let's see if we can catch Jesus doing something wrong." They watched Him very closely. If only they could catch Jesus healing somebody, they could accuse Him of working on the Sabbath. But Jesus knew what the Pharisees were thinking. So He invited a man with a crippled hand to stand up. Then Jesus faced the crowd and said, "On the Sabbath should we do good deeds or bad deeds? If we can save a life, shouldn't we do it?" But none of the people said a word. Jesus was disappointed. He felt sorry for them because they still did not understand. "Stretch out your hand," He said to the man. The man obeyed and his crippled hand was healed. "Jesus is a criminal," the Pharisees said to each other. "He healed someone on the Sabbath!" So they began to plot against Him.

JESUS' HEALINGS AND MIRACLES

DAY 278
Jesus Heals Two Blind Men
Matthew 9:27-31

Jesus was walking along when two blind men started to follow Him. They were shouting, "Have pity on us, Son of David!" Jesus started to go indoors, but the blind men did not go away. So Jesus turned around and asked them, "Do you believe I can make you well?"

"Yes, Lord," they answered.

So Jesus laid His hands on their eyes. He said, "Because of your faith, you are healed." Then He took His hands away. The men looked around and saw everything. "Praise God, we're healed!" they shouted with joy. Jesus told them, "Don't tell anyone about what I have done." But the men were too excited to listen. They ran off and told everybody they could find about how Jesus healed them.

JESUS' HEALINGS AND MIRACLES

JESUS' HEALINGS AND MIRACLES

DAY 279
A Sick Woman
Mark 5:21-34

Jesus went to teach by the shore of Lake Galilee. A man named Jairus had come to see Jesus. He had a sick daughter. He told Jesus, "Please come back to my home! My daughter may die any minute." So Jesus went with him, and all Jesus' followers came too. While they were walking, a woman tried to get Jesus' attention. But there were so many people around Him that it was hopeless. She was very sick. She had spent all her life going to doctors. Not one of them could heal her sickness. "If I can just touch His clothes," she said to herself, "I will get well." So she brushed her hand along His robe. In an instant, all her sickness left her, and she was well.

Jesus felt power go out from Him. "Who touched My clothes?" He asked. His disciples told Him, "Jesus, there are so many people here. How can You ask who touched You?" But the woman knew that Jesus was talking about her. She started to tremble as she knelt down before Him. She told Him about her sickness and why she had touched His clothes. So Jesus said to her, "You had faith, and your faith is what healed you!"

The woman smiled. She was not afraid anymore.

JESUS' HEALINGS AND MIRACLES

DAY 280
A Dying Girl
Mark 5:35-43

Some men came from Jairus's house and told him, "It's too late. Your daughter is dead." But Jesus didn't listen to them. He told Jairus, "Don't worry. Just have faith!" Then He went to the house. The little girl's family was sitting around crying. "Why are you so sad?" Jesus asked them. "The girl is only asleep."

Jesus went into the girl's bedroom. He picked up her hand and said, "Talitha koum!" which means, "Little girl, get up!" Suddenly the little girl opened her eyes and sat up. She got out of bed and started walking around. Her parents were amazed. Jesus told them to give the little girl something to eat. "But keep this miracle that you have seen to yourself," Jesus added. "Don't tell anyone." Then He left.

JESUS' HEALINGS AND MIRACLES

DAY 281
Jesus Calms the Storm
Mark 4:35-41

Jesus was with His disciples on Lake Galilee. The sky was growing dark, and Jesus said, "Let's cross to the east side." While they were crossing, a windstorm started to blow. Waves splashed and filled the inside of the boat with water. The boat got heavier and heavier and started to sink. "Jesus, help us!" the disciples cried. But Jesus was asleep at the back of the boat. He didn't hear them. The storm was growing worse. So they shook Jesus and woke Him up, "Teacher," they said, "don't you care that we are about to drown?"

When Jesus woke up, He didn't panic like the disciples. He stood up and held out His hand.

JESUS' HEALINGS AND MIRACLES

Then He told the waves, "Be quiet!" And He told the wind, "Be still!" All at once the sea stopped thrashing, and the wind stopped howling. It was calm and peaceful again.

Jesus turned back around to His disciples and said, "Why were you afraid? Don't you have faith?" But the disciples became even more afraid. "Who are You?" they asked. "Who is this? Even the wind and the waves obey Him!"

JESUS' HEALINGS AND MIRACLES

DAY 282
The Wild Man in the Graveyard
Mark 5:1-20

Jesus and His disciples crossed Lake Galilee in their boat. They started to get out when they spotted a man running toward them. He had been living in the graveyard. He was dirty and covered in cuts and bruises. People from the town had tried to lock him away. They put chains around his legs and arms, but he always broke them.

JESUS' HEALINGS AND MIRACLES

When the wild man saw Jesus, he came and knelt down before Him. "What's your name?" Jesus asked him. "My name is Lots—because I've got lots of evil spirits inside of me." Jesus wanted to help the man. But the man said, "Don't get rid of my evil spirits, just send them into those pigs!" He pointed at a herd of pigs up on the hill. So Jesus sent the man's evil spirits into the pigs. The whole herd went wild and rushed down the hill straight into the lake. All the pigs drowned. The pig farmers couldn't believe it. They went into town to tell the people. But the man bowed before Jesus. "Please let me come with You," he said. Jesus told him, "Go home to your family. Tell them how much the Lord has done for you."

The man spent the rest of his life teaching people about Jesus.

JESUS' HEALINGS AND MIRACLES

DAY 283
Herodias Takes Revenge
Mark 6:14-29

King Herod married a woman named Herodias. But she was his brother's wife. John the Baptist told the king, "It isn't right for you to marry your brother's wife." Herodias didn't like John. "Who are you to judge the king and queen?" she said to him. Then she asked Herod to kill him. But Herod knew that John was a holy man. He didn't want to kill him, so he just threw him in jail.

On Herod's birthday he threw a big party. The daughter of Herodias came in and danced for the guests. They all smiled and clapped after she was done. "Dear girl," said Herod, "you've made us so happy. Ask for anything you want, and I will give it to you." The girl didn't know what to say, so she ran back to her mother. Herodias told her, "Ask the king for the head of John the Baptist."

So the girl went back and told Herod what she wanted. The king bowed his head. He was sorry for what he had said. But he kept his promise. "Cut off John's head," he told his jail guards. And when this was done, the girl took the head of John the Baptist to her mother. Herodias was very pleased. But John's followers were sad, and Jesus was too. They took his body and put it into a tomb.

JESUS' HEALINGS AND MIRACLES

DAY 284
The Work of Jesus' Followers
Luke 10:1-20

The Lord picked seventy-two followers to go out and spread His message. He sent them two by two to every town and village. He told them, "Don't take anything with you, not even sandals. If people invite you into their home, say, 'God bless this home with peace.' If they are kind to you, your prayer of peace will bless them. Eat whatever they give you and heal anyone who is sick. Tell them, 'God's kingdom is coming soon!'"

Jesus' followers obeyed. When they came back, they were very excited and ran to Jesus. "Lord," they told Him, "even the evil spirits listened to us when we spoke Your name!" Jesus smiled. "Are you so surprised?" He asked. "If you believe in Me, nothing can harm you. But don't be happy because evil spirits obey you. Be happy because you belong to God's kingdom."

DAY 285
Jesus Thanks His Father
Luke 10: 21-24

When Jesus' followers told Him about their travels, He felt joy for them. He knew that God was with the people. So He got down on His knees and prayed, "My Father, thank You for what You have done. You have hidden Your wisdom from the ones who think they know everything. Instead You've given Your wisdom to the humble people. They are the ones who please You. My Father has given Me everything. The only one who knows the Father is the Son. But the Son wants to tell others about the Father. When they know Him like I do, they will feel the same joy that is within Me."

Then Jesus told His followers, "Many prophets and kings would love to see what you see. But you are the ones that God has chosen. You are really blessed!"

JESUS' HEALINGS AND MIRACLES

DAY 286
Jesus Seeks a Quiet Place
Mark 6:30-33, 44

The disciples were sitting with Jesus. They were telling Him about their day and all the things they had done and taught. People were walking by with noisy carts and animals. So Jesus said, "Let's go find a quiet place. We can be alone and get some rest."

They left town and went down to the lake. Then they got in their boat to look for a quiet place. But the people from town saw them leave. They said to each other, "Come on. Let's go with Jesus!" People from other villages left what they were doing and came too. A few of them had an idea of where Jesus and the disciples would go. So the whole crowd ran on ahead and got there first. There were more than five thousand people.

JESUS' HEALINGS AND MIRACLES

DAY 287
The Hungry People
Mark 6:34-38; John 6:5-9

When the disciples saw the big crowd, they groaned. But Jesus didn't mind. He felt compassion for them. They were like sheep without a shepherd. So He told them to come closer, and then He began to teach. Afternoon rolled around and the disciples were hungry. "Let's take a break," they told Jesus. "The people

JESUS' HEALINGS AND MIRACLES

can go back to their villages and eat something."

But Jesus said, "Why don't you give them something to eat?"

"That's impossible," they replied. "It would cost a fortune to feed all these people!"

The disciple Andrew said, "Well, there is a boy here with some food. He has five loaves of bread and two fish. But that's not enough to feed five thousand people."

JESUS' HEALINGS AND MIRACLES

DAY 288
Five Loaves and Two Fish
Mark 6:39-44; John 6:10-14

Jesus told His disciples to have faith. "Tell the people to find a nice spot in the grass and sit down," He said. So the disciples obeyed. Once the people quieted down, Jesus stood up and took a loaf of bread in His hands. He bowed His head and gave thanks to God. Then He broke the bread and gave it to the people. He continued to pass the bread around until every single person had a piece. Then He did the same with the fish.

There was plenty of food, and the people couldn't eat it all. Jesus told His disciples to not let anything go to waste. So they went around and gathered up the extra food in big baskets. The people were amazed when they saw Jesus' miracle. "How did He make so much food out of so little?" they asked each other. "He is a miracle-worker!"

JESUS' HEALINGS AND MIRACLES

DAY 289
Jesus Walks on Water
Mark 6:45-50

When the day was done, Jesus told His disciples to go home without Him. He wanted to be by Himself for a while. They said good-bye and got in their boat. When all the crowds had left, Jesus climbed up to the side of the mountain and prayed.

That evening Jesus was still by Himself on the mountainside. He could see the lake from where He sat, and He spotted His disciples in their boat. The winds were very strong, and they were having trouble rowing. So Jesus went down to help them. He started to walk on top of the water toward them. But when the disciples saw Jesus, they were scared. "It's a ghost!" they cried out. They clung to each other and trembled.

"It's Me!" Jesus told them. "Don't be afraid."

JESUS' HEALINGS AND MIRACLES

DAY 290
Peter Lacks Faith
Matthew 14:28-33

Peter gathered his courage and spoke, "Lord, if it's really You, show me. Let me walk out to You on the water."

Jesus answered, "Come on, Peter. Don't be afraid."

Peter walked toward the edge of the boat. Then he stepped out onto the waves. He didn't sink, so he began to walk toward Jesus. But the wind picked up, and Peter got nervous. He started to look down at his feet. "I'm sinking, Jesus!" he cried. "Save me!"

Jesus reached His hand out to Peter and lifted him up again.

"Where did your faith go?" Jesus asked him. "If you had trusted Me, you wouldn't have fallen. Why do you doubt?"

Then Jesus and Peter walked back together toward the boat. The other disciples had been watching the whole thing. "You really are the Son of God!" they said. They bowed down at Jesus' feet and worshipped Him.

DAY 291
A Woman's Faith
Matthew 15:21-28

Jesus was traveling with His disciples. A Canaanite woman walked behind them crying, "Lord, please have pity on me! I have a daughter, but she is full of evil spirits. Can you save her?" Jesus didn't say a word. The disciples told Jesus to send her away. But He said to her, "I have come to help the Israelites. They are like lost sheep. But you are a Canaanite."

"Please help me," she said again.

"Would it be right to take away food from children and give it to the dog instead?" Jesus asked her.

The woman replied, "You are right, Lord. But even dogs get the crumbs that fall from their owner's table."

Jesus rejoiced in His heart. He knew that she truly trusted Him. "Dear woman," He said, "you do have faith after all! Go home—I've already given you what you asked for."

JESUS' HEALINGS AND MIRACLES

DAY 292
Jesus Heals a Blind Man
Mark 8:22-26

At Bethsaida the disciples saw some people coming toward them. It was a blind man being led by some of his friends. "Please heal this man," they asked Jesus. So Jesus took the man's hand and led him a little ways out of the village. Then He spit on the man's eyes. He put His hands over them, and then He took His hands away. "Can you see anything?" Jesus asked him.

"Yes, Lord! I see some people, but they look like trees walking around." So Jesus placed His hands on the man's eyes again.

"And can you see anything now?" Jesus asked him, as He took His hands away. The man just stared. He saw everything clearly, and his eyes were full of wonder.

"You can go home now," Jesus told him. "But don't go through the village."

346

JESUS' HEALINGS AND MIRACLES

DAY 293
Simon Shows True Faith
Matthew 16:13-19

Jesus and His disciples were near the town of Caesarea. While they were walking Jesus asked, "Who do people say that I am?"

His disciples answered, "Some people think You are John the Baptist raised from the dead. Other people think You are Elijah or Jeremiah or some other prophet."

Then Jesus asked, "Who do You think I am?"

Simon Peter said, "You are the Son of God!"

Jesus smiled. "Simon, you are blessed. You could not have known this on your own. My Father in heaven told you. So I will change your name. It will be Peter, which means rock. And on that rock I will build My church. After you die, the church will go on. But I will give you the keys to My kingdom. God in heaven will be with you!"

JESUS' HEALINGS AND MIRACLES

DAY 294
The Ten Lepers
Luke 17:11-19

Jesus was on his way to Jerusalem. He went through a village and saw ten men with leprosy. They cried out to Him, "Jesus, have pity on us!"

Jesus went over to them and said, "Go to the priest and ask him for help." They obeyed Jesus and left. On their way to the priest, Jesus healed them.

They left to celebrate. But one man came back to Jesus. He was a Samaritan. He sang God's praises the whole way. When he saw Jesus, he bowed down at His feet. "Thank You, Lord. You have healed me," he said.

"Where are the others?" Jesus asked him. "You are a foreigner, and yet you are the only one who has come back to thank God. You can go now. Your faith has healed you."

JESUS' HEALINGS AND MIRACLES

JESUS' HEALINGS AND MIRACLES

DAY 295
Moses and Elijah Appear
Luke 9:28-36

Jesus went up on a mountain to pray. He brought Peter, John, and James with Him. While Jesus was praying, the other three fell asleep in the grass. Suddenly Moses and Elijah came down from heaven and spoke with Jesus. His plain clothes turned bright white. The three of them spoke about Jesus' death and what it would mean.

Peter, John, and James heard their voices and woke up. They saw Jesus, Moses, and Elijah in all their glory. They were amazed. But Moses and Elijah knew it was time for them to go. "Don't go," Peter begged. "Let us make shelters for the three of you! We can all stay here together."

But Peter didn't understand why they had really come.

God sent a dark cloud that passed over all of them. Then a voice spoke, saying, "This is my Son. Listen to what He tells you." Suddenly Moses and Elijah disappeared. Only Jesus was left. So the disciples stayed quiet. They didn't tell anyone about what happened.

DAY 296
Jesus Heals a Woman on the Sabbath
Luke 13:10-17

On the Sabbath Jesus was teaching in a meeting place. A woman was there whose back was bent. She could hardly see Jesus because she was forced to hunch over. "Come over here," Jesus told the woman. He put His hands on her, and the woman's back straightened. "You're well now!" Jesus said. The woman thanked God. But the man who was in charge of the meeting place was angry. He said to Jesus, "You can't heal someone on the Sabbath. There are six other days You can heal her. Why do You have to do it today?"

So Jesus said, "If you had a thirsty donkey, you would give it a drink. If it were the Sabbath, would you let it go thirsty? This woman belongs to God. But she has been suffering eighteen years. I will heal her no matter what day of the week it is."

These words made the man feel ashamed. But everyone else in the crowd felt happy. They knew that Jesus was doing wonderful things.

JESUS' HEALINGS AND MIRACLES

DAY 297
The Death of Lazarus
John 11:1-15

Mary and Martha had a brother named Lazarus. He was one of Jesus' good friends. But one day Lazarus got very sick. He couldn't get out of bed. So Mary and Martha sent a message and told Jesus to come. Jesus got the news, but He didn't go right away. He knew that Lazarus would be all right.

Two days later Jesus told His disciples to come with Him to see Lazarus. "But he lives in Judea," they answered. "Why do You want to go?"

Jesus answered, "Our friend Lazarus is asleep. I want to wake him up."

"Can't he wake up on his own?" the disciples asked. But they didn't understand what Jesus meant. "No, Lazarus is dead," He explained. But he will come back to us. I'm glad I didn't go sooner, because now you will have a good reason to put your faith in Me. Let's go, and I'll show you."

JESUS' HEALINGS AND MIRACLES

JESUS' HEALINGS AND MIRACLES

DAY 298
Jesus Brings Lazarus to Life
John 11:10-44

Martha saw that Jesus was coming. She ran out to meet Him. Jesus said, "I am the one who can raise the dead! Anyone who puts their faith in Me will live, even after death. Do you believe this, Martha?"

"Yes, Lord!" she replied. "I know that You are the Son of God."

Then Mary came out. She went to Jesus and kneeled down in front of Him. "Lord, our brother is dead. If You had come sooner, I know he would've lived."

Jesus started to cry. Then He walked over to Lazarus' tomb. "Roll the stone away," He told them. But Martha said,

JESUS' HEALINGS AND MIRACLES

"Lord, he's been dead for four days. There will be a bad smell." The stone was rolled away. Jesus prayed, "Father, answer My prayer and let these people see that I am truly Your Son."

Then Jesus said, "Lazarus, come out!" A man came out of the tomb wrapped in burial cloth from head to foot. Jesus took the bandages off, and everyone saw it was Lazarus. Jesus had raised him from the dead!

JESUS' HEALINGS AND MIRACLES

DAY 299
The Cripple by the Water
John 5:1-9

Jesus was on His way to Jerusalem for a festival. As He came into the city, He walked by a large pool of water. The pool was surrounded by many sick, blind, and crippled people. They were lying on decks around the pool. Some of them were swimming. Jesus saw a man lying near the edge of the water. He had been sick for thirty-eight years. Jesus felt compassion for him.

"Do you want Me to heal you?" he asked the man.

"Lord," the man replied, "I only want to go swimming in the pool. I have no one to carry me in. And when I try to go by myself, I am so slow that someone always gets there before me." Jesus told him, "Pick up your mat and walk!"

At that moment, the man was healed.

JESUS' HEALINGS AND MIRACLES

DAY 300
Little Man Zacchaeus
Luke 19:1-10

Zacchaeus collected people's taxes and made a lot of money. He heard that Jesus was coming to Jericho on His way to Jerusalem. But Zacchaeus was a little man. He couldn't see Jesus because there were too many people. So he found a tall sycamore tree and climbed up into its branches. Then he listened to Jesus while He spoke. Jesus spotted Zacchaeus in the tree. "Come here, Zacchaeus!" He said to him. "I want to stay with you today."

Nobody liked Zacchaeus because he was a tax collector. "Why does Jesus want to stay with a sinner like him?" they said. But Zacchaeus was very excited. He came down the tree and invited Jesus to his home. After spending the day together, Zacchaeus was like a new man. He said to Jesus, "I'm giving up all my riches. I will give what I have to the poor. And I will pay back four times as much to everyone I cheated."

Jesus said, "Because of this, you and your family are saved. You have heard My message in your heart. Taking from people made you rich. But giving to people is what brings true joy."

DAY 301
The Big Parade
Luke 19:28-38

Jesus was nearing Jerusalem. He sent two of His disciples ahead of Him. "Go into the next village," He instructed them. "There you'll see a donkey tied to a pole. Untie the donkey and bring it back to Me. If anyone asks why you are taking it, tell them the Lord needs it."

The disciples went and found the donkey Jesus was talking about. As they began to untie it, the owner of the donkey snapped at them, "What do you think you're doing?" But the man let them go when they told him the Lord needed it.

They brought the donkey to Jesus, and He climbed on its back. Then He rode down the Mount of Olives toward Jerusalem.

The people were waiting for Him down below. They had taken large palm tree leaves and waved them like flags. They also put their clothes down on the ground to make a path for Jesus. The disciples cheered and sang praises alongside the people. "Blessed is the King our Lord! Peace in heaven and glory to God!"

JESUS' LAST DAYS

DAY 302
Jerusalem! Jerusalem!
Luke 19:39-42

As Jesus rode into Jerusalem, the people cheered so loudly that the noise shook the buildings. They praised God with all their might. But the Pharisees were irritated. "Make those people stop shouting," they demanded. Jesus said to them, "Even if they kept quiet, the stones themselves would begin to sing!" And so the people went right on singing God's praises.

Then Jesus cried out, "Jerusalem! God has come to save you, but still the truth is hidden from your eyes. You don't know the true meaning of peace. If you know Me, then you will know peace."

JESUS' LAST DAYS

DAY 303
Healing in the Temple
Matthew 21:14-16

The first thing Jesus did in Jerusalem was visit the temple. Many people followed Him. He healed every blind, sick, or crippled person that came to Him. But the teachers and the priests in the temple were angry at this. "Who gives You the right to perform miracles in our temple?" they asked Him. Just then the sound of singing came from outside. The teachers and the priests went to see what was going on. A group of children were jumping up and down singing, "Praise the Son of David!"

"Do You hear what those children are saying?" they grumbled to Jesus.

"Yes, I hear them," Jesus said. "Don't you remember what the Scriptures say? 'Children and babies will sing praises!'"

JESUS' LAST DAYS

DAY 304
Judas Betrays Jesus
Matthew 26:1-5, 14-16

That night Jesus was with His disciples. He told them, "Two days from now is the festival for Passover. That's the day your Lord will be taken from you. On that day My enemies will nail Me to a cross."

Meanwhile, the leaders of Jerusalem had come together to plot against Jesus. They met in secret and planned Jesus' death. "We can't do it during the festival," they said to one another. "There are too many people, and they might riot!" So they schemed about where and when they would arrest Jesus. Just then Judas Iscariot, one of Jesus' twelve disciples, walked in the door. "If you pay me," he told them, "I will help you get Jesus." The leaders agreed and paid Judas thirty silver coins.

JESUS' LAST DAYS

DAY 305
A Special Meal Is Prepared
Luke 22:7-13

The day of Passover came. All of Israel woke up early and prepared for the big day. Jesus told Peter and John, "Go make our Passover meal."

"But Jesus," they said, "we have no home where we can cook our food."

"Don't worry about that," said Jesus. "Go into Jerusalem and look for a man with a jar of water. Follow him home. The owner of the house will take you upstairs to a big kitchen. You can make our meal there."

So Peter and John left for Jerusalem. They found a man with a water jar and they followed him back home. Then the owner of the house led them upstairs to a big kitchen. Everything happened just as Jesus said. They made the meal and then went back to Jesus.

JESUS' LAST DAYS

DAY 306
The Leaders Shall Serve
Luke 22:14, 24-30

Jesus and His disciples sat down to eat the Passover meal. While they were talking, one of them asked, "Who is the greatest among God's people?" All the disciples had a different opinion. They began to argue. Jesus told them, "Some of you may think a ruler is the greatest because he orders people around. But don't be like that. The greatest person is the one who serves others. I have been a servant to you. Soon I will be gone. If you can serve others as I have served you, then you be with Me in My kingdom. Each of you will have a throne, and you will eat and drink at My table."

JESUS' LAST DAYS

DAY 307
A New Command
John 13:31-35

Jesus told His disciples, "I will have to leave you all soon. You will look for Me, but I won't be there. God is going to bring glory to His Son! My time has come to go and be with My Father. But I will leave you with a new command. My command is that you love each other just as I have loved you. If you do as I say, then I will know that you are truly My followers."

DAY 308
Jesus Promises the Holy Spirit
John 14:15-20

Jesus said to His disciples, "If you love Me, you will do as I have told you. Then I will ask the Father, and He will give you another teacher, who will stay with you always. He is the Holy Spirit, and He will teach you the whole truth. The people of the world cannot understand Him, because they cannot see Him or know Him. But you know Him, because He is with you and is living in you.

"I am leaving, but you will not be left alone. I will come back to you. In a little while the world will see Me no more, but you will still see Me. I live, and you also will live. Then you will know that I am one with My Father and that you are one with Me, just as I am one with you."

DAY 309
The Lord's Supper
Mark 14:18-25

Jesus told His disciples, "One of you dining with Me is going to betray Me." The disciples hung their heads. They felt sad. "Surely You don't mean me?" each of them asked Jesus. "I would never do a thing like that," each of them said. Jesus told them, "One of you twelve will turn your back on Me. I will die and go to the Father. But the man who betrays me will feel terrible. He will wish he had never been born.

Then Jesus picked up the loaf of bread from the table. He said a blessing and then broke the bread in two. "Take this bread and eat it," Jesus told them. "It is My body." Then Jesus passed around the wine. "Take this wine and drink it. It is My blood." So the disciples ate and drank. Jesus told them, "I will give up My body for you so that your sins may be forgiven."

JESUS' LAST DAYS

DAY 310
Jesus Washes the Disciples' Feet
John 13:1-9

The disciples were all sitting around the table. But Jesus stood up. He took off His robe and wrapped a towel around His waist. Then He filled a bowl with water and went back to the table. He knelt down at the disciples' feet and began to wash them. Then He dried them with the towel. The disciples were speechless. But Simon Peter spoke up. He said, "Lord, why are you washing our feet?"

"You don't understand right now, but you will soon," Jesus answered.

Peter didn't want the Lord to do something only a slave would do. He said, "Jesus I won't let You wash my feet."

But Jesus told him, "If I don't wash your feet, then you don't belong to Me."

So Peter let him wash his feet along with the other disciples.

DAY 311
Jesus Sets the Example
John 13:12-17

After Jesus had finished washing the disciples' feet, He sat back down. "Do you know why I have done this?" He asked them. But the disciples were silent. "You call Me 'Lord' and that is what I am! I have served you by washing your feet. This is to show you that the most important one should be like the least important. Learn from My example and serve one another. I love you to the very end, and I am willing to do anything for you. Do the same for each other. Now that you know these things, God will bless you if you do them."

JESUS' LAST DAYS

JESUS' LAST DAYS

DAY 312
His Father's Work
John 14:8-14

Philip said, "Lord, show us the Father. That is all we need."

Jesus answered, "Philip, for a long time I have been with you all, and you still don't know who I am? If you have seen Me, you have seen the Father also. Why do you then say, 'Show us the Father?' Philip, trust Me when I say that I am one with the Father and the Father is one with Me. If you cannot do this, believe Me at least because of the things you see Me do. It's absolutely true that those who trust Me will do the same things that I am doing. Yes, they will do even greater things, because I am going back to the Father. Ask Me, and I will do whatever You ask. This way the Father will be honored through the Son. Please ask Me, and I will do whatever you ask."

JESUS' LAST DAYS

DAY 313
Peter Will Deny Jesus
Mark 14:26-31

The disciples finished their meal. They sang a hymn and left to find a place to relax. They went to the Mount of Olives. While they were there, Jesus told them, "I will die, and each one of you will turn your back on Me. You will be scattered and lost like sheep. But this won't be the end. I will come back and lead you again."

"Lord," Peter said, "Even if the others turn their backs on you, I never will."

But Jesus knew the truth. He said, "You will reject Me this very night. Before the rooster crows you will say that you don't know Me three times." Peter didn't believe Him. "No, I will never do that," he replied. All the other disciples said the same thing.

JESUS' LAST DAYS

DAY 314

A Home in Heaven

John 14:1-6

The disciples felt sad and Jesus could see it in their faces. So He told them, "Don't worry! Just have faith in God, and have faith in His Son too. It's true that I cannot stay with you. But there are many rooms in God's house. I am going ahead of you to prepare a place where we can be together. I wouldn't tell you this if it weren't true."

"Lord," the disciple Thomas replied, "we don't know where You're going. How can we follow You if we don't know the way?"

Jesus told him, "I am the way, the truth, and the life! No one comes to the Father except through Me."

JESUS' LAST DAYS

DAY 315

Jesus Prays for His Followers

John 17:1–18:1

After Jesus finished speaking with His disciples, He went off to pray by Himself. "Father, you have given Me many followers. They have believed in Me. They know that I am Your Son. Now I am coming home to You, but help My followers who are still in the world. Protect them by Your power, and bring them closer to Your Word. Keep them safe. I also pray for those who will believe in Me through their message. Let them be as one people the way the Father and Son are one that the world may believe that You have sent Me."

Jesus finished His prayer and went with His disciples into the Garden of Gethsemane.

DAY 316
The Disciples Fall Asleep
Mark 14:33-42

Jesus felt sad and lonely. He knew that He was going to die soon. "Will you stay awake and pray with me?" He asked His disciples. Then He walked a few steps away and knelt in the grass. "Father," He prayed, "I am suffering. You can do anything, so don't let this happen to Me. But You must do what You want, and not what I want."

Jesus went back over to His disciples. They had all fallen asleep. This made Jesus feel lonelier than ever. He said to Peter, "Can't you stay awake with Me for one hour?" But they couldn't keep their eyes open. They just mumbled and fell asleep again. So Jesus prayed by Himself. When He was finished, He went back to the disciples.

"Aren't you through with resting?" He said to them. "Wake up! It's time for Me to be taken away from you. The one who has betrayed Me is already coming this way into the garden." The disciples looked around and wondered what Jesus was talking about.

375
JESUS' LAST DAYS

DAY 317
Betrayed With a Kiss
John 18:2-8; Matthew 26:48-50

Judas Iscariot told the Roman soldiers where they could find Jesus. "He will be in the garden with the disciples," Judas told the men. "And you will know who Jesus is because I'll give Him a kiss on the cheek." The plan was settled. They lit their torches and carried their weapons. Then they followed Judas to the Garden of Gethsemane.

Jesus saw them coming. "Who are you looking for?" He asked them.

"We've come to arrest Jesus," they answered.

"I am Jesus," He said. The soldiers seemed surprised, and they stumbled backward. So Jesus asked them again, "Who are you looking for?"

"We've come for Jesus," they answered.

"Leave My disciples alone. I am the one you want," Jesus said. Then Judas walked up to Jesus and kissed Him on the cheek. The soldiers tied up Jesus' wrist and started to take Him away.

DAY 318
Jesus Is Taken Away
John 18:10-11; Luke 22:51-53

Peter burned with anger. He wanted to save Jesus. So he pulled out a sword and swung it at the priest's servant. He chopped off his ear, but Jesus stopped him before he could do any more and said, "Put that weapon away, Peter." He touched the servant's ear and made it whole again. Then He turned to the soldiers and the police who had come to arrest Him. "Why are you treating Me like a criminal? You have come with swords and clubs. Once, we worshiped together in the temple. You never wanted to hurt Me then. But I know that this is your time. You don't understand what you are doing. There's a darkness covering your eyes, and you can't see the truth."

JESUS' LAST DAYS

DAY 319
Peter's Denial
John 18:12-14; Luke 22:54-62

Jesus was taken to the high priest's house. Peter tried to go with Him, but he had to wait outside. Some people had made a fire in the courtyard. Peter went over and sat down next to it. "Aren't you the man who came with Jesus?" a servant girl asked him.

"No, I don't even know Him," Peter replied.

A little while later someone else said, "You are Jesus' disciple!"

But Peter said, "No, I'm not."

"You must be with Jesus," another man said. "You come from Galilee just like He does."

"I don't know what you're talking about," Peter growled.

Then in the distance a rooster crowed. Peter remembered what the Lord had said: "You will deny Me three times before the rooster crows."

Peter knew Jesus had been right all along. He felt so bad that he couldn't stop crying.

DAY 320
Jesus Is Questioned
Mark 14:53-65; 15:1

The high priest met with the leaders of Israel. "What has Jesus done?" he asked them. "He's a liar!" they shouted. "He told us He would tear down our temple and rebuild it in three days."

The priest turned to Jesus and said, "Why don't You speak up for Yourself?"

But Jesus didn't say a word.

"Are You the Son of God?" the priest asked Him.

"Yes, I am!" Jesus answered. "And soon I will be with My Father in heaven."

The priest turned to the leaders. "Aha!" he exclaimed. "Did you hear Him say He was God? That's reason enough to kill Jesus." They blindfolded Jesus and tied Him up with rope. They beat Him and spit in His eyes. Then they took Him to Pilate.

DAY 321
Jesus Is Sent to Herod
Luke 23:7-11

Pilate did not want to deal with Jesus. He decided to let another ruler judge Him. So the soldiers took Jesus to King Herod. Herod was very curious about Him. He had heard many stories about Jesus' miracles and wonders. He wanted to see if Jesus could do them again. But Jesus did not do anything for Herod. He didn't even speak. "What is Your crime, Jesus?" Herod asked him. Jesus didn't say a word, so some of the leaders spoke up instead. "He thinks He's the Son of God!" they shouted. Herod sneered at Jesus, "So You think You're God? Well then we'd better put You in some better clothes!" He brought out a fancy robe and put it on Jesus. Herod's soldiers snorted with laughter. They made fun of Jesus for a long time. Finally Herod said, "Send Him back to Pilate. I have no reason to kill Jesus."

JESUS' LAST DAYS

DAY 322
Pilate Tries to Free Jesus
John 18:28-40; Matthew 27:20-23

Jesus was led back to Pilate's palace. There was a huge crowd that had gathered outside Pilate's door. They had come to rally against Jesus. "Why are you so angry?" Pilate asked the people. "What has Jesus done wrong?" The mob began to shout all kinds of lies about Jesus. Pilate could hardly understand what they were saying, so he asked, "Why don't you punish Him?" But the people cried back, "It's against the law for us to crucify Him. We need you to do it!" So Pilate went back inside to Jesus. "Are you the king of the Jews?" he asked him. "Do you believe I am?" Jesus replied.

"The people are saying that You call Yourself a king," Pilate said.

"My kingdom does not belong to this world," Jesus replied. "If it were, the people would have stayed true to Me."

"So," Pilate said, "You admit to being a king!"

"It's You who say I am a king," Jesus replied. "I was born to tell the truth."

Pilate was frustrated. He didn't want to kill Jesus, but the mob was growing angrier every minute. He went out to them and said, "Jesus doesn't seem guilty. And after all, it's Passover today. Why don't I set Him free?"

The mob yelled back, "No! Nail Him to a cross!"

JESUS' LAST DAYS

DAY 323
Jesus Is Sentenced to Death
John 19:1-16

Pilate tried to calm the mob. But more and more people kept shouting and crowding around his door. "Tie Jesus up, and we'll whip Him," Pilate told his soldiers. "That should make the people happy." So they whipped Jesus and put a crown of thorns on His head. But the people were not satisfied. "Crucify Him! Crucify Him!" they chanted.

Pilate went over to Jesus. "Where do You come from?" he asked. But Jesus was silent. "Why don't You answer me? Don't You know I have the power to free You?"

Jesus lifted His wearied head and replied, "Only God has the power to free Me. Without Him, you couldn't do anything at all to Me."

Pilate asked the mob again, "So, you really want me to kill your king?"

"He's not our king," the people yelled back. "Only the emperor is king."

Pilate finally gave in and handed Jesus over to be killed.

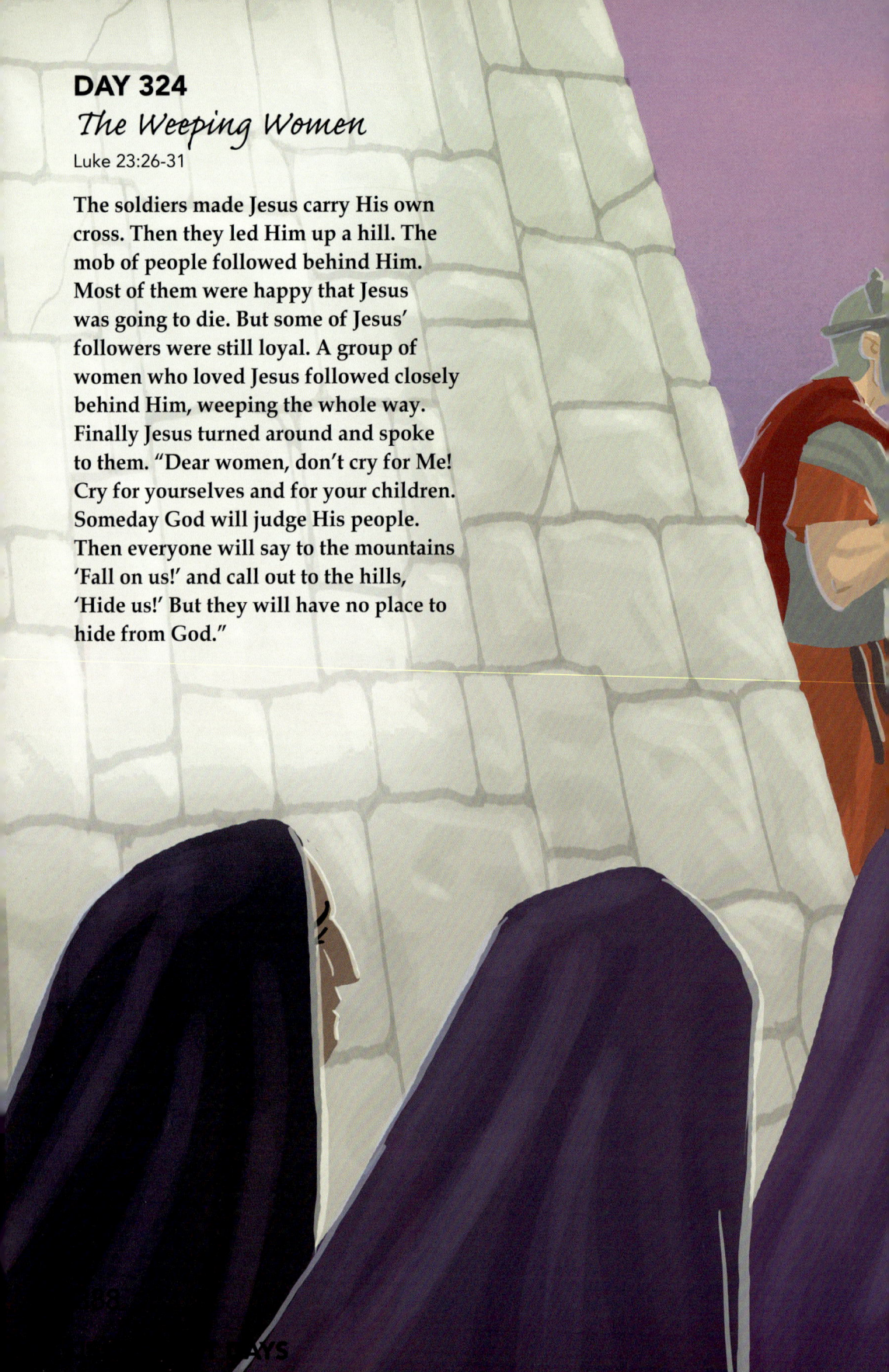

DAY 324
The Weeping Women
Luke 23:26-31

The soldiers made Jesus carry His own cross. Then they led Him up a hill. The mob of people followed behind Him. Most of them were happy that Jesus was going to die. But some of Jesus' followers were still loyal. A group of women who loved Jesus followed closely behind Him, weeping the whole way. Finally Jesus turned around and spoke to them. "Dear women, don't cry for Me! Cry for yourselves and for your children. Someday God will judge His people. Then everyone will say to the mountains 'Fall on us!' and call out to the hills, 'Hide us!' But they will have no place to hide from God."

DAY 325
Jesus Is Nailed to a Cross
Luke 23:32-38

They nailed Jesus to a cross. There was a sign above His head that read: The King of the Jews. Then the soldiers crucified two other criminals alongside Jesus. The people watched from down below. Some of them made fun of Jesus and called Him names. "Why can't you save Yourself?" the soldiers taunted Him. "I thought You were the Lord!" Then they gambled for His clothes. While Jesus was waiting to die, He prayed, "Forgive these people, Father! They don't know what they're doing."

JESUS' LAST DAYS

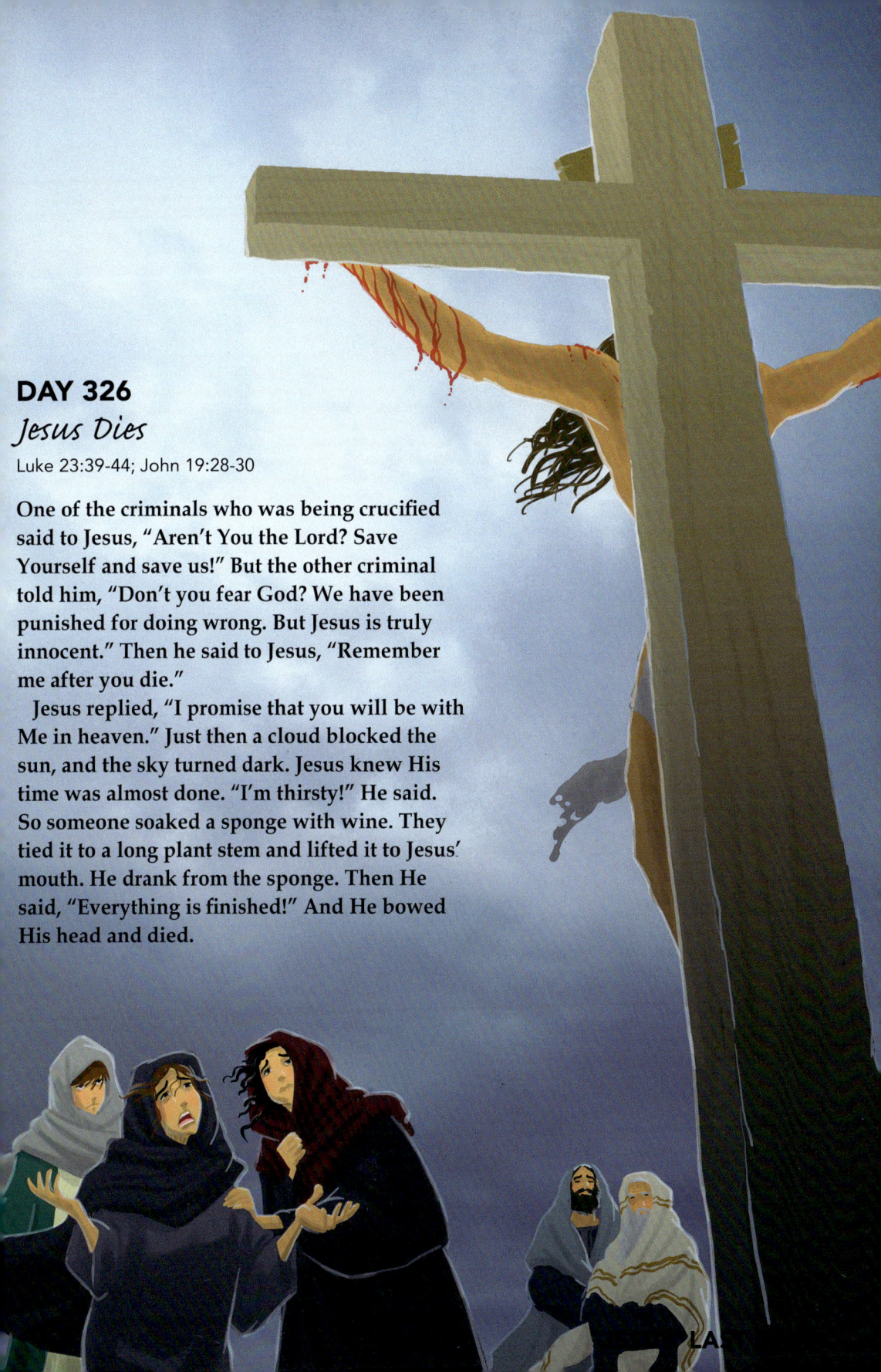

DAY 326

Jesus Dies

Luke 23:39-44; John 19:28-30

One of the criminals who was being crucified said to Jesus, "Aren't You the Lord? Save Yourself and save us!" But the other criminal told him, "Don't you fear God? We have been punished for doing wrong. But Jesus is truly innocent." Then he said to Jesus, "Remember me after you die."

Jesus replied, "I promise that you will be with Me in heaven." Just then a cloud blocked the sun, and the sky turned dark. Jesus knew His time was almost done. "I'm thirsty!" He said. So someone soaked a sponge with wine. They tied it to a long plant stem and lifted it to Jesus' mouth. He drank from the sponge. Then He said, "Everything is finished!" And He bowed His head and died.

DAY 327
The Earth Trembles
Matthew 27:51-56

The moment Jesus died, the curtain in Jerusalem's temple tore in two. Then an earthquake came and split even the heaviest rocks in two. The graves of Jesus' followers opened up. And when Jesus had risen to life again, His dead followers came up out of their graves to go and see Him in Jerusalem. Many of the soldiers and leaders of Israel were scared when all these things happened. They thought to themselves, "Jesus must have truly been the Son of God!"

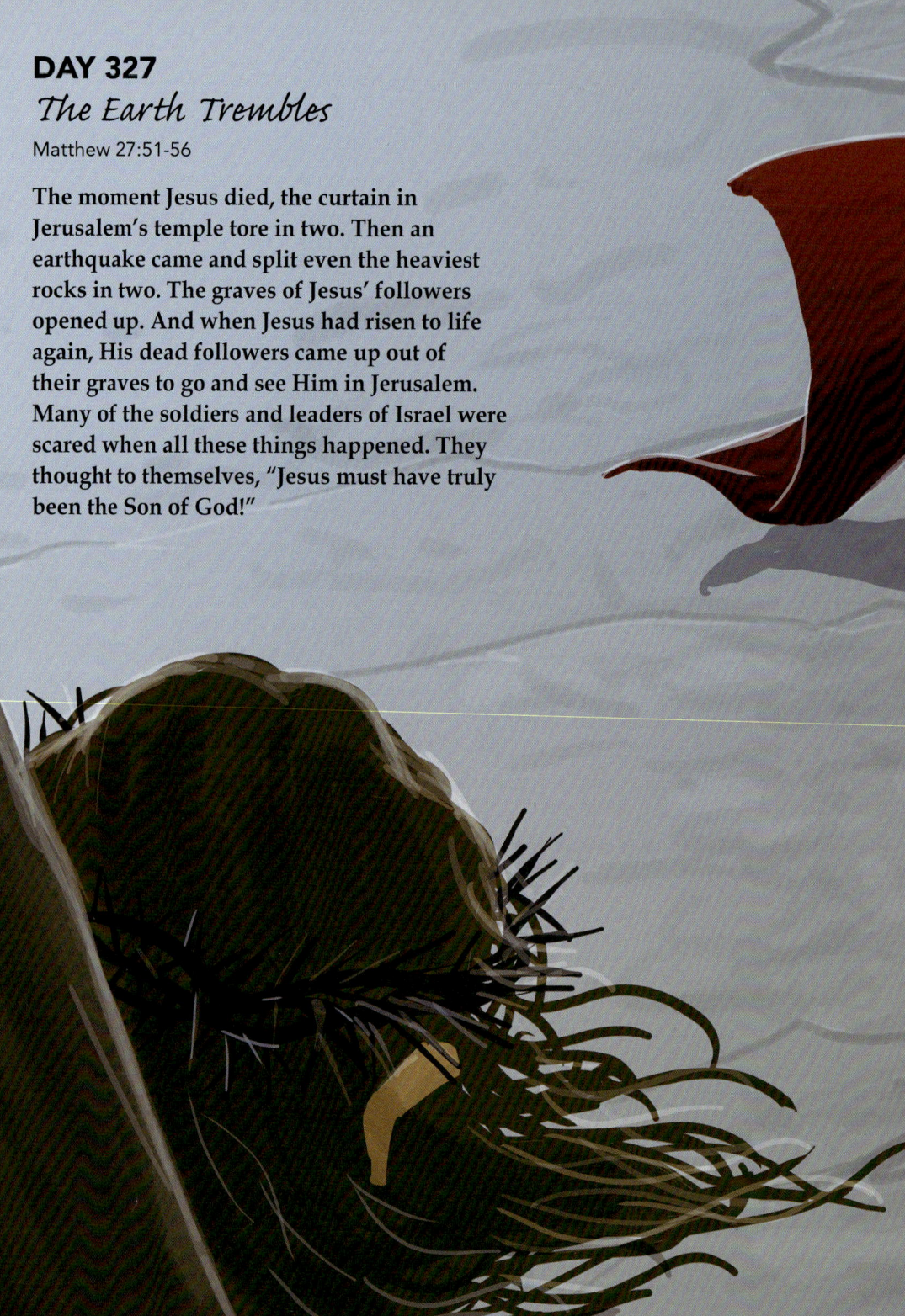

JESUS' LAST DAYS

DAY 328
Jesus Is Buried
John 19:31-34; Matthew 27:57-66

The next day was the Sabbath. The people wanted the bodies to be taken down from the crosses on this special day. So the soldiers took down Jesus' body. But one of Jesus' followers named Joseph came running up to them. He asked the soldiers if he could bury Jesus himself. The soldiers asked Pilate, and Pilate said he could. So Joseph took Jesus' body home. He cleaned it and wrapped it in white linen. Then he put Him in a tomb that had been cut out from the rocks. He rolled a heavy round stone over the entrance door and left. But two soldiers stayed and guarded the tomb.

DAY 329

Jesus Has Risen
Matthew 28:1-10

Mary Magdalene went to visit Jesus' tomb with the other Mary. But as soon as they arrived, an earthquake rumbled and shook the ground. The soldiers guarding the tomb were so frightened that they both fainted. Then an angel of the Lord came down from heaven. His clothes were bright white, and his face was shining. "Don't be afraid," the angel told the women. "I know you've come to be with Jesus. But He isn't here. God has raised Him to life!" The women were speechless. They started running back to town—full of joy and excitement. They couldn't wait to tell everybody what the angel had said. Then suddenly Jesus came out and greeted them. "Don't be afraid," Jesus said with a smile. "It's Me! Go and tell My disciples that I will meet them in Galilee."

JESUS' RESURRECTION

397

JESUS' RESURRECTION

DAY 330
The Empty Tomb
John 20:2-18

Mary Magdalene found Simon Peter and said, "The Lord has risen! The tomb is empty!" Peter had to see it with his own eyes. He immediately got up and ran toward the tomb. Another disciple went with him and got there before Peter. But he was too afraid to go inside. So Peter went in first. Jesus wasn't there! The only thing he saw was a folded pile of linen that Jesus' body had been wrapped with. The other disciple finally came inside too. He saw the empty tomb and believed. The two of them went back to tell the other disciples. It was true! Jesus had risen!

JESUS' RESURRECTION

DAY 331

Jesus Appears to the Disciples

John 20:19; Luke 24:37-45; John 20:21-23

The disciples were afraid of the leaders of Israel. They didn't want to be killed like Jesus. So they hid out in a room and locked the door. While they were sitting there, Jesus appeared before them! "Hello, friends," He said. But the disciples thought He was a ghost. They huddled together and clung to each other's arms. "Why are you afraid of Me?" Jesus asked them.

"Don't you see My wounds?" Jesus showed His wrists where the nails had been. "It is You, Lord!" they answered in surprise.

"Do you have something to eat?" Jesus asked. One of the disciples handed Him a piece of baked fish, and He ate it. Then He said, "The Father sent Me to earth. But My time is over. Now I am sending you." He breathed on the disciples and said, "Receive the Holy Spirit. If you forgive anyone's sins, they will be forgiven. But if you don't, then they won't be forgiven."

JESUS' RESURRECTION

DAY 332
Thomas Touches Jesus' Wounds
John 20:24-29

One of the twelve disciples had not seen Jesus. Thomas was not in the room with the other disciples. So they went to him and said, "We have seen the Lord!" But Thomas didn't believe them. "I must see Jesus' wounds myself and touch them with my own fingers. Then I will believe you." A week later all twelve disciples were together again in one room. They locked the door. But Jesus appeared to them just like He had before. He went over to Thomas. "Here, touch My scars. It's Me!" Jesus said. So Thomas took

JESUS' RESURRECTION

Jesus' hands and touched His wounds. "You are my Lord!" Thomas replied. He was happy to see Jesus again. But Jesus asked him, "Why did you doubt Me? The ones who believe without seeing are the blessed ones."

JESUS' RESURRECTION

DAY 333
A Net Full of Fish
John 21:1-14

Jesus appeared to His disciples a third time.

Peter wanted to go fishing on the lake. So the other disciples said, "We'll go with you." But the entire day and night they didn't catch even one fish. Early the next morning Jesus stood waiting for them on the shore. The disciples saw Him from the boat, but they didn't realize it was Jesus. "Have you caught anything?" Jesus asked them. "No," they answered. Jesus told them to let their nets down on the other side of their boat. The disciples decided it wouldn't hurt to try. They could hardly believe their eyes as they watched the nets fill with tons of huge fish! The nets were so heavy that the disciples huffed and puffed as they were pulling them in. Peter realized it was Jesus and jumped out of the boat to swim to Him while the others rowed to shore.

Jesus was waiting for them next to a small fire. He had some bread and some fish cooking over the flames. "Bring over your catch," Jesus called to them. "Let's have some breakfast!" The disciples recognized Jesus. But they didn't dare say anything. Jesus handed a piece of bread and some fish to each one of the disciples. Then they ate together.

DAY 334
Jesus and Peter
John 21:15-19

After Jesus and His disciples finished eating, Jesus asked Peter a question. "Do You really love Me more than the others?"

"Yes Lord, You know I love You!" Peter answered.

"Good," Jesus replied. "Then take care of My sheep."

Jesus asked him a second time, "Do you really love Me?"

Again Peter answered, "Yes Lord, You know I love You!"

"Then take care of My sheep," Jesus said.

Jesus asked Peter a third time, "Do you love Me?"

Peter's feelings were hurt. He thought Jesus doubted his love. But he answered, "Lord, You know everything. You know I love You."

JESUS' RESURRECTION

"Good," Jesus replied. "Then feed My sheep and follow Me!"

Jesus asked Peter if he loved Him three times, just as many times as Peter had denied Him. He wanted to make sure Peter was ready to be His follower again.

Finally Jesus looked into Peter's eyes and said, "Simon, when you were young, you used to get ready and go wherever you wanted to go. But when you are old, you will stretch out your hands, and others will lead you where you don't want to go."

DAY 335
Jesus Returns to God
Acts 1:3-11

Jesus stayed with His disciples forty days after He had risen from the grave. He spoke about the kingdom of God with them. He also told them, "Stay in Jerusalem until the Father gives you the Holy Spirit. John baptized you with water, but in a few days God will baptize you with His Spirit." The disciples had a lot of questions for Jesus. "Are You going to give us a king?" they asked. But Jesus said, "Don't worry about those things. They are in God's hands. But the Holy Spirit will give you power. Spread the news and tell everyone in the world about Me!" Then Jesus went up to heaven in a cloud.

Long after Jesus had disappeared, the disciples still stood staring up in awe at the sky. An angel stood next to them smiling. "What are you looking at?" he asked. The disciples glanced over at the angel in surprise. Then the angel said, "Jesus is in heaven now! But He will come back someday. And He will come the same way that you saw Him go."

DAY 336
The Day of Pentecost
Acts 2:1-13

After Jesus went back to heaven to be with God, His disciples came together in Jerusalem and wondered what to do now. While they were gathered, something incredible happened. A strong wind started whistling in the sky. The wind tore through the windows of the house, blowing little flames of fire inside! This was the Holy Spirit of Jesus coming down to His people. The flames settled on the people, and they began to speak in different languages as if the Holy Spirit was speaking through them.

Meanwhile, some other people living in Jerusalem started to hear all the noise coming from the house. "What is going on?" they wondered. "How are these people speaking in languages they do not know?" Then someone said, "They must be drunk!" The apostle Peter overheard this remark. He could see that the people watching did not understand what was going on, so he turned to speak with them.

THE EARLY CHURCH

DAY 337
Peter Speaks to the Crowd
Acts 2:14-36

"Friends, you are wrong to think these people are drunk," Peter spoke. "Something special happened here today. Listen to what I have to say. Long ago God told His prophet Joel this very thing would happen! God said, 'I will pour out My spirit to My people.' David also foresaw these things when he said, 'For You God will not leave my soul or allow the Lord to rot in the grave.'

"People of Jerusalem," Peter continued, "the words that have been spoken by the old prophets are true! God sent us His only Son, Jesus. Jesus worked miracles and wonders. All of you know this. Then Jesus was rejected by His people and hung on the cross. But Jesus has risen again! He is with the Father in heaven. Jesus is also with us—His Spirit has come. His miracles and wonders will go on through His people. The people you see here have been filled with the Holy Spirit! That is how they do these things."

THE EARLY CHURCH

DAY 338
The Fellowship of the Disciples
Acts 2:37-39, 41-47

Word got around Jerusalem about the miracle that had happened in the meeting hall. People began to turn their hearts to Jesus. They looked to the apostles to answer their questions, saying, "We believe in Jesus! What shall we do now?" Peter explained to them that Jesus taught love and acceptance. He told them they should share the things they have with others and give away what they do not need. He explained

THE EARLY CHURCH

how Jesus cared for all people. They, too, should care for others, even their enemies. Then Peter told them that if they obeyed God and trusted Him with their whole hearts, they would receive the Holy Spirit.

After hearing these things, many people were baptized. They started to meet with the apostles in the temple every day to pray and worship God. They cooked and ate meals together, sharing their food with the hungry and the sick. They loved one another. They laughed together. They prayed for each other and spread the good news about Jesus to others who did not know Him.

DAY 339
A Lame Man Is Healed
Acts 3:1-8

One day, Peter and John were on their way to the temple for the afternoon prayer. A crippled man whose legs were gnarled and weak was sitting by the temple door begging for coins. When Peter and John came up to the door, the crippled man held out his begging bowl. He was too ashamed to even look up at them. He pleaded, "Please have pity on me and give me a few coins."

Peter answered, "Why don't you look up at us?" So the crippled man lifted his gloomy face toward them.

Peter said, "I have no coins to give you. But I have something better." Peter saw the look of trust in the crippled man's eyes. Then Peter said, "In the name of Jesus, get up and walk!" Peter took the crippled man's hand and helped him to his feet. The man's legs strengthened and stretched out. He could walk! He jumped up and down in excitement and his face broke out into a smile of joy. "Praise God!" he cried out. Peter and John smiled. They invited the man to pray with them in the temple.

THE EARLY CHURCH

DAY 340
Faith in Jesus
Acts 3:9-26

People began to hear about the miracle that had just happened to the crippled man. They ran to the temple to see if it were really true. Soon the temple was packed with people trying to catch a glimpse of the crippled man whose legs were now as strong as ever.

Peter looked around curiously. Then he spoke out above the crowd, "Tell me, have you all come to stare at this crippled man who can now walk? Why are you surprised? You must think that the apostles and I have special powers. Don't you know that the Holy Spirit heals those who have faith? Jesus leads people to new life! But you people rejected Jesus, and He was crucified. Now He has shown you that He lives on. He has performed this miracle here today." The crowd was amazed. Many of them accepted Jesus that day.

THE EARLY CHURCH

DAY 341
Peter and John Are Arrested
Acts 4:5-21

Some of Jerusalem's powerful men, including the high priest, refused to listen to Peter and the apostles. When they heard about the miracle that had happened to the crippled man, they were suspicious. They had Peter and John arrested. Then they brought them in to a council meeting for questioning.

"You healed a crippled man! How did you do it?" the council demanded to know.

Peter replied confidently, "The power of Jesus." Then he added, "Only Jesus has the power to heal, and He has done it. You put Jesus on the cross, but God has raised Him to life again!"

The men shook their heads in frustration and said to one another,

THE EARLY CHURCH

"What will we do with these followers of Jesus? Word will get around about this miracle. The people might rebel against their leaders!" Then the men turned back to Peter and John and told them they could go free, as long as they never taught about Jesus again.

But Peter answered, "Do you think God wants us to obey you or to obey Him? We will not be quiet about Jesus!"

The men threatened Peter and John again but finally had to release them.

DAY 342
Rescued by an Angel
Acts 5:17-32

Another time, the high priest had the apostles put in jail. But this time, an angel of the Lord came to them. The apostles watched in amazement as the shackles around their wrists burst apart. Then the door to their cell swung open. The angel said to them, "Go to the temple and continue to teach people about the good news of Jesus!"

They did as the angel had told them and went back to the temple where the people were. They knew that the Lord was with them so they were not afraid.

They told the people, "The Lord has showed us His mighty power! He is with us in everything we do. Obey Him. Continue the good works that Jesus taught. Trust and have faith that God will take care of you!"

THE EARLY CHURCH

DAY 343
Stephen Is Arrested
Acts 6:8-15

Stephen had a special gift for speaking. Whenever he spoke about Jesus, he would speak with such grace and sincerity, people would come just to hear him give a lesson. But some men were jealous of Stephen's gifts. They tried to start an argument with him. Stephen was filled with the Holy Spirit, and he could not be made angry. This made the jealous men even angrier! They decided to start rumors about Stephen.

Stephen was dragged before the Jewish council. The people who wanted to hurt him said, "Stephen says some horrible things about the temple and the Law. He is teaching against the old ways."

The council members just stared at Stephen. They saw that his face looked like the face of an angel.

THE EARLY CHURCH

DAY 344
Stephen Is Killed
Acts 7:1, 51-59

The high priest found Stephen and asked him, "Are these rumors about you true?"

Stephen answered, "The people who tell the truth have always been put down and mistreated. Jesus died for it. Now Jesus' disciples are here to continue to tell the truth. Why are you and your people always disobeying God?"

The high priest and the other officials fumed at these words. They picked up big rocks and hurled them at Stephen. Stephen knew he would be killed. He prayed to God, "Take my spirit to heaven and forgive my enemies. They don't know what they are doing." And with those last words, Stephen died.

THE EARLY CHURCH

DAY 345
Saul on the Road to Damascus
Acts 8:1-3; 9:1-9

Saul was a strong believer in the Jewish ways. He wanted to round up all the believers of Jesus and throw them in jail. One day he went to Damascus to do these things. As he rode, trotting along on his horse, a light shone and burned in his eyes. The light got brighter until Saul could not see anything! He fell right off his horse onto the dirt.

A voice called out from above, "Saul, why are you fighting against Me?"

Saul was frightened. With a quivering voice he asked, "Who—who are You?"

The voice replied, "I am Jesus! Get up and go to Damascus. I will tell you what to do when you are there." But Saul had been blinded by the Lord's light. He had to stumble and fumble his way into the town of Damascus.

DAY 346
Saul Is Baptized
Acts 9:10-19

A man named Ananias was waiting for Saul in Damascus. Ananias went to Saul and laid his hands atop his head. Then Ananias said, "Saul, the Lord has sent me to bless you. You once rejected the Lord, but now He wants you to spread the good news about Him. He has saved you, and He is filling you with the Holy Spirit. Now open your eyes and see!"

Saul opened his eyes. He could see again! And yet it seemed to Saul that the world was clearer, more colorful and brighter than it had ever appeared before. Saul fell on his knees and prayed, "Thank You, God. Forgive me for my sins. I am Your servant."

Saul was baptized and stayed for several days with the followers of Jesus in Damascus.

DAY 347
Saul Begins to Preach
Acts 9:20-31

Saul went to the places where the Jews would meet and eagerly told people that Jesus is the Son of God. People were amazed and said, "Isn't this the man who used to hate Jesus' followers in Jerusalem and drag them to the chief priests? Now he is trying to prove that Jesus is the Messiah!" The Jewish people in Damascus were completely confused.

Later, when Saul arrived in Jerusalem, he wanted to join the followers. But they were afraid of him, because they couldn't believe he had become a Christian. Then Barnabas took him to the apostles, and Saul explained how he had seen the Lord and how the Lord had spoken to him. Barnabas also told the apostles how Saul had spoken about Jesus in Damascus.

The church now had a time of peace and kept on worshiping the Lord. The followers became stronger, as the Holy Spirit encouraged them and helped them grow.

THE EARLY CHURCH

DAY 348
Peter Brings Dorcas Back to Life
Acts 9:36-43

There was a good woman named Tabitha who lived in the town of Joppa. Her Greek name was Dorcas, which means "deer." Everybody loved Tabitha. They admired her because she could sew beautiful clothes. She made things for the poor and always did good deeds for people. But one day Tabitha got sick and died. The whole town was full of grief and sadness. When they heard that the apostle Peter was staying in a neighboring town, they ran and found him. "Peter," they cried, "come as quickly as you can!"

They took Peter to where Tabitha was

laying on her deathbed. Peter knelt down and prayed in front of her. Then he said, "Tabitha, get up!"

Tabitha opened her eyes and looked at Peter. Peter helped her to her feet. Everyone rushed in to see—was it true? Tabitha had been raised from the dead! The people of Joppa were overjoyed. They ran to hug and kiss Tabitha. Then they turned their eyes in awe and wonder toward Peter. Peter explained that it was the Lord's miracle he had performed. The Lord had given Tabitha back her life!

Then Peter decided to stay on in Joppa and teach the people more about Jesus. Peter gained many followers for the Lord there.

SIMON PETER'S MINISTRY

DAY 349
A Sheet Full of Animals
Acts 10:1-16

Captain Cornelius was a man who lived in the town of Caesarea. He was a good man, and he loved God with all his heart. But Cornelius was a Gentile, not a man from the people of Israel.

One day Cornelius had a vision. An angel came to him and said, "God has heard your prayers. He has seen the good things you have done. Now I want you to send a group of your men to the town of Joppa. A man named Peter is living there, and he has some good news to share with you." Cornelius immediately sent two of his servants and one of his trusted soldiers off to Joppa to find Peter.

Meanwhile back in Joppa, Peter was also having a vision. In Peter's vision he saw the sky open up. Out of the sky, a sheet full of animals was lowered down. The voice of God spoke, "Peter, take these animals and eat them."

Peter was stunned, "But those animals are unclean," he cried out. "Snakes and birds? They are not right for eating!"

But God replied, "Don't worry about that. It is better to listen to what I tell you."

Then the vision faded away, and Peter found himself in his own house once again. He wondered, "What could that dream possibly mean?"

SIMON PETER'S MINISTRY

DAY 350
Peter Visits an Army Officer
Acts 10:19-48

The Holy Spirit came to Peter again and said, "I have sent three men to you. Hurry now and meet them!" So Peter left his house and wandered through the streets until he came upon the three men Cornelius had sent.

"Are you Peter?" the three men asked.

"Yes. Why have you come?" answered Peter.

"We were sent by our captain," they explained. "He is a Gentile and a believer in God. An angel asked him to send for you." Peter welcomed the men to stay for the night in his home.

The next day the men took Peter back with them to Caesarea. There the captain had been waiting with his friends and family for Peter to come. When he saw Peter he fell on his knees. But Peter said, "Stand up! I am a man just like you. But I have good news to give you." Then Peter told Cornelius and his family all about Jesus. Peter saw the faith in Cornelius's face. He thought for a moment and then he said aloud, "I see now what is meant by the vision God gave me. In the vision, God asked me to eat all kinds of animals that I thought were unfit to eat. But God does not want us to decide what is fit and unfit. He wants us to obey Him. God has asked me to preach to all His people, whether they are Jews or Gentiles!" Then Peter baptized Cornelius and his family.

SIMON PETER'S MINISTRY

DAY 351
Peter Is Arrested Again
Acts 12:1-9

Herod was the king of Israel. He was a strict ruler, and he punished anyone who believed in Jesus. Soon he began to hear stories about Peter. He heard that Peter was turning hundreds of people toward Jesus. He also heard of the miracles Peter was performing such as healing the sick and raising the dead. Herod would not stand for this. He demanded to have Peter arrested and thrown in jail.

Peter was thrown into a dingy, damp prison cell and bound with heavy chains on his wrists and his ankles. There was a guard on the left of Peter and another on the right, including two guards at the door to make sure he didn't escape. But that did not stop God from saving Peter. An angel of the Lord came to Peter while he was asleep and poked him. "Peter! Quick, get up!" the angel said. "Put on your shoes and your clothes." Peter felt the chains fall away from his body, and he saw that the guards were fast asleep. Then the angel said, "Now come with me." The prison doors opened, and the angel led Peter outside into the empty street.

DAY 352
Peter Escapes from Prison
Acts 12:9-17

Peter, heavy in a daze, just stood out in the street. When he looked around, the angel was no longer there. But he was free! "The Lord has allowed me to escape," he said under his breath. Then

Peter snuck quietly over to the house of a woman named Mary. Mary was the mother of Peter's friend John. Inside Mary's house a group of people had come together to pray for Peter.

Peter knocked at the door. "Let me in! It's Peter!" he said. The servant woman, Rhoda, was walking toward the door and recognized Peter's voice. She was so excited, she ran straight back to the others.

"Peter is at the door!" she cried out.

But the others said, "Stop being so silly, Rhoda! Peter is in jail."

Peter was still at the door waiting to be let in. He knocked louder this time. "Open the door! It's me, Peter!" When the others heard this, they rushed to Mary's front door and opened it. When they saw Peter standing there, they gasped in surprise. "But how did you escape?" they asked. Peter shushed them, for he knew if anyone heard them he would be caught. Peter pushed them back inside and told them about God's angel who had set him free.

DAY 353
Barnabas and Saul in Cyprus
Acts 13:1-12

Saul, who had once fought against Jesus, was like a new person ever since God had come to him. His name was changed to Paul. He was filled with bold love for Jesus, and he was devoted to telling the world about the good news of the Lord.

Paul sailed to the island of Cyprus with his companion Barnabas. There he stood on the street corners and the squares and spoke about Jesus. But the governor of Cyprus had a man who worked for him named Bar-Jesus. Bar-Jesus did not like Paul and tried to keep him from teaching about Jesus. Bar-Jesus told the governor, "This Jesus that Paul talks about is nonsense! Do not believe him."

When Paul heard the lies Bar-Jesus was spreading, he went to him. He looked Bar-Jesus straight in the eye and said, "You are speaking lies about me! But I was once like you. I could not see the truth. So the Lord blinded me! Now He will do the same with you until you can see rightly again." Suddenly Bar-Jesus' sight became like a black cloud. He became blind and reached out for someone to take his hand.

The governor was watching all this. What Paul said had come true, and so the governor believed and turned his heart to Jesus.

DAY 354
Paul and Barnabas Are Worshiped As Gods
Acts 14:8-20

Paul and his companion Barnabas traveled to the city of Lystra. The people there believed in many gods. One day Paul was preaching on the outskirts of the city. One of his listeners was a crippled man.

Paul said to him, "Stand up and walk!"

But when the people saw this, they began to shout, "Look at this! The gods have turned into humans! Paul surely is a god!" Then they said, "We must give him the name of a god and sacrifice something for him."

Paul was very worried and upset. "I am not a god!" he said. "I am only a human like all of you. Don't make any sacrifices to me. Instead give up your foolish beliefs and turn to God who has made everything you see!"

The people thought Paul was making fun of them. They said, "Paul is saying our beliefs are foolish!" So they threw stones at him until they thought he was dead.

But some of the people who believed in Jesus helped pick Paul up again, and he was able to walk back into the city.

PAUL'S MINISTRY

DAY 355
Paul and Silas in Jail
Acts 16:16-24

Even though he was mistreated, Paul continued to do the Lord's work.

One day he came upon a slave girl in the marketplace where he was walking with his companion Silas. The slave girl was yelling and howling curses everywhere she went. She had an evil spirit inside her. The girl's owners were glad she was possessed by an evil spirit. It gave her the ability to see into the future and tell fortunes. They made a lot of money off of her this way. Paul put his hand on her and said, "In the name of Jesus, let this girl be herself again!"

Just then the girl turned calm and peaceful. But the girl's owners were infuriated. The girl had lost her ability to tell fortunes, and they could no longer make money off of her.

The girl's owners went all around the city of Lystra yelling bad things about Paul and Silas. Then they told the city officials, "These Jews are making nothing but trouble in our city!"

So the city officials arrested Paul and Silas. Then they beat them and threw them into the dungeon where thieves and crooks were kept.

DAY 356
Singing in Jail
Acts 16:25-34

Paul and Silas did not let the pitifully cold, dark dungeon keep them from doing God's work. They sang songs of worship, and their voices echoed throughout the labyrinth of jails underground. Other prisoners began to perk up and listen to the songs. The place filled with the Holy Spirit. Then, all of a sudden, the ground began to shake, and the chains that bound them rattled furiously. God was sending an earthquake! The chains burst and broke, and the doors were opened!

The jailer was frightened. He thought all the prisoners would escape; then he would be in big trouble. In his panic, he reached for his sword to kill himself.

But Paul cried out, "Stop, jailer! We have not run away. There is no need to harm yourself!"

The jailer was full of gratitude. He bent down at the feet of Paul and said, "What do I have to do to be saved?"

Paul answered, "Believe in the Lord."

The jailer took Paul and Silas to his house and cooked them a fine meal. Then Paul baptized the jailer and his whole family.

DAY 357
Paul and Silas in Thessalonica
Acts 17:1-9

Paul and Silas continued traveling and preaching the word of God to new people. They came to a town called Thessalonica. A friendly man named Jason lived there. He let Paul and Silas stay in his home while they were visiting. The next day Paul visited the local temple and preached to the people. He urged them, "Follow the ways of the Lord, for He has died for your sins!" By that afternoon, a big crowd had gathered to listen to Paul. The leaders in the town began to feel envious. More people were listening to Paul than to them!

The leaders went to the city officials and said, "Paul and Silas are big troublemakers! The gossip is that they have been kicked out of every city they visit! Now they are in our city, and Jason has let them stay in his home!"

The city officials planned to have Paul and Silas arrested. But the two had already left town, so they arrested Jason instead. They made Jason pay a big fine for allowing Paul and Silas to stay in his home.

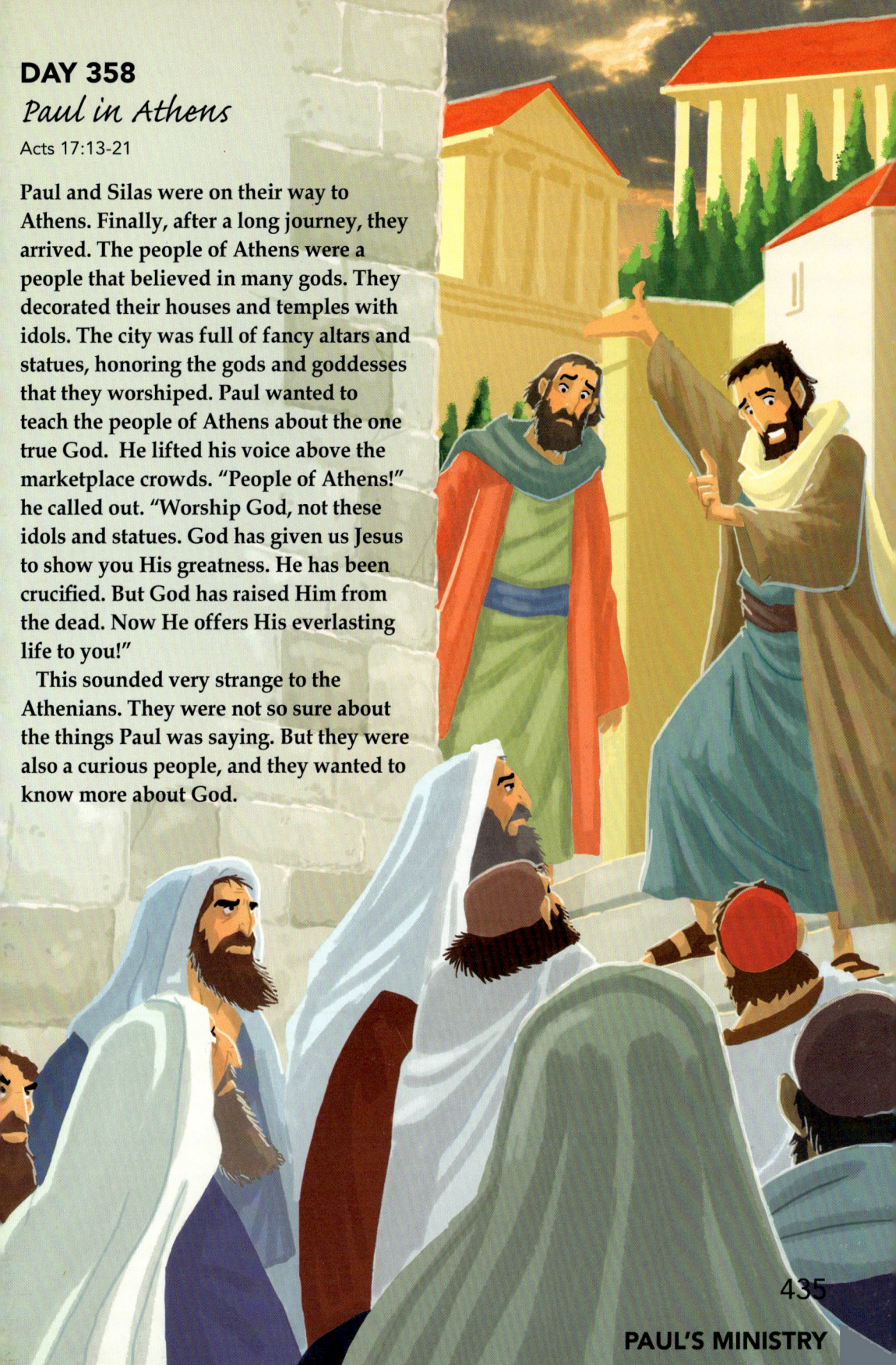

DAY 358
Paul in Athens
Acts 17:13-21

Paul and Silas were on their way to Athens. Finally, after a long journey, they arrived. The people of Athens were a people that believed in many gods. They decorated their houses and temples with idols. The city was full of fancy altars and statues, honoring the gods and goddesses that they worshiped. Paul wanted to teach the people of Athens about the one true God. He lifted his voice above the marketplace crowds. "People of Athens!" he called out. "Worship God, not these idols and statues. God has given us Jesus to show you His greatness. He has been crucified. But God has raised Him from the dead. Now He offers His everlasting life to you!"

This sounded very strange to the Athenians. They were not so sure about the things Paul was saying. But they were also a curious people, and they wanted to know more about God.

PAUL'S MINISTRY

DAY 359
Paul Speaks at Areopagus
Acts 17:22-34

The Athenians called Paul out for a meeting on a hill called the Areopagus. They wanted to hear more about the things Paul was saying about Jesus.

Once they were gathered, Paul gave a speech. He said, "I see that you are religious here in Athens! I was walking through your streets, and I spotted an altar inscribed 'To an Unknown God.' It must be difficult to worship a God you know nothing about. Let me tell you what I know about God. God is great! He has made the world and everything in it. He has made you and me, and we are his children. But God is not in the idols you keep or in the silver or gold models of the temples. He is greater than that! He sent down His only Son, Jesus, to teach us about His greatness. Jesus was nailed to the cross. But He rose up from the dead!"

Paul looked around and saw that many people listening began to laugh at this.

The people interrupted Paul and said, "We will have to talk about this with you some other time. All your talk about Jesus being raised from the dead is too hard to believe." But there were a few people who considered what Paul said. They turned their hearts to Jesus.

PAUL'S MINISTRY

DAY 360
The Riot in Ephesus
Acts 19:23-30

Demetrius was a silversmith who lived in Athens. He had a job making silver models of the temple of the goddess Artemis. His business brought in good money because the people of Athens liked to decorate their homes with the things he made.

Demetrius was suspicious of Paul. He called all the silversmiths together and said to them, "This foreigner is trying to destroy our business! If people listen to him, they will no longer worship our goddess Artemis. Then who will buy our models of the temple? Paul will put us right out of work!"

Demetrius spoke with such passion that soon he had all the silversmiths in a rage. They started to riot—screaming and shouting insults about Paul throughout the streets. A big mob formed in the square. They swung their fists in the air and waited for Paul to come so they could attack him.

Just then Paul was on his way to the square to speak to the people about Jesus. Someone quickly ran to him and warned him about the mob that had formed, so Paul stayed away and didn't get hurt.

DAY 361
Paul Is Warned
Acts 20:17-38

It was too dangerous for Paul to stay in Athens. He called his friends and followers together to tell them he planned to leave, saying, "I have done Jesus' work and told people the good news I've learned about God. I have told them to have faith in Jesus no matter where they come from or what religion they may be. Now it's time for me to leave Athens. I can do no more here, and I might be thrown in jail. I'm going to Jerusalem, and who can say what will happen to me there? But I don't care! As long as I am teaching people about Jesus, nothing else matters!"

Paul's friends and followers cried at these words. They knew he was brave. They kissed and hugged him, and they waved goodbye to him as he sailed away toward Jerusalem.

PAUL'S MINISTRY

DAY 362
A Mob Turns Against Paul
Acts 21:27-36; 22:23-24

Paul reached Jerusalem where he met with his old friends and some of the church elders. They were glad he had come. But some people were not. A few people in the streets recognized Paul. They whispered to one another, "That is the man that travels to other lands and says bad things about his people!"

Then another person would point and say, "That's the man who brings shame on our people by welcoming Gentiles into Jewish temples!" Paul could hardly go out into the streets without people snickering and staring at him.

One day Paul was attacked by a mob of people. They began grabbing his clothes

and yelling in his face. The Roman army commander heard the uproar and found Paul being pushed and shoved by a group of angry people.

The army commander yelled out, "What has this man done?"

Everybody began to shout at once. "He's a liar!" one said.

"He's a friend of our enemies!" said another.

Then others in the crowd began to yell different things. The voices turned into a great big clamor of noise. The army commander could not make out what any of them were saying. But he decided he must do something, so he had Paul arrested and whipped to satisfy the angry crowd.

DAY 363
Paul Speaks Before the Governor
Acts 24:24-27; 25:8-12

At this time, a man named Felix was serving as Jerusalem's governor. Felix visited Paul while he was in jail. "Tell me," he said, "what are these things you teach that make the people so angry?" Paul was always willing to speak about Jesus. He told Felix about Jesus' crucifixion and how He rose again. He told Felix how to follow Jesus through kindness and good works. He told Felix that it was not right to be greedy or selfish. But Felix did not want to hear these things. Felix was hoping Paul would offer him money in exchange for his freedom. But Paul never bribed him, so Felix left.

Two years later, a man named Porcius took the place of Felix as governor of Jerusalem. One day Porcius came to Paul and asked him if he was ready to be judged and charged for his crimes. Paul answered, "I have not done anything wrong. If I had done something deserving death, I would accept it. But I will go anyway and be judged by the emperor of Rome who has the highest authority."

Porcius replied, "If you want to be tried by the emperor, then it's off to Rome with you!" Porcius sent Paul out on the next ship bound for Rome.

PAUL'S MINISTRY

DAY 364
A Stormy Voyage
Acts 27

Paul boarded the ship to Rome with some other prisoners and the captain and crew.

They sailed along smoothly until they came to a harbor called Fair Havens. There Paul felt a tinge of cold in the air. He suggested to the captain that they stay in Fair Havens until the winter had passed. Paul knew there might be dangerous storms at sea this time of year. But the captain insisted they sail on.

One night as they were sleeping in their bunk beds, a torrent of wind began to blow and rage. Everyone who was sleeping woke up to the sounds of the creaking and groaning of the ship as it crashed up and down on the waves. A storm was brewing.

The wind grew stronger until big black waves pounded against the ship. The ship flooded with water. The captain of the ship spotted a cove of sand off in the distance. But before they could reach the cove, the crashing waves had grown too fierce, and the ship began to sink! The waves wrecked the ship, and the wind tore the sails. The captain ordered all on board to abandon ship and swim toward the cove.

DAY 365
Rome at Last
Acts 28

Paul and the others swam with all their might against the angry sea. Finally they reached the sandy cove and collapsed on the shore.

They had come to an island called Malta. The islanders of Malta welcomed the shipwreckers. They built a fire to help them get warm. Paul was gathering some wood when suddenly a snake came out and bit him on the finger.

The islanders cried out, "That's a poisonous snake. You will die!"

But Paul just shook the snake off, and he didn't die. The islanders were stunned. They were certain Paul was a god. Who else could survive a poisonous snakebite? But Paul told them, "I am not a god. I am a follower of Jesus. He has given me His Holy Spirit!"

The islanders had never heard the good news about Jesus before. They were interested in everything Paul had to teach them.

Once spring arrived and the sea was calm again, Paul and the others boarded another ship and finally arrived in Rome. Paul stayed in a house while he waited for the emperor to call him into court to be judged. Many people in Rome had heard about Paul. Paul kept his door wide open and invited strangers and friends alike to come and talk about Jesus with him. His house became a popular meeting place for all the followers of Jesus.

PAUL'S MINISTRY